D1014698

THE LOGIC OF EVIL

The Logic of Evil

The Social Origins of the Nazi Party, 1925–1933

W I L L I A M   B R U S T E I N

Yale University Press   New Haven and London

Published with assistance from the foundation established in memory of Philip Hamilton McMillan of the Class of 1894, Yale College.

Designed by James J. Johnson and set in Stemple Garamond type by Tseng Information Systems, Inc., Durham, North Carolina.
Printed in the United States of America by Edwards Brothers, Inc., Ann Arbor, Michigan.

Library of Congress Cataloging-in-Publication Data

Brustein, William.
    The logic of evil : the social origins of the Nazi Party, 1925-1933 / William Brustein.
       p.   cm.
    Includes index.
    ISBN 0-300-06533-7 (alk. paper)
    1. Nationalsozialistische Deutsche Arbeiter-Partei.   2. National socialism—Germany.
3. Germany—Social conditions—1918-1933.   4. Political parties—Germany—History—20th century.   5. Germany—Politics and government—1933-1945.   6. Germany—Economic conditions—1918-1945.   I. Title.
DD253.25.B76   1996
943.086—dc20   95-47263
                                                                            CIP

A catalogue record for this book is available from the British Library.

The paper in this book meets the guidelines for permanence and durability of the Committee on Production Guidelines for Book Longevity of the Council on Library Resources.

10 9 8 7 6 5 4 3 2 1

To Yvonne, Arielle, and Maximilian

Contents

Figures, Tables, and Map

Figures

Tables

Map

Preface

My earliest recollections of discussions of Hitler and Nazism date from my childhood: I grew up in a Jewish family in Connecticut during the 1950s. My relatives would frequently recount the gruesome details of the Nazi campaign to eliminate European Jewry. Nazism became for me another word for *evil*. I remember wondering who these Nazis were and how they could have committed the most heinous crime in human history. I turned to the dictionary to understand the meaning of the word *evil*. It instructed me that evil is that which is morally bad or injurious or causes suffering, misfortune, or disaster. It took no great leap of logic to realize that if we were to consider twentieth-century phenomena to which the definition of evil applies, Nazism would stand out as the most egregious example.

But as my curiosity to fathom the Nazi phenomenon heightened, I encountered a gnawing paradox: I had been taught that human beings are not essentially evil. How then could so many Germans, nearly fourteen million adults (37.3 percent of the electorate), have voted for the Nazi Party in a free and open election in July 1932—for the party that gave new meaning to the human capacity for evil and whose contributions to the twentieth century included genocide, massive physical destruction, racial and religious bigotry, and totalitarianism? I searched for an answer to my dilemma in the vast literature on the rise of Nazism but came away unsatisfied. Where the literature focused on the motivations of the Nazi rank and file, it stressed the naïveté, gullibility, and bigotry of the Nazi constituency. This traditional view did not sit well with me, for I could not accept that a party that promoted hate could attract so many people to its ranks.

The search for an answer to why millions of average Germans turned to the Nazi Party before 1933 has inspired me to join forces with Jürgen W. Falter (University of Mainz) to conduct the most extensive and representative examination to date of pre-1933 individual Nazi Party membership data, derived from the official Nazi Party membership file (NSDAP master file) housed at the Berlin Document Center, and ultimately to write *The Logic of Evil*.

In this examination of who became Nazis, and why, I hope to shatter some reigning myths about the rise of the Nazi Party, much as Hannah Arendt did in the early 1960s when she popularized the term *the banality of evil* in reference to the mundane motives and the averageness of Nazi administrators such as Adolf Eichmann. But rather than spotlight the motives of Nazi administrators, I focus here on the reasons that millions of ordinary Germans may have had for joining the Nazi Party before 1933. My central thesis is that the mass of Nazi followers were motivated chiefly by commonplace and rational factors—namely, their material interests—rather than by Hitler's irrational appeal or charisma. In this way Nazi supporters were no different from average citizens elsewhere, who usually select a political party or candidate they believe will promote their interests. Thus, I suggest that *evil* as an *outcome* may have very logical origins and that evil is not always easily discerned—a chilling recognition.

If my suggestions provoke readers to reexamine why the Nazis triumphed in 1933 or to ponder the origins of other political movements commonly assumed to represent evil, then I will feel that I have succeeded. Answers to the questions of which people became Nazis and why are more relevant today than ever. Indeed, the present period shares some frightening parallels with the post–World War I era. Since the end of World War II, no period has rivaled the present for revival of fanatical xenophobic movements. Like the 1920s and 1930s, the 1980s and 1990s have witnessed significant worldwide economic shocks and political and social turbulence. Newspapers abound with reports of the activities of xenophobic and hypernationalist groups such as the White Aryan Resistance in the United States, the neo-Nazi skinheads in Germany, the Hindu extremist Bharatiya Janata Party (BJP) in India, Zhirinovsky's Liberal Democrats in Russia, and Le Pen's National Front in France. Whereas some of these movements are estimated to have a following in the hundreds, others, like the National Front in France, the Liberal Democrats in Russia, or the BJP in India, can muster millions of votes in national elections.

It is perhaps necessary to state clearly what this book is and is not. This book is not a historical treatment of the rise of the Nazi Party, for that history has been well and often rehearsed. I am a social scientist interested in applying and testing general theoretical explanations of macropolitical phenomena. This work is the first serious attempt to apply to the social origins of the Nazi Party (up to 1933) a model of political behavior founded on the assumption that political affiliation is based on self-interest, and to test that model empirically.

The organization of the book is quite simple. I choose to concentrate on the period between 1925 and 1933 principally because 1925 marks the reconstitution of the Nazi Party and the entry date of the first Nazi membership cards in the BDC master file, and 1933 marks Hitler's appointment as chancellor of Germany and the end of the period in which Germans could freely choose to oppose the Nazi Party. In Chapter 1 of this book, I examine the major theories of the sociology of Nazism and conclude with a discussion of my theory that people joined the Nazi Party largely out of material self-interest. From that perspective, in Chapters 2 through 4 I analyze the programs of the major Weimar political parties between 1925 and 1933 and the degree to which the competing political programs responded to the material interests of Germany's two principal classes: the middle and working classes. Using my Nazi Party membership sample in this part, I show that the Nazi Party program appealed more to some segments of the middle class and working class than to others. Among the important empirical findings of this part is that the NSDAP won the support of a surprisingly large number of blue-collar laborers, contrary to previous assumptions about the sociology of Nazism. In the last chapter I examine the incentives and disincentives for joining the Nazi Party before 1933. Interestingly, studies of the early Nazi Party often ignore the numerous personal costs and risks that the act of joining the party entailed.

Over several years, I have accumulated many debts in the writing of this book. I am especially indebted to Michael Hechter, who encouraged me to tackle the big puzzles, and to Jürgen W. Falter, who during 1989 graciously accommodated me and my Minnesota team of research assistants in Berlin and introduced me to the rich literature based on empirical accounts of the rise of Nazism. For their many helpful suggestions I owe a debt of appreciation to Ronald Aminzade, Brian Ault, Harmut Esser, Conan Fischer, Debra Friedman, Joseph Galaskiewicz, Walter Goldfrank, John R. Hall, David Knoke, Margaret Levi, Siegwart Lindenberg, Günther Mai, Barry Markovsky, Jeylan Mortimer, Detlef Mühlberger, John O'Loughlin, Karl-Dieter Opp, Paul Reynolds, Joachim Savelsberg, W. Phillips Shively, Karol Soltan, and Rainer Zitelmann.

This study would not have been possible without the efforts of people in both Minneapolis and Berlin who helped organize and carry out a massive collection of Nazi Party membership data at the Berlin Document Center. I give special thanks to Heidrun Suhr, who helped recruit my Minnesota research team, Gregory Shattuck, who designed our software program, and William Barthelmy, Mark Brose, Steen Gilberston, Jana Jakub, Lisa Kemper, Kristi Kinney, Isabelle Schallreuter, and Cheryll Solstad, who made up my Minnesota research team and worked long days at the Document Center. I owe a great debt of thanks to Hartmut Bömermann, Bettina Husemann, Marguerite Kleist, Achim von Malotki, Torsten Schneider-Haase, and Jürgen Winkler, all participants in the Berlin research group supervised by my dear colleague Jürgen W. Falter. Brian Ault, Mark Brose, Bettina Husemann, Jana Jakub, Torsten Schneider-Haase, Achim von Malotki, and Jürgen Winkler had the unenviable tasks of cleaning, restructuring, coding, and analyzing the Nazi Party membership data; I deeply appreciate their work. Thanks as well to Mynda Grimaldi and Robert Zweifelhofer, who spent weeks during the summer of 1991 in Berlin analyzing the contents of the principal Weimar political party newspapers, to Colin Flint and Yu Zhou for their technical assistance in digitizing Weimar county units, and to Tamara Lubic and Susan Abel for their helpful editorial suggestions. And special thanks to John Covell, my editor at Yale University Press, whose steadfast support I truly value.

I also want to thank the staff of the Berlin Document Center who assisted us in our six-month data collection project. I deeply appreciate the efforts of Daniel Simon, former director of the Berlin Document Center, who granted me access to the NSDAP master file, and to David Marwell, the last American director, who went out of his way to ensure that our data collection proceeded without a hitch.

I have benefited greatly from the assistance of institutions as well. Administrative and material support for my research and writing came from the University of Minnesota's Western European Area Studies Center, directed by J. Kim Munholland, and the department of sociology at the University of Minnesota. At different stages, my research was funded by a Fulbright Western European Regional Research award, two Andrew W. Mellon awards from the University of Minnesota Western European Area Studies Center, three Grant-in-Aid of Research fellowships from the University of Minnesota Graduate School, six University of Minnesota Undergraduate Research Opportunity grants, a University of Minnesota Bush Sabbatical Award, and two National Science Foundation grants (#SES-9009715 and SES-9270211).

Most important, I wish to thank my wife, Yvonne, without whose support and encouragement I would never have completed this book.

THE LOGIC OF EVIL

1

Who Became Nazis and Why?

For more than sixty years, the world community has struggled to understand who became Nazis and why. What was it that impelled apparently sane, rational individuals to support an organization that advocated the destruction of a people? Scholars have concentrated primarily on the "who," because voting results, party membership files, and the records of Nazi Party paramilitary organizations provide some clues about which people joined. Still, the curious and diligent have arrived at no consensus about the composition of the Nazi rank and file, and the debate continues, as new research periodically emerges that strengthens or undermines earlier explanations. Answers about *why* people adhered to Nazi Party precepts are less common and less conclusive, because voting records and party membership files shed little light on the matter. Today we rely on exit polls or survey research to assess individuals' motivations for making political choices, but these information-gathering tools were nonexistent in the 1920s and 1930s.

Who became Nazis, and why, are the principal questions I will consider in this book. Though the questions are not new, the answers and supporting evidence are. My central argument is that the Nazi Party's emergence between 1925 and 1933 as the most popular political party in Germany resulted largely from its superlative success at fashioning economic programs that addressed the material needs of millions of Germans. The explanations are based on a unique and exceptionally rich sample of more than 42,000 individuals who joined the Nazi Party between 1925 and 1933.

Note: A preliminary version of parts of Chapter 1 was published in William Brustein and Jürgen Falter, "Sociology of Nazism: An Interest-Based Account," *Rationality and Society* (1994) 6: 369–99, and William Brustein and Jürgen Falter, "Who Joined the Nazi Party? Assessing Theories of the Social Origins of Nazism," *Zeitgeschichte* (1995) 22: 83–108.

Prevalent Explanations for the Social Origins of Nazism

The breakneck rise of the Nazi Party from its beginnings as one of forty-two racist and ultranationalist fringe groups in 1923 to its position as the most popular German political party in 1932 has been a focus of attention for more than sixty years. Were Germans attracted to Nazism because of the party's irrationalist appeals or because of the extent to which the party's programs responded to their discernible interests? Did the Nazi Party comprise primarily lower-middle-class voters, or was it a catch-all party of protest? Did Nazis come mainly from villages and small towns, or were they the rootless inhabitants of major urban agglomerations? Was the Nazi Party a party of Protestant northern Germany, or did its appeal transcend regional and religious affiliations? Each of these characterizations of Nazi supporters has at one time or another since the late 1920s appeared in the literature. Four of the most prevalent explanations of the social origins of Nazism emphasize respectively its irrationalist, lower-middle-class, confessionalist, and cross-class appeal.[1] Each of these major explanations contains theoretical and empirical shortcomings, which are summarized below. An alternative explanation of the social origins of Nazism, the theory of interest-based adherence, will be discussed in detail later on.

The Irrationalist Appeal

In the aftermath of World War II, as the world became increasingly aware of the heinous crimes perpetrated against humanity during Hitler's Third Reich, it seemed only natural to emphasize the irrationalist nature of the movement. The irrationalist interpretation, that individuals and institutions act on deep and frequently unaccountable impulses, uninfluenced by critical judgment,[2] found favor among many scholars as an explanation for the characteristics and motivations of Nazi Party supporters, for the programmatic appeal of the party, and indeed for the overall political and social climate of Weimar Germany.

One of the best-known variations on the irrationalist explanation is the mass-society theory of political behavior. Drawing on the works of Tarde, Sighele, Le Bon, and Pareto, such mass-society theorists as Arendt, Bendix, Ortega y Gasset, Lederer, and Kornhauser focused on the irrational, anti-intellectual, and visceral nature of the Nazi appeal to the masses.[3] Here is Arendt's classic description of the support base of extremist movements:

"It was characteristic of the rise of the Nazi movement in Germany and of the Communist movement in Europe after 1930 that they recruited their members from this mass of apparently indifferent people whom all other parties had given up as too apathetic or too stupid for their attention. The result was that the majority of their membership consisted of people who never before had appeared on the political scene."[4]

Underlying the mass-society theory is the Durkheimian notion that modernization has intensified the anomic character of society by cutting the masses loose from their traditional and communal moorings. In the absence of sufficient social integration and regulation, people are likely to exhibit deviant (pathological) behavior.[5] For Bendix and Kornhauser, those most vulnerable to the irrationalist appeal are the victims of societal atomization. These people (usually young urban dwellers) lack the necessary intermediate ties to social networks and social institutions such as churches, professional associations, and workers' clubs.[6] The isolated and powerless are particularly susceptible to the promises of shrewd demagogues such as Adolf Hitler, proponents of the mass-society thesis argue.[7]

According to the mass-society theory, social isolation and anomie should increase in times of severe economic crisis, because growing numbers of individuals fall victim to prolonged unemployment and thus become detached from their primary- and secondary-group affiliations. Mass-society theorists see a connection between the rise of National Socialism and the defeat of Germany in World War I, the unfinished revolution of 1918–1919, the hyperinflation of 1922–1923, the agrarian crisis of 1927–1929, and the onset of the Great Depression in 1929.[8]

Ritter notes that the masses are readily persuaded by the impassioned appeals of demagogues to seek quick solutions based on their own sentiments rather than on rational considerations.[9] Stachura sees the German electorate's immaturity as facilitating Hitler's rise to power; Moeller views the German peasants during the Weimar Republic as pawns of politically sophisticated outsiders;[10] and Mühlberger, in an examination of local and regional Nazi Party membership records, concludes with this remark: "Acceptance of the fact that irrational political behaviour is not the prerogative of any particular class, but of sections of all class groupings, is an essential step to the ultimate understanding of the very complex social response on which Nazism was based."[11] The common thread in these assessments is that individuals' attachments are not rational. People are quick to follow without thinking about the content of party appeals.

For some scholars the irrationalist appeal also seemed to help describe the Nazi Party's programmatic appeal. In *Ideology and Utopia,* first published in 1929, Mannheim alerted the public to the irrationalist nature of Nazi ideology, observing that not programs but unconditional subordination to a leader mattered in Nazism and that the purely intuitive, mythological component took priority over any political or historical knowledge.[12] The sensational success of the Nazi Party, according to Broszat, had less to do with the party's programmatic content than with its ability to captivate the masses through its parades, ceremonial blessing of banners, marching columns, bands, and uniforms.[13] Stachura adds that the principal attraction of Nazi propaganda lay not in the party's economic programs, which offered only vague promises to all groups, but rather in its emphasis on the mystical Führer cult, chauvinism, anti-Semitism, and anti-Marxism [14] — themes that appealed to the racist and nationalist prejudices of the gullible German middle classes.[15] Bessel refers to the Nazi Party program as a grab bag of contradictions, a collection of absurdities that was nevertheless able to entice voters who were confused and susceptible to calls for radical change.[16] The theme of the irrationalist character of the Nazi Party program appears also in Madden's study on the social composition of the party. Madden observes that the Nazis tailored their program to take advantage of people's tendency to blame a group of conspirators for their own misfortunes.[17] Finally, in a recent book comparing the lives of Hitler and Stalin, Bullock describes Nazism as "a movement that was deliberately designed to highlight by every manipulative device — symbols, language, ritual, hierarchy, parades, rallies culminating in the Führer myth — the supremacy of the dynamic, irrational factors in politics: struggle, will, force, the sinking of individual identity in the collective emotions of the group, sacrifice, discipline." [18]

Irrationalism has been employed to describe not only the motivations of Germans and the programmatic appeal of the Nazi Party but also the general political, social, and cultural climate of the Weimar period. Although it is never clearly stated by proponents of this thesis, their argument appears to rest on the belief that an irrationalist political doctrine like Nazism can arise only in an irrationalist context.[19] In writing about the last quarter of the nineteenth and the first quarter of the twentieth century, historians such as Meinecke and Croce focused on the cultural fragmentation and moral relativism of the era and saw the massive dislocations of World War I as aggravating Europe's spiritual collapse and social and cultural anomie. Cole, among others, contends that the German military defeat in World War I nurtured feelings of frustration and a fanatical belief in German superiority [20] — sentiments that the Nazis cultivated successfully. Kohn comments on how, during the interwar period, distrust of reason and glorification of life gave birth to a host of political witch doctors adept in the use of mass hypnosis.[21] Dawidowicz frames Weimar politics and culture as "a world intoxicated with hate, driven by paranoia, enemies everywhere, the Jew lurking behind each one." She adds: "The Germans were in search of a mysterious wholeness that would restore them to primeval happiness, destroying the hostile milieu of urban industrial civilization that the Jewish conspiracy had foisted on them."[22]

Lower-Middle-Class Reaction

Another explanation is that interwar European fascism developed in response to the mistrust among the lower middle class (independent artisans, shopkeepers, farmers, and white-collar employees) of the growing influence of big labor and big business. As early as 1930, the German sociologist Theodor Geiger described the basis of Nazism as panic among the middle class (the *Mittelstand*).[23] In the aftermath of World War II, the thesis caught on with a great many scholars, including S. M. Lipset. Lipset posits that associated with every social class or stratum is an extremist form of political expression: communism or Peronism with the working class, traditional authoritarianism with the upper class, and fascism with the lower middle class. Regarding the inclination of the lower middle class to support fascist movements, Lipset asserts: "The petty bourgeoisie of these sections not only suffer deprivation because of the relative decline of their class, they are also citizens of communities whose status and influence within the larger society is rapidly declining. From time to time, depending on various specific historical factors, their discontent leads them to accept diverse irrational protest ideologies — regionalism, racism, supranationalism, anticosmopolitanism, McCarthyism, fascism."[24] Proponents of this thesis hold that the stresses of modernization in late nineteenth- and early twentieth-century Germany, with the attendant concentration and centralization of production, led the German lower middle class to embrace Nazism.

Building on Lipset's argument, Hagtvet and Kühnl[25] observe that the precariousness of lower-middle-class social existence nurtured a longing to return to a precapitalist corporatist society based on small business and agriculture and ruled by a strong state that could secure the lower-middle-class position in society. According to Winkler and Lepsius, the lower middle class followed the Nazis because of the party's promise to reconstitute that world and eliminate all organizations and ideologies promoting narrow, class-based interests.[26]

During the Wilhelmine period, Petzina observes, the lower middle class had held a relatively privileged position and enjoyed the effects of a flourishing economy and identification with the power and glory of imperial Germany. The Weimar Republic symbolized the end of the old order and the birth of a threatening new world in which the lower middle class had limited prospects. Hitler's movement promised an end to the paralyzing hopelessness associated with Weimar.[27]

Loomis and Beegle suggest that Nazism did best among the lower-middle-class groups suffering most acutely from the economic insecurity and anxiety that accompanied the loss of social solidarity. Loomis and Beegle add that during periods of rapid change, Nazism made its greatest inroads among groups whose basic values and organizational experience derived from the Gemeinschaft, Volk, or family and whose formal, contractual, bureaucratic obligations and affiliations had been insignificant. Because of their feelings of insecurity, frustration, and longing for the good old days, members of these groups were more likely to become Nazis than others were.[28]

Other scholars cite the economic downturns of the late 1920s and early 1930s, which led to underemployment, indebtedness, bankruptcies, foreclosures, and decline in agricultural prices, as important factors in lower-middle-class attachment to the Nazis.[29] The economic crises made the position of the lower middle class even more precarious, causing its members to turn away from their traditional allegiances, toward a party that promised to restore them to their former position.

The tremendous electoral support that the Nazis won in Germany's small towns and rural areas, the bastion of the lower middle class, is cited as evidence of lower-middle-class backing for the party.[30] Gerschenkron notes that Hitler himself was well aware of the Nazi debt to Germany's rural areas and claimed: "Our revolution would not have been possible at all if a certain part of the nation had not lived on the land. If we review the revolution soberly we must admit that it would not have been possible to accomplish this revolution from the cities. In the urban communities we could not have reached a position which gave to our policies the weight of legality."[31]

Political Confessionalism

Many critics emphasize that whereas lower-middle-class citizens did suffer from the effects of German modernization and the Great Depression, not all of them became Nazi supporters. Why some in the lower middle class turned to Nazism while others stayed away is the focus of Burnham's important article on political immunization and political confessionalism. For Burnham, lower-middle-class grievances do not in themselves suffice to explain electoral support for the Nazi Party. He points out that in times of social and economic instability, social groups deprived of a political church are likely to fall prey to extreme right- or left-wing movements. In effect, Burnham combines elements of the mass-society thesis with speculations about lower-middle-class support. Like the mass-society theorists, he posits that people who lack social ties are most susceptible to political extremism. Like Lipset, he sees among the lower middle class a particular propensity toward Nazism. But Burnham believes that the German lower middle class fell to the Nazis because it lacked a preexisting political structure to provide social integration and regulation and thus immunize it against the Nazi virus. Burnham states: "It can be said of such strata that they are less actors than acted upon by social transformations which threaten without enlightening them; that they are dependent, vulnerable, and politically reactive under stress; and that, lacking a preexisting political church which explains their plight to them, their instinctive response to dangerously stressful social change is to support those candidates and movements who can most effectively promise them that such change will be stopped."[32]

Burnham's thesis regarding political confessionalism offers one explanation for the often stated claim that German Catholics and many German workers remained immune to the Nazi appeal. According to this line of reasoning, the Catholic Center Party and the Social Democratic Party, the two principal political umbrella groups for German Catholics and German laborers, sheltered their followers from the extremist contagion, wrapping their members in a dense network of formal and informal organizations. Consequently, when Germany fell victim to the severe crises of the 1920s and 1930s, German Catholics and many German workers remained active adherents of their political parties. By contrast, middle-class German Protestants had traditionally aligned themselves with liberal parties such as the German People's Party (DVP) or the German Democratic Party (DDP), which lacked the pull that political churches like the Catholic Center Party exerted on the German Catholic constituency or that the Social Democratic Party exerted on the socialist labor movement. According to the political-confessionalism model, in times of crises German middle-class Protestants were more likely than German Catholics to abandon their parties.[33]

A Catchall Party of Protest

An increasing number of scholars have viewed the Nazi Party as a remarkably successful catchall party.[34] Though more a statement about the social heterogeneity of the Nazi movement than an explanation for the rise of Nazism, the characterization of Nazism as a protest choice (of more than the lower middle class) implies that as people became disaffected by the Weimar system and experienced increasing deprivation, they embraced Nazism. Childers, for example, thinks that the Nazi Party succeeded in transcending its pre-1930 lower-middle-class origins to become the party of the entire middle class, as well as of blue-collar workers in handicrafts and small-scale manufacturing, in both Protestant and Catholic regions.[35] Like Childers, Stachura notes that the Nazi Party becomes increasingly a general party of protest after 1928, with the electoral support of artisans, small businessmen, salaried white-collar employees, lower-level civil servants, small farmers, pensioners, and fixed-income groups; in 1932 the inclusion of upper-middle-class groups such as the propertied bourgeoisie and educated professionals and academicians followed.[36] Mühlberger and Madden insist that the makeup of the Nazi Party was more predominantly working class than proponents of the theory of lower-middle-class support believe. Mühlberger cites as evidence of working-class involvement his study of several local and regional Nazi Party organizations. Madden employs membership data from the official NSDAP master file to bolster his argument that the working class accounted for between one-fourth and one-third of Nazi Party members for every year from 1925 to 1933.[37]

Conceptual and Theoretical Shortcomings

All the treatments of the social origins of Nazism discussed so far stress the Nazi Party's ability to serve as a reservoir of hope for people with grievances. The theorists thus place a disproportionate emphasis on Nazi followers' *reactive* response, while ignoring the degree to which individuals' support for the Nazi Party stemmed from their desire to improve their material condition. Consider the conventional interpretation that Nazism appeared to many Germans a bulwark against communism. The Nazi Party's anticommunism alone could not have generated much popular support: anticommunism did not distinguish the Nazi Party from most other major political parties. Germans who feared communism could just as easily have adhered to the German Nationalist People's Party, the German People's Party, the German Democratic Party, or the Catholic Center Party.

Similarly, scholars have seen support for the Nazi Party largely as a protest vote: individuals chose the Nazis by default, when they felt that the more mainstream parties had failed them. The assumption is that people generally voted *against* mainstream parties rather than voting *for* the Nazis. But the sheer magnitude of Nazi popularity—the party gained nearly 38 percent of the popular vote in July 1932 (almost 14 million votes)— should suggest that the Nazi mandate cannot be attributed solely to the protest vote. Germans who desired to use their votes as a protest could also cast their ballots for the German Communist Party, the German National People's Party (after 1930), or the Wirtschaftspartei (Economic Party)—or they could simply abstain from voting. The Nazi Party undoubtedly did capture protest votes; however, we should acknowledge that millions of Germans might have voted for the Nazis because the party offered a program that included measures to improve their material situation.

Analysts have for the most part failed to distinguish between levels of commitment. It is often not clear whether certain theorists seek to explain why individuals voted for the Nazis or why they became members of the party. Failure to distinguish between voting and joining may be attributable to problems associated with the data, as I will discuss shortly. It would be unwise to assume that all those who voted for the Nazi Party joined the party: the Nazi Party received more than fourteen million votes in 1932 but had fewer than one million active members. As Kater[38] observes: "Scholars have often wrongly assumed that sociographic trends based on voting behavior may be readily used to make inferences about the characteristics of the party's membership structure." It would be equally erroneous to assume that people's motivations for joining the Nazi Party were the same as their motivations for voting for it. Indeed, the factors that led many people to vote for the Nazis before 1933 probably contributed to but do not fully explain the decision by some to become more committed and join the party.

In addition to the general conceptual and theoretical problems shared by all four of the prevalent explanations of the social origins of Nazism, three of the four approaches also contain specific theoretical stumbling blocks. Proponents of the thesis about Nazism's appeal to irrationalism, for example, have largely ignored the Nazi Party's appeal to people's material interests and have underestimated the degree to which Nazi Party support emanated from groups with strong institutional ties.[39] Certainly, emphasis on nonrational and irrational motivations seems justified in light of the result: the systematic genocidal extermination of the European Jews and Gypsies and the immeasurable destruction brought down on Germany and the rest of Europe as a result of Nazi Germany's initiation of World War II. We should not conclude, however, simply because the collective outcome of Nazism was irrational, that individual supporters behaved less than rationally. Rational behavior certainly includes selecting alternatives that appear relatively advantageous for achieving certain goals. Instead, the collective irrationality of Nazism may be a product of numerous rational calculations by individuals. This may seem illogical if we assume that individual motivations in aggregate explain a collective phenomenon or that the sum of individuals' intentions should equal the general outcome. But a collective phenomenon is also the product of multiple individual *interactions.*

Nazi Party membership files kept between 1925 and 1933 document that approximately 40 percent of all those who joined the Nazi Party before 1933 also left the party before 1933. If the irrationality thesis is correct, then we must assume that thousands of previously irrational people suddenly became rational by 1933. Few will find this a very compelling explanation for the eventual turnover in the party. A more plausible explanation may be that people calculated the costs of party membership as exceeding the benefits and decided to leave the party—behavior that is more rational than irrational.

Proponents of the claim that German Protestants were more likely than German Catholics to become Nazis have largely failed to explain the reasons for the overwhelming attachment to the Nazi Party among the Protestant population. Why did Protestants turn to the Nazi Party rather than to some other extremist movement? The close correlation between the two groups—Nazi supporters and Protestants—may point to a convergence between the content of the Nazi Party program and the material interests of German Protestants.

Finally, the characterization of the Nazi Party as a catchall party of protest is less a theory than a description of the group's makeup. It puts forth no explicit propositions regarding people's motivations for adhering to the Nazi Party. A viable theory of the social origins of Nazism should explain, for instance, why workers, independent farmers, merchants, artisans, and educated professionals turned to the Nazis rather than to other political parties and why the Nazi Party did not draw its adherents equally from all social groups.

Methodological and Empirical Shortcomings

Evidence can be marshaled to support each of the explanations of the pre-1933 Nazi constituency just discussed. That evidence includes autobiographies of prominent and not so prominent Nazis, case studies of towns and villages, Nazi propaganda, investigations of the social composition of various Nazi organizations, and sophisticated voting studies of Weimar-era elections (1919–1933).

Modern Studies of Weimar Voting Patterns

Social scientists have increasingly relied on aggregate-level analyses of Weimar electoral and census data (that is, analyses for territorial units such as counties or communities) to assess the empirical validity of competing explanations of the social origins of Nazism. The electoral studies of the Weimar Republic are for the most part based on statistical correlations between electoral votes at the community or county level and census data from 1925 and 1933.

Modern studies of Weimar voting patterns have undermined important claims of the irrationalist model of Nazism, such as that the unemployed easily fell prey to the Nazis. Falter finds a negative correlation between unemployment and the pro-Nazi vote but a positive correlation between unemployment and the Communist Party (KPD) vote.[40] Childers concurs with Falter, finding that rising unemployment in a town or city generally presaged a rising communist, not Nazi, vote.[41]

Studies of Weimar voting patterns have also challenged at the empirical level the notion that Nazi voters came primarily from the lower middle class. These critiques do not attempt to refute the claim that the Nazis drew votes heavily from the lower middle class but rather to show that the Nazis gained significant support from other social strata as well, and that lower-middle-class adherence to the NSDAP was furthermore not solely a result of the economic decline. Hamilton furnishes evidence that Protestant farmers, whether lower middle class or wealthy, voted solidly for the Nazis.[42] Falter and Zintl find that whereas Protestant lower-middle-class and blue-collar workers evidenced significant electoral support for the Nazi Party, the Catholic lower middle class displayed considerably less sympathy toward the party. Even within the lower middle class, the self-employed supported the Nazis substantially more than the salaried white-collar stratum did. Other critics see only an imperfect correlation between rising lower-middle-class economic grievances and Nazi electoral support. Tilton cites cases of villages, relatively untouched by the agricultural crisis, in which the Nazis received more than 70 percent of the vote in 1932. Falter offers empirical evidence that no statistical correlation (either positive or negative) can be shown between the level of agrarian debt and the electoral success of the Nazi Party in Catholic rural counties.[43]

Studies of Weimar-era voters have been kinder to the theory of a correlation between confessional affiliation and Nazi support. Although the evidence indicates that Nazi voters came largely from Germany's Protestant regions, the pattern was not uniform.[44] Zofka found, in his examination of the July 1932 Reichstag elections in the predominantly Catholic Bavarian county of Gunzburg, for example, that in five of the county's sixty-five communities the Nazi Party gained a majority of the votes. All told, the Nazi vote in Gunzburg county ranged from 10 to 90 percent.[45] Moreover, Pridham's study of Catholic Bavaria reveals that the town of Passau, with a Catholic population of 95 percent, gave the Nazi Party 31 percent of the vote in the 1930 Reichstag election; the national average was 18.3 percent.[46] Not all Catholic communities rejected the Nazis; conversely, not all Protestant voters jumped on the Nazi Party bandwagon. In separate studies of the rise of Nazism in the northern Protestant state of Lower Saxony, Noakes and Farquharson note considerable divergences in local Nazi electoral success rates in the 1930 Reichstag election.[47] Similarly, Faris finds in his examination of the 1929 state elections in Baden that in the predominantly Protestant village of Kurnbach the Nazis obtained 10 percent of the vote, whereas four kilometers away in the equally Protestant and rural Zausenhausen the Nazi Party gained 64 percent of the vote.[48] These authors take issue with the claim that differences in Nazi voting preferences were occasioned solely by religion.

Recent studies have also challenged the premise that the working class remained immune to Nazism. Hamilton, Childers, and Falter have clearly demonstrated a sizable working-class Nazi constituency between 1925 and 1933.[49]

All the explanations outlined thus far are based on statements about the behavior of members of certain groups (for example, that most Nazi voters came from the lower middle class). Yet these theories rely principally on aggregate-level voting data for empirical verification. Aggregate-level data analyses, however, can provide neither direct information on the political preferences among specific social strata or occupational groups nor knowledge of the specific characteristics of individual Nazi Party supporters. We cannot assume that because individuals in a particular set of geographical units with a particular pattern of social and demographic characteristics behaved in a particular way, all people in those geographical areas who possessed most or all of the same characteristics behaved in the same fashion. This is the so-called ecological fallacy. Simply stated, an association that holds true at one level may disappear at another, or the association may even be reversed.[50]

How have scholars tried to circumvent the problems with ecological inference about Nazi mobilization? By reducing the degree of heterogeneity of the population studied, both Hamilton and Falter have attempted to counteract the ecological fallacy. In the hope of establishing a relationship between class and the Nazi vote without resorting to correlations between voting patterns and census data on occupations, Hamilton examines the record of Nazi votes for a number of large German cities, focusing on districts whose residents belonged predominantly to one particular class. Falter has employed ecological regression analysis to make certain inferences about the social base of the Nazi electorate.[51] Hamilton's and Falter's studies have succeeded in compensating for the ecological fallacy; however, because their research still relies on aggregate-level data on voting behavior, we must bear in mind the limitations of our knowledge about the specific individual characteristics of Nazi voters. Nor can these studies of voting behavior offer a profile of the more committed Nazis, the ones who joined the party's organizations.

Modern Nazi Party Membership Studies

Although most empirical studies of the sociology of the Nazi movement have employed aggregate-level Weimar voting results, some recent studies have examined specific Nazi organizations. Because membership studies of Nazi Party organizations rely on individual-level data and thus avoid problems of ecological inference, they often offer a more adequate test of the theories of Nazism. Two superb recent studies of Nazi Party organizations are those of Fischer and Ziegler. Fischer has looked at various samples of the S.A. (Nazi storm troopers), while Ziegler has focused on the elite S.S. (Nazi Security Guards).[52] Given the relatively restrictive recruitment policies of the S.A. and the S.S., however, these two studies are unable to present a truly accurate profile of the popular Nazi constituency that studies of the Nazi electorate or Nazi Party membership reveal.

Examinations of the pre-1933 Nazi Party membership have the potential to offer excellent insight into the social composition of the Nazi constituency. Furthermore, a study of Nazi Party membership should provide a more accurate profile of the kinds of individuals who were most committed to the movement. By January 30, 1933, a total of 1,435,530 Nazi Party membership cards had been issued.[53] Though the party required a formal enrollment procedure and nominal dues, admittance was unquestionably less restrictive than it was in the S.A. or S.S. For example, neither the S.A. nor the S.S. allowed female members, but the Nazi Party was open to males and females eighteen years of age and older. The wealth of information about the social composition of the Nazi Party before 1933 stored in Nazi Party membership records has remained virtually untapped. Unlike Weimar voting returns for German counties and communities, which are readily available, national party membership data are exceptionally difficult to obtain and examine. The three principal sources of national Nazi Party membership data for the Weimar period are the 581 Abel autobiographies, the 1935 Nazi Party three-volume publication of the *Partei-Statistik*, and the NSDAP master file housed at the Berlin Document Center.[54]

The Abel autobiographies collected in 1934 are a valuable source of data on the life histories of early Nazis. Abel, a professor of sociology at Columbia University, offered small cash prizes to party members who had joined the Nazi Party before January 1, 1933, for the "most detailed and trustworthy accounts" of why they joined the Hitler movement. The autobiographies varied in length from one to eighty pages. In addition to information on each respondent's education, employment, membership in various associations, place of residence, marital status, and wartime service, these autobiographical essays contain important information on each member's first contacts with the party and principal reasons for joining the party.[55] Merkl has extensively examined these autobiographies to tap into the possible motivations of those who joined the party before 1933.[56] The Abel autobiographies are on file at the Hoover Institution at Stanford University. Though they offer a rich and insightful account of life histories of Nazi adherents, the autobiographies fall far short as a reliable source of

information on the Nazi Party's rank and file because the collection is too
small to furnish a statistically representative sample of membership, the respondents were self-selected, the party may have influenced the content of
the essays as well as handpicked those which were eventually submitted, to
promote a favorable picture, and the content of the autobiographies, rather
than presenting an accurate account for joining, may instead have reflected
respondents' desire to impress party officials.

The Partei-Statistik was amassed by the Nazi Party for internal purposes from the thirty-two German *Gaue* (Nazi administrative districts),
which roughly corresponded to the thirty-two Weimar electoral districts
or *Wahlkreise*.[57] It provides aggregate data on the occupation and age of
members who joined the party after 1925 and who were still members in
1935. One problem with the Partei-Statistik is that it reflects stable membership, rather than showing how the social structure of the party varied
at different intervals between 1925 and 1933. Because the turnover rate in
the Nazi Party between 1925 and 1933 was approximately 40 to 50 percent,
the Partei-Statistik offers a less than complete view of the party's social
composition.[58] To discover who the Nazis were before 1933 would require
a thorough examination of the *evolution* of the Nazi Party's social composition, and that is impossible to carry out using the Partei-Statistik. A
second reservation regarding the Partei-Statistik is its high level of aggre-
gation. The German *Gau* is too large and heterogeneous a base unit; the
internal variation in the key attributes of party joiners is thus tremendous.[59]

The primary and richest source of information on Nazi Party membership is the NSDAP *Zentralkartei,* or master file, containing approximately
7.2 million original and official individual German Nazi Party membership
cards,[60] dating from the reconstitution of the party in February 1925 to
its demise in May 1945. The cards are arranged alphabetically. The master
file is thought to be nearly 90 percent complete.[61] Some cards are believed
to have been destroyed by Nazi Party officials before being captured by
the U.S. military. The master file, which is housed at the Berlin Document Center (BDC) in Germany, actually comprises two separate files.
The larger is the *Ortskartei;* the *Reichskartei,* from which more cards are
missing, is smaller. They were intended to duplicate one another and were
cross-referenced. The Ortskartei was originally arranged alphabetically by
Gau and then within each Gau alphabetically by county, local group, and
member's last name. The Reichskartei was arranged alphabetically by last
name regardless of membership location. When these files were captured

by the U.S. military in Munich in 1945 they were moved to Berlin, where the Ortskartei files were rearranged alphabetically by last name, regardless of geographical designation.[62]

In contrast to the Partei-Statistik, the master file contains the membership records of all Nazis, no matter whether they left the party before 1935 or remained members. Moreover, each membership record includes the individual's first and last names, party number, birthplace, birth date, marital status, occupation, residence at time of joining (and subsequent residences), local membership affiliation, Gau affiliation, dates and location of joining, exiting, and rejoining, and remarks on the member by party leaders. (Gender of members can also be deduced from first names.) As a source of information on the social origins of the Nazi Party members, the master file is incomparable.[63] Why then has this invaluable source of information on the Nazi Party gone relatively unused? The underutilization of the NSDAP master file can be attributed to (1) the unsuitability of the Berlin Document Center for large-scale research endeavors, (2) the failure to microfilm the contents or make them computer accessible, (3) the sheer magnitude of the two files, (4) the difficulty in deciphering the contents of pre-1933 cards, which were frequently entered by hand and in old German script, and (5) the massive effort required to draw a representative sample, given that the cards have been rearranged alphabetically by member's last name and last names in pre-World War II Germany were strongly associated with particular geographical locations. (To control for this phenomenon, all letters of the alphabet must be sampled in order to obtain a representative sampling for all of Germany.)

Until recently, there have been two studies of the NSDAP master file for Germany covering the years 1925 to 1933.[64] Although both the Kater and Madden studies of Nazi Party membership have contributed to our understanding of the social composition of the Nazi Party, they both contain shortcomings that may render their findings problematic for the pre-1933 Nazi Party.[65] Kater's study relies on a sample of roughly 18,000 Nazi Party members who joined the party between 1925 and 1945. Because nine-tenths of all Nazi Party members joined only after Hitler came to power in 1933 and because Kater drew a strictly proportional sample of the Nazi Party membership records, his sample includes fewer than two thousand cases for the period of 1930 to 1932, and fewer than five hundred cases for the early years, 1925 to 1929. Furthermore, Kater did not record the information concerning the day and month of joining and whether and when joiners left and rejoined the party before 1933. This information is necessary to analyze how important political events or Nazi Party policies shaped membership decisions and whether key constituencies left the party at certain times in disproportionate numbers.[66]

Like Kater, Madden drew a sample of Nazi Party membership from the NSDAP master file. Unlike Kater, however, who sampled membership cards from across the entire German alphabet, Madden sampled single letters for the period from 1925 to 1930. Given the pronounced regional clustering of names in Germany, his sampling method probably biased his sample with regard to region, confession, occupation, date of entry, and so on.[67] Furthermore, he misspecified certain occupations and underrepresented particular social categories like skilled labor.[68]

Aware of the significance of the NSDAP master file for a study of the Nazi Party as well as of the lacunae in earlier examinations of the file, J. W. Falter and I in 1989 jointly organized and supervised the largest and most systematic collection of Nazi Party membership data from both the Ortskartei and the Reichskartei. Our total sample of pre-1933 members consists of 42,004 observations.[69] Our sample contains nearly three thousand cases for each of the early years (and for 1933) and roughly eight thousand cases for each of the years 1930 to 1932.

To understand what kinds of individuals became Nazis and why they joined the party, it is important to know in what kinds of social milieux joiners resided. Regrettably, the membership cards contain no information on members' religion, formal education (except if joiners belonged to certain professions requiring academic training or had doctorates), social class or status, or union membership. For example, an individual Reichskartei record cannot tell us if the member resided in a small village or a large city, in a Catholic or Protestant region of Germany, in a livestock-raising or grain-growing district, or in an area of high or low unemployment. These factors are all important because they can provide the context in which individuals made their decisions about joining the Nazi Party, and context is generally a force in shaping political choices. During a three-year effort, however, we were able to code occupations according to several schemes of categorization.[70] We combined the membership data according to place of residence and birthplace with two sets of community- and county-level Weimar election data compiled earlier by Falter.[71] I am thus able to work with hundreds of contextual variables, such as political traditions, unemployment figures, city size, region, geographical location, and confessional, occupational, and economic structure of locality.[72]

The Brustein-Falter sample of Nazi Party members, combined with

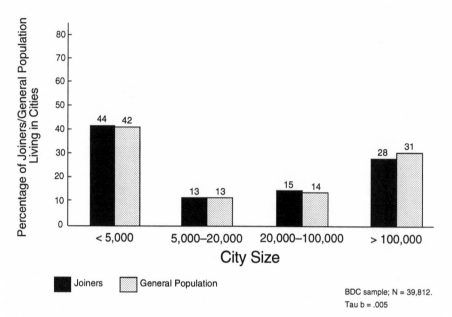

1.1   Nazi Party Joiners Living in Cities, 1925–1932

the contextual data in the Weimar Republic County Data Collection (WRCDC) and the Weimar Community Data Set (WCDS) constitute the richest source of information to date for testing competing explanations of who became Nazis.

Figures 1.1 through 1.4 present results of tests of the four views on the sociology of Nazism discussed earlier—those emphasizing the party's appeals to irrationalism, to lower-middle-class interests, to confessionalism, and to a cross-class protest sentiment. These test results call into question the empirical validity of key tenets of the corresponding explanations. For example, an important proposition of the irrationalism thesis is that atomized, uprooted Nazi Party joiners must have come largely from cities. Our test results do not support this premise. Figure 1.1 provides a breakdown by size of city of residence for Nazi Party joiners between 1925 and 1932. The findings show that only 28 percent of Nazi Party joiners came from

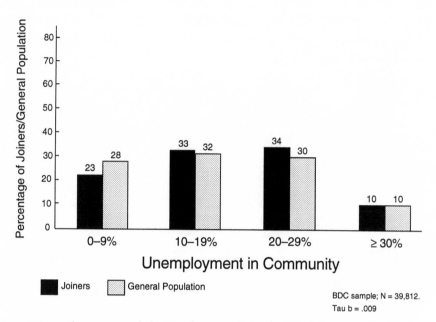

1.2 Unemployment and the Tendency to Join the Nazi Party, 1925–1932

large urban agglomerations (population over 100,000). By contrast, 43 percent of Nazi Party joiners resided in predominantly rural areas (population less than 5,000).[73] Furthermore, compared with the general population, party joiners were underrepresented in cities but slightly overrepresented in rural areas.

An additional hypothesis of the explanation based on joiners' irrationalism is that the unemployed were overrepresented among Nazi Party joiners. The membership cards contain no information on whether a joiner is unemployed (only on his or her occupation). The WRCDC and the WCDS contain contextual evidence on unemployment levels, however. Figure 1.2 presents a breakdown of German communities between 1925 and 1932 by percentage of unemployment with the corresponding proportion of Nazi Party joiners. The data in figure 1.2 do not provide convincing confirmation that the unemployed were overrepresented among Nazi

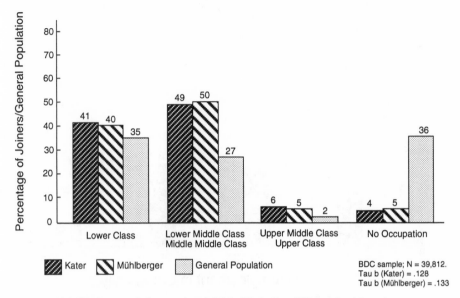

BDC sample; N = 39,812.
Tau b (Kater) = .128
Tau b (Mühlberger) = .133

Note: If the "no occupation" category is excluded, the following Kater-Mühlberger Population comparisons obtain: Lower Class, 43%–42%–55%; Lower Middle Class/Middle Middle Class, 51%–53%–42%; Upper Middle Class/Upper Class 6%–5%–3%.

1.3   Nazi Party Joiners and Class, Using Kater and Mühlberger Schemes, 1925–1932

Party joiners. In the communities with the highest level of unemployment (greater than or equal to 30 percent) the percentage of unemployed Nazi Party joiners was equal to the percentage of unemployed in the general population. Only in the two middle categories (those for communities with unemployment rates between 10 and 19 percent and with unemployment rates between 20 and 29 percent) were Nazi Party joiners overrepresented.

The principal claim of the second explanation of Nazism we considered is that joiners came primarily from the lower middle class. The data in figure 1.3 clearly show, however, that this was not the case. Employing both the Kater and the Mühlberger schemes of classification by social class for Nazi Party joiners and the general population between 1925 and 1932, in figure 1.3 we see that lower-class joiners accounted for 42 percent of joiners overall according to Kater's classification scheme, or 40 percent according to Mühlberger's. The lower middle class combined with the middle middle

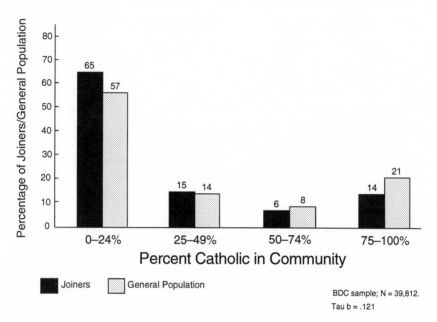

1.4 Nazi Party Joiners According to Confessional Context, 1925–1932

class constituted 49 percent (according to Kater's scheme) and 50 percent (according to Mühlberger's scheme). The upper middle class combined with the upper class comprised 5 or 6 percent of Nazi Party joiners; 4 or 5 percent of the joiners reported no occupation. These results show a strong overrepresentation of each class.[74] That the German lower class made up 40 or 42 percent of Nazi Party joiners between 1925 and 1932 challenges any claim that Nazi Party joiners came primarily from the lower middle class.

The theory that German support for the Nazis can be charted along confessional lines has as its central proposition that people's immersion in the Catholic milieu or the socialist working-class milieu should have immunized them against National Socialism. Moreover, if that theory holds true, politically "unchurched" middle-class Germans should have moved toward the far right (Nazi Party). In figure 1.4 German communities are broken down according to their predominant religious confession. The results of figure 1.4 generally confirm that Nazi Party joiners were underrepresented in predominantly Catholic communities. The differences are not as convincing, however, as proponents of the theory of confessionalism would claim, given that party joiners are only slightly overrepresented in communities with the fewest Catholics.[75]

The findings generally confirm that the Nazi Party between 1925 and 1932 served as a catchall party for the dissatisfied. But this description offers no theoretical explanation for the sociology of Nazism. The literature that emphasizes that the Nazi Party attracted its members from diverse classes—the working class, old middle class, and new middle class—fails to designate *what kinds* of workers, farmers, and white-collar employees were most likely to join the Nazi Party and, most important, *why* these groups, more than other groups, joined the Nazi Party. To answer these questions, I will present and test an explanation of Nazi affiliation that emphasizes its appeal to people's self-interest.

An Account of Interest-Based Nazi Affiliation

Why should we think that people living in Germany during the period between 1925 and 1933 would have been thinking about mass destruction or the invasion of Poland? Why should we think that the reasons people had for joining the Nazi Party would be any different from their reasons for joining any other party or organization?

Let's try for a moment to treat the rise of this party as we would the rise of any party. My principal hypothesis is that individuals who joined the Nazi Party calculated that the benefits of joining would exceed the costs. Calculations about the net benefits of joining the Nazi Party before 1933 were largely shaped by individual self-interest. To account for variations in Nazi Party support, I will employ a general theory of individual choice. "Joining party x" and "not joining party x" may be treated as alternative courses of action between which individuals must make a choice.[76]

According to this new approach, individuals' decision to join a party, in this case the Nazi Party between 1925 and 1933, is a two-stage process. In the initial stage people select the political party that they perceive will provide them with the greatest benefits. If a party is to attract members, it must confront people's natural desire to get a free ride—that is, to enjoy the benefits the party offers without contributing to the production of those benefits.[77] In the second stage of decision making, individuals whose interests are compatible with a party's program will join, but only if they think that doing so will give them access to "goods" or rewards if the party comes to power, *or* if they perceive the costs or disincentives of joining to be no greater than the costs of voting for the party.[78]

Compatibility of Interests and the Decision to Join a Political Party

Joiners' political preferences reflect their interests; they determine those interests by calculating the benefits and costs associated with supporting party A over party B. If individuals' self-interests more nearly correspond to the political programs of party A than to the programs of party B, we should expect to see those individuals joining party A.[79] In my application, perceived utility takes the form of material or economic preferences. In this approach to interest-based action, actors' preferences are inferred from their requisites for economic survival. Thus, laborers prefer wage increases to policies stabilizing wholesale grain prices; landowners prefer market price increases to policies establishing collective ownership. In general, the degree of preference for an outcome corresponds to the magnitude of the expected benefits.

This explanation further posits that individuals' material preferences are largely shaped by structures (for example, particular jobs or living conditions) that help specify the interests as well as constrain them. In the face of these constraints, individuals should, theoretically, act rationally; that is, they should employ the most efficient means to reach their goals.

Nevertheless, people's choice of political party may not perfectly correspond to their self-interests in every situation. Friedman and Hechter observe that individuals with similar preferences may behave differently.[80] Take the case of citizens who are uninformed about the particular programs of competing parties: they select the party whose program they think best reflects their interests, whereas in reality another party's program does. Or people may join a particular party on the basis of its publicly advocated positions, but its actual positions may vary from those considerably.

Because people's perceptions of costs and benefits are shaped by the amount and kinds of information they receive, their choice of political party programs may appear to deviate from their actual interests. In some cases citizens possess adequate information about the programs of rival political parties and still join a party seemingly at variance with their self-interest. In late nineteenth-century rural Brittany, for example, many poor peasants voted for the conservatives rather than for the center-left parties —parties that campaigned to improve the poor peasants' economic and social livelihood by instituting land redistribution, progressive taxation, and wage reforms.[81] One should not assume automatically that these poor French peasants were unaware of the positions of the rival political parties. The peasants may have realized that because of their dependence on others, their long-term and short-term interests differed. If dependent individuals act on their long-term interests, they may jeopardize their present livelihood. The lack of a truly secret balloting process before 1913 in France enabled the conservative elites to effectively threaten tenants, sharecroppers, and agricultural laborers with eviction or loss of employment if they did not cast their votes for the conservative party.[82] Consequently, the peasants may have perceived their interests as being similar to those of the people on whom they depended: without independence, they could not follow their *actual* self-interest. It should be emphasized that in voting, however, this dependency and deflected self-interest are conditional; an effective threat to withdraw the dependent persons' access to resources if they cast the wrong vote rests on the providers' ability to monitor the act of voting effectively. Without that power, resource providers are unable to enforce voting compliance.

In other situations citizens find that the parties' programs differ only negligibly regarding issues of interest to them, the voters. We should not forget that leaders of political parties also behave according to rational and self-interested motives and thus, when possible, move to the positions that voters demand. For example, what if party A and party B equally advocated tax reduction? Let's assume for the sake of argument that to the voters no other issue in this particular election mattered significantly. On what grounds might rational citizens select between party A and party B? In this model, many citizens are likely to consider which of the two parties appears to them to be more credible on the tax issue and which party has the greatest likelihood of winning the election. Citizens are unlikely to join a party that they estimate lacks an active commitment to the issue. Rational individuals may review each party's previous voting record on taxes or they may ask themselves which of the two parties has contributed resources to the efforts to reduce taxes. The party that appears to citizens to expend more of its resources for the cause should be the more likely recipient of their support.

Moreover, if two parties differ only negligibly regarding issues of interest to voters, rational citizens are unlikely to join the political party with little chance of coming to power.[83] If they perceive party A's probability of success as greater than party B's, they should choose party A over party B.[84] One way a political party can enhance perception of its commitment to activism while at the same time augmenting the perception of its probable success is to focus on local goals and goods with immediate payoffs. Such a strategy can serve to shorten the time that elapses before benefits are received.[85]

In summary, although people will generally join the political parties that they perceive to respond most closely to their interests, political choices may not in every situation perfectly correspond to actual self-interest because they are also affected by access to information on a candidate's or party's positions, the extent of individuals' dependency on others for resources, the candidate's or party's probability of success, and the extent of a party's or candidate's commitment.

Selective Incentives and Disincentives: Joining a Political Party

Compatibility between individuals' interests and preferences and a party's programs is a necessary condition for joining the Nazi Party but not a sufficient one. Compatibility of interests was largely responsible for millions of German votes for the Nazi Party. Although roughly 14 million Germans voted for the Nazi Party in July 1932, however, only 1.4 million Germans had joined the Nazi Party by January 30, 1933. Membership in the Nazi Party clearly entailed greater costs than did vote-casting. We can safely assume that many Nazi adherents decided against active membership because they believed that the personal costs were too high and the personal benefits too few. It is easy to understand why, all else being equal, more people support a party with votes than with membership. If compatibility of interests or resolution of grievances were the sole condition for joining a party, rational individuals should choose to remain free riders. From my theoretical perspective, joining and working for a political party make little sense to a citizen who can receive the identical benefits merely by casting a vote. In the case of the Nazi Party, the free rider may have hoped to benefit from the party's program without having to engage in any actions that were potentially more costly, time consuming, or sanctionable than voting. Riding free would have presented obvious problems for the party: if all supporters decided to ride free—that is, to vote for but not join and work for the party, then the party would have collapsed.

We know that if party supporters could get benefits without joining and yet if not all supporters took such a free ride, then we should find that there were additional incentives and/or a reduction in disincentives for active membership. Incentives increase the utility of participation in supporters' eyes; disincentives lower the utility to them of participation.

Selective incentives are goods that an organization has the capacity to supply to or withhold from individual members selectively.[86] These may include jobs, property, information, affirmation of behavior, friendship, and social activities.[87] If individuals view membership in a particular party as their sole means to maintain or gain access to selective incentives, they will be less reluctant to express their support through joining.[88] Also, if individuals require the resources that selective incentives provide, and if the costs of obtaining them elsewhere are high, individuals will depend on the supplier. Hence, if the supplier of valued resources is a political party, individuals are likely to join the party if membership ensures uninterrupted access to the resources. Individuals' dependence on the party for resources should correlate strongly with the party's monopolistic control of the resources. If alternative parties or institutions possess valued resources and have the capacity to distribute them, individuals' dependence on any single group to provide them is reduced. By contrast, if the party is the sole provider of valued resources, it should be in a stronger position to demand participation by making it a condition for access to the resources.[89]

Selective incentives to join a party can originate from outside the party. Preexisting networks can serve as a major source of incentives. Individuals are unlikely to join a party in the absence of social support—that is, without the participation of members of their social networks. Social networks may include families, friends, co-workers, and resource providers. They are a major source of solidarity and of influence on our actions.[90] Social networks affect participation by creating social pressures that may act as selective incentives for participation or disincentives for nonparticipation. If groups provide relatively strong positive incentives for participation to their members, participation should be high, whereas if groups impose relatively high costs on participation, we should expect to find low member participation.[91] Olson observes that people desire companionship and the esteem of their colleagues and fear public ostracism. These are powerful incentives that a group can use to motivate individuals to participate in concerted action. But the motivation exists only if the social networks are tightly knit and capable of exerting social pressure on their members.[92]

Joining the Nazi Party brought with it both a high personal risk of public ostracism and high costs in expenditure of time. Rational individuals sought to divide among many people such risks and obligations stemming from party membership. Therefore, people were likely to make their own participation conditional on the behavior of others. Rational individuals may have decided to ride free unless they could be confident that members of their networks were also likely to join. This tactic is akin to what Taylor and Hardin refer to as conditional cooperation or to what Sen and Lindenberg call assurance games: each individual is willing to participate provided that others do likewise.[93] Members of a community have the capacity to monitor the behavior of other community participants and sanction it socially over extended periods.[94] Such monitoring is effective because people's livelihood and social life depend on maintaining good relations with other members of the community.

While much of the current literature on social networks appears to emphasize social relationships based on strong horizontal interpersonal ties, it should be noted that tightly knit social networks can also emerge from social arrangements based on vertical interpersonal ties.[95] Clientelistic systems, for instance, have the capability to offer positive incentives to clients who support parties of patrons and disincentives to clients who support alternative political parties.

If a party's capacity to allocate selective incentives (private goods) is sufficient to promote membership, is there any reason to consider the party's ability to redress people's grievances (a collective good), as I did earlier? According to Tullock, incentive of public goods is of relatively little importance in the decision to participate in a revolution.[96] But if this were true, individuals' motivations for joining the party would have little to do with the political issues at stake. In the case of Nazi Party membership, we would expect to find socialists and communists joining the Nazis if the Nazi organizers simply provided beer and sausage to its members.[97] Yet we know that the socialists and communists were not attracted to the Nazi Party initially, because its program did not address their particular constellation of grievances.

Persons who are committed to a particular party program and thus likely to vote for the party may not join it unless the disincentives associated with membership are lowered. Rational individuals would be unlikely to risk involvement if they calculated that participation might result in loss of employment, imprisonment, physical harm, or loss of friendship. Additionally, people may be reluctant to participate if they calculate that others would be opposed to it or unlikely to involve themselves. Many fear that participation would come at the cost of high risk to their liveli-hood. Disincentives to joining an extremist political party frequently take the form of (actual or anticipated) official punishment, threats or punish-ments from opposition movements, costs in time, energy, and money, and group reprisals for participation.[98]

In brief, a necessary initial condition for joining a high-risk party like the Nazi Party is the belief that the party offers solutions to people's griev-ances. Individuals are more likely to join a political party that promises to improve their situation than one that supports the welfare of others. Re-dressing individuals' grievances cannot, by itself, constitute the basis for joining a party, however, given that party membership involves greater costs to individuals than voting. Individuals who are predisposed to vote for a party may calculate that it is in their best interests to ride free rather than join. Thus, to explain membership in high-risk political movements, we must locate factors that reduce the tendency to catch a free ride. This necessity has led me to consider the role played by selective incentives and disincentives and to propose that parties can lower the likelihood of free rides and encourage joining by providing positive incentives to prospective joiners and eliminating disincentives for prospective joiners.

No theory applies universally, however. For my purposes, the model of interest-based adherence is assumed to apply under certain "scope condi-tions." These are that actors (1) are presented with a choice between two or more alternative courses of action; (2) associate a unique set of outcomes with each alternative action; (3) assign a utility to each outcome; and (4) as-sign a probability to the occurrence of each outcome that is conditional on the course of action chosen.

In the following chapters I will attempt to demonstrate the appropri-ateness of the interest-based model for the rise of the Nazi Party by ex-plaining how the Nazi Party became the logical choice for millions of Ger-mans. In Chapters 2–4 I shall survey the political programs of the principal Weimar parties and the material interests of the major social classes in Ger-many between 1925 and 1933. The reader will discover that a large part of the Nazi Party's success at attracting skilled blue-collar workers, livestock farmers, and independent artisans and the party's failure to capture the allegiance of many semi- and unskilled laborers, female white-collar ser-vice employees, and grain-growing farmers can be attributed to the content of the Nazi Party's economic programs and the degree to which those eco-nomic programs corresponded to the material interests of the groups mentioned. As economic conditions deteriorated in Germany after 1925, many Germans would begin to look favorably at the Nazi Party economic orientation that represented for Germany a third path between Marxist centralized state planning and laissez-faire capitalism—an orientation that integrated elements of nationalist-etatist thinking and Keynesian economics.

2 Weimar Political Parties

For a political party to gain a sizable constituency in Weimar Germany it would have had to make substantial inroads into Germany's two principal classes, the middle and working classes. The Nazi Party did just that; it fashioned programs that millions of middle- and working-class Germans perceived could substantially improve their material situation. Yet it would be inaccurate to claim that all segments of these two classes saw the Nazi Party's programs in a favorable light, for many middle- and working-class Germans believed that other Weimar political parties better represented their material interests. Chapters 2 through 4 present an overview of the material interests of the middle and working classes in Germany and the particular political programs that the competing Weimar parties fashioned to address these interests. My decision to focus exclusively on the interests of the middle class and working class is warranted for at least two important reasons. First, the middle class and the working class together made up more than 90 percent of both the active population in Germany and the Nazi Party membership during the Weimar era. Second, in their political discourse, leaders of the major Weimar political parties customarily spoke to Germans as members of social classes.

The German middle class included both old and new middle classes. The old middle class comprised largely farmers, independent artisans, self-employed professionals, and merchants engaged in what might be broadly defined as "preindustrial" occupations. The new middle class consisted of salaried (white-collar and civil service) employees involved generally in clerical or service work. Germany's largest class was the working class, the blue-collar labor force engaged in manual tasks.

A note of caution: the decision to employ class categories to study the Nazi Party is largely heuristic; one must not assume that class location (relationship to property) is the only or even chief determinant of political choices. An explanation of political behavior strictly along class lines fails to capture the significant intraclass differences and interclass commonalities in people's interests and political behavior. Although both independent German grape growers and livestock farmers owned property, for example, these groups frequently held divergent views on important issues such as free trade and tariffs. Similarly, blue-collar workers who held jobs in export-oriented industries did not necessarily have the same political interests as their counterparts who held jobs in domestic-oriented industries. Indeed, many livestock farmers and domestic-sector industrial workers opposed free trade and supported political parties that opposed it, whereas many wine-producing farmers and export-sector industrial workers favored free trade and supported political parties advocating that position. I would propose that market location plays as important a role in shaping political choices as does social class.

Following the brief description of the principal Weimar political parties and their general ideological orientations in Chapter 2, I provide a more in-depth examination of the material (economic) interests of Germany's middle classes and working class and a look at the specific class programs of the major Weimar political parties in Chapters 3 and 4.

The political landscape of Weimar Germany was dotted with political parties. I choose to examine the parties that maintained a political presence throughout the Weimar era and that appealed to a national rather than a local or regional constituency. The parties examined are the German Nationalist People's Party (DNVP), the German People's Party (DVP), the German Democratic Party (DDP), the Catholic Center Party, the Social Democratic Party of Germany (SPD), the German Communist Party (KPD), and the National Socialist German Workers' Party (NSDAP).[1] In this chapter I present an overall view of the programmatic orientations of each of these major Weimar political parties.

The German Nationalist People's Party

The DNVP entered the Weimar period as an assembly of pre–World War I conservative remnants, including the German Conservative Party, the Free Conservative Party, the Völkische (anti-Semitic) movement, the Christian Social movement, the Pan-German Association (Alldeutscher Verband), and some pre-war right-leaning National Liberals. (See Appendix C.) With the collapse of the empire, the DNVP at first pursued a more liberal program endorsing a parliamentary form of government, civil liberties, land reforms, expansion of welfare programs, and unionization. By 1920, in light of the perceived Marxist threat, more conservative elements of the party won out and called for a return to authoritarian monarchy under the Hohenzollerns, opposition to a democratic or republican form of government, rejection of land reforms, resistance to Marxism and planned economy, and advocacy of a strong Prussia within the new German state.[2] Not all the party's remnants agreed on the program, however. The Christian Social movement, for instance, whose strength lay in the west and south, opposed any return of the monarchy. Nevertheless, the DNVP did exceptionally well in the June 1920 Reichstag election, winning 71 out of 459 seats.

The DNVP leadership was strongly influenced by both big agriculture and heavy industry. Yet surprisingly, the party managed in the early years of Weimar to construct a mass constituency comprising small farmers, shopkeepers, artisans, white-collar employees, and workers in cottage industries, through its ties with numerous occupational organizations and pressure groups, such as the Agrarian League and the Deutschnationaler Handlungsgehilfenverband (DHV).[3]

The year 1920 also marked a turning point in the DNVP's strategy to achieve power. The party had endorsed the failed Kapp putsch in the spring of 1920 to seize power in the Reich and Prussia. In light of the failed coup, the party leadership abandoned the extraparliamentary road to power and turned to mobilizing mass support at the ballot box. Campaigning on a platform of subsidies for agriculture and small business, demands for a return to the principles of "Christian and patriotic education," and an undivided and undiminished Prussia and stressing antidemocratic, anti-Semitic, anti-Catholic themes, the DNVP gained wide popular support in the February 1921 Prussian Landtag election.[4]

For the DNVP the early 1920s brought constant internal bickering among the party's rival constituencies. By 1922 the moderates in the party had gained the upper hand and kicked out the radical anti-Semitic groups advocating the violent overthrow of the government.[5] The position of the moderates within the DNVP was strengthened considerably between 1924 and 1925 when the party became the largest faction in the Reichstag and Hindenburg was elected president of the republic.

Between 1924 and 1928 the DNVP held ministerial positions—in the Luther cabinet in 1925 and in the government headed by Marx in 1927-1928. Internally the DNVP continued to be split between a moderate pragmatic wing led by Kuno Westarp, which favored government involvement, and an ideological Pan-German nationalist wing led by Alfred Hugenberg, which opposed the Weimar Republic. The lack of philosophical coherence within the DNVP displayed itself in the party's inability to muster voting compliance even from its parliamentary deputies, as in the Reichstag vote on the Dawes Plan.[6] The party's internal strife boiled over in 1928 after the DNVP lost nearly two million votes, or one-third of its voters, in the May election. Both the moderates and the Pan-German nationalists within the party blamed the other group for the party's poor electoral showing. The DNVP withdrew from government, citing its opposition to a Social Democratic chancellorship and to Weimar foreign policy.[7] The Pan-German nationalists under the leadership of Hugenberg saw the party's misfortune as resulting from its participation in republican governments. In July 1928 the leader of the moderate wing, Westarp, resigned. The Pan-German nationalists gained the upper hand, and with Hugenberg's ascension to the party's leadership, the DNVP steered a course of antiparliamentarianism. Under Hugenberg's leadership, the DNVP decided to work only with parties sharing anti-Marxist and anti-free trade positions. Hugenberg favored strong protection of agriculture through total opposition to "fulfillment politics" and reparations payments. Hugenberg's policies forced out many of the party's more moderate elements. In the first fifteen months of Hugenberg's leadership the party lost forty-three of seventy-eight Reichstag deputies. The Christian Social movement left the party to form a new party and the Christian National Peasants' and Rural People's Party campaigned under the name of the Deutsches Landvolk in the 1930 Reichstag elections.[8]

Under Hugenberg's leadership the DNVP formed the National Opposition in 1929 to attack Chancellor Müller's Grand Coalition. Hugenberg enlisted support from leaders of the Stahlhelm, the large nationalist ex-servicemen's organization; Dr. Schacht, the president of the central bank; and Hitler. The National Opposition organized a national campaign against the Young Plan (a redrafting of Germany's reparation payments). The National Opposition drafted a bill "against the enslavement of the German People," which repudiated any payments to foreign powers on the basis of the Versailles treaty.[9] Hugenberg's campaign reached a national audience in large part as a consequence of his control of the Scherl publishing house.[10] Hugenberg took pride in his attempts to rid the DNVP of moderates. In April 1930 he announced that no political leader could be to the right of him.[11] The results of the 1930 Reichstag elections did not reverse the popular decline of the DNVP.[12] Heinrich Brüning's (Catholic Center Party) appointment as chancellor by Hindenburg in 1930 was initially greeted favorably by the DNVP, because the party saw it as a step toward the elimination of the parliamentary system. The two wings of the party became irreconcilably split in July 1930, however, over the moderates' charge that Hugenberg aspired to become a dictator and over the moderates' support of the implementation of Article 48 giving the president authority to enact laws without Reichstag consent.[13] The party's Pan-German nationalist wing called for the creation of a new German Conservative Party (Konservative Volkspartei)—a party free of any leftist tendency and supportive of a new Germany that would evince a will to be strong and would transcend class divisions.[14]

The German People's Party

The Liberal parties in pre-1918 Germany were a heterogeneous group comprising libertarians, progressives, and conservatives. With the founding of the Weimar Republic, the liberals and progressives split off from the National Liberal Party to form the German Democratic Party, while the conservatives of the former National Liberal Party established the German People's Party.[15] Unlike the DDP, the DVP joined with the DNVP in opposition to the 1918 revolution and the establishment of a parliamentary democratic system of government. In its early years the DVP pursued a policy of estrangement from the republic, rallying support from those who favored a restoration of the monarchy and an end to socialist influence over the government. Within the Reichstag in 1919 the DVP joined the DNVP in opposition to the terms of the armistice and the Versailles treaty. The 1920 Reichstag election, which was a high-water mark for conservative parties in Germany, saw the DVP winning 65 out of 459 seats. Support for the DVP came from the Protestant middle class and especially from high-level civil servants, large landowners, and major industrialists.[16]

The Kapp putsch marked a real watershed in the DVP's evolution. The party abandoned its right-wing antirepublican stance and began to pursue a more moderate political policy. Under Stresemann's leadership the DVP turned its back on a possible alliance with the DNVP and decided to enter Weimar government, no longer refusing to participate in governance with the Social Democrats.[17] At least until 1929 the DVP continued to support the Weimar Constitution.[18]

Throughout the 1920s the DVP's political platform showed unrestrained support for classic laissez-faire free enterprise and German nationalism. Party leaders placed considerable importance on expanding Germany's international trade opportunities, arguing that Germany had to trade with other nations to get what it could not produce on its own.[19] Thus, it comes as no surprise that the party was perceived as the party of Germany's industrial bourgeoisie, especially the industrialists engaged in competitive export-oriented high-technology industries that produced chemicals and electrical equipment, for example. Interestingly, both the DVP and the DNVP vied for support from Germany's large industrialists. The DNVP's economic philosophy, which included criticism of nineteenth-century liberal economic theory, enabled the party to do better among German industrialists who favored protection of the domestic market, whereas the DVP's advocacy of free trade helped that party gain adherents among industrialists who favored expanding foreign trade.[20]

Though Gustav Stresemann is best known for his adroit guidance of German foreign policy during the late 1920s, he also, in his capacity as DVP's party chairman, steered the DVP along a moderate path within German politics. The DVP pursued positions that were consistent with its liberal philosophy on economics and social issues. For instance, the DVP in 1926 joined the other middle-class parties in opposing the Left's attempt to pass a referendum favoring the appropriation of the properties of the former German ruling houses. The DVP saw the measure as interference with the right of private property.[21] Many of the positions that the DVP took derived directly from its roots in the pre-1918 German liberal movement. Foremost among the positions it advocated were the clear separation of church and state and protection of such individual freedoms as speech and religious practice.[22]

Under Stresemann's moderate leadership the DVP tried earnestly to build a popular mass constituency. Stresemann believed that the party's future lay in an equilibrium between big business and Germany's white-collar working force. To this end he worked closely with the four million-strong National Association of Commercial Employees (DHV) union to push for social and liberal welfare programs in 1928 and 1929.[23] Stresemann supposed that by curbing the influence of big business in the DVP he could attract large segments of the white-collar class and working class to the party. Stresemann's death in October of 1929, however, seriously dampened the party's prospects of expanding its influence among the middle and lower classes. By the beginning of 1930 the DVP began to fall apart. A large part of the responsibility for the party's downfall belonged to the new party leader, Ernst Scholz, who steered the party toward the interests of big business and heavy industry. Scholz and his allies endeavored to defeat organized labor.[24] The industrial wing aimed to purge the party of its more moderate elements and to highlight the party's anti-Marxist positions. The party was additionally convulsed by a struggle between hard-liners, who opposed participation in Brüning's government, and moderates, who favored it. Thanks to Scholz, the party was also instrumental in bringing down the Grand Coalition headed by Müller, the Social Democratic chancellor, in early 1930.[25] After the DVP's poor electoral performance in the 1930 Reichstag elections, Scholz's stewardship ended. Eduard Dingeldey became party head in November 1930. Dingeldey, a moderate, had hoped to guide the party back toward the place it had occupied under Stresemann but could not diminish the dominance of the industrial wing within the party. Under both Scholz and Dingeldey the DVP supported the Brüning government until mid-1931, when the party leaders sensed that their support for Brüning's austerity measures was hurting the party among the middle class and that big business interests had lost faith in Brüning's policies to revive the German economy.[26]

By 1932 the DVP's electoral fortunes had plummeted. The number of elected Reichstag deputies, which had stood at thirty in 1930, fell to eleven after the November 1932 Reichstag election. The DVP based its 1932 electoral campaigns largely on defense of the economic order against socialistic tendencies and rejection of the Weimar parliamentary system. The leadership sought to shore up the party by presenting joint electoral lists with the DNVP. The DVP's embrace of a more politically conservative agenda and its flirtation with the DNVP led to an exodus of many moderates from the party and the collapse of its remaining links with the white-collar labor movement.[27]

The German Democratic Party

The German Democratic Party (DDP) emerged after the disintegration of the pre-1919 National Liberal Party. The DDP grew out of the merger of Progressives and the left wing of the National Liberal Party. At the outset, the DDP proclaimed itself a liberal, democratic, and republican party. The party's chief regional base of support was southwest Germany, especially the states of Baden and Württemberg.[28] More than any other Weimar political party, the DDP was a loose association of German notables. Such German luminaries as Friedrich Naumann, Conrad Haussmann, Walther

Rathenau, Hugo Preuss, and Theodor Wolff identified in one way or another with the German Democratic Party. Ironically, all of these men died or left the party by 1925.[29] The DDP in 1919 tried to woo every group in the nation except large landowners and heavy industry.[30] Along with the SPD, the DDP played the most instrumental role in framing the Weimar Constitution, as is clearly seen in the inclusion of voting rights for women and young people, proportional representation, and Article 48, which gave the president emergency powers, and in the fight to include the use of the initiative and referendum in the constitution.[31] The party's 1919 program contains references to equal rights for people of all classes, occupations, and religions. The program goes on to favor states' rights and oppose dictatorship.[32]

The party portrayed itself as a nonsocialist democratic party. But like the DNVP and the DVP, the DDP had to contend with rival wings. The better financed right wing consisted of businessmen and industrialists; the left wing included intellectuals and pacifists. The DDP reached its electoral high point in 1919 with the election to the Reichstag of 75 deputies (out of 439). Thereafter, the DDP tried unsuccessfully to become the principal party of Germany's urban middle class. The perception that the German Democrats were too willing to compromise with the Social Democratic Party on social and economic issues and unwilling to take a firmer stand against the Versailles peace treaty undermined their base of support in the German middle class. By 1920 the DVP replaced the DDP as the dominant liberal party in Germany, as the number of DDP deputies fell to 39.[33]

During the early 1920s the German Democratic Party promoted the protection of individual rights, the defense of democracy and the Weimar Constitution, social legislation to improve the condition of the laboring class, support for the League of Nations, peaceful adjudication of international disputes by international organizations, and the expansion of foreign trade. Unlike the German People's Party, the DDP supported Social Democratic efforts to introduce legislation to improve the lot of Germany's working class and poor. The DDP backed legislation that included assistance to women and children as well as measures affording rights to trade unions and support for an eight-hour workday. The DDP leaders also called for the confiscation of war profits and welcomed the breakup of the great landed estates.[34]

In the tradition of European liberalism, the DDP stood steadfastly for the separation of church and state. The party pushed for a uniform, national, and secular school system.[35] In Reichstag debates the DDP often

joined with the DVP and SPD to sponsor legislation aimed at the secu-
larization of schools. The DDP often found itself on the opposite side of
issues from the Center Party. For instance, the DDP played an instrumental role in the fight against the national school law and the Reich Concordat
sponsored by the Center Party in 1926-27. The DDP initiated efforts to
undermine attempts by the Center Party and the Bavarian People's Party to
gain state funding for parochial schools and religious education.[36] The two
Catholic parties sought to make the parochial school the rule and insisted
that clerics have the right to provide religious instruction during regular
school hours. Basing its opposition to state aid for parochial schools and
religious instruction during regular school hours on the principle that religion was a private concern, the DDP joined with the DVP and SPD to
oppose the Catholic parties.[37] The German Protestant church was also a
favorite target of the DDP, especially when party officials thought that
the church was interfering in German politics, such as in November 1928,
when party leaders accused the Protestant church of supporting the rightist Stahlhelm and advocating intolerance toward the Weimar Republic.[38]

The German Democratic Party portrayed itself as a strong advocate
of free trade and improved relations with its western neighbors. DDP
delegates argued consistently for lower tariffs and claimed that through
expanded foreign trade Germany could shake off the economic malaise resulting from World War I. Party officials went on to call for the creation
of a "United States of Europe" in which every European nation would rid
itself of senseless chauvinism and antiforeign sentiment.[39]

During the mid-1920s, as a consequence of the periodic failure of the
German Democratic Party's right and left wings to find a common ground
on economic issues, the DDP's Reichstag delegation tried to mobilize
popular support around noneconomic issues. The party played a key role
in the debates surrounding state public education and proposed a plan to
fundamentally reform Germany's federal structure. In the 1928 Reichstag
electoral campaign the DDP leadership highlighted the party's interest
in improving relations with Germany's European neighbors, defending
Germany's republican system, reducing the duplication of governmental
services at the federal and state levels, and blocking the Catholic Center
Party's effort to pass its school bill. Noticeably absent in the 1928 electoral campaign were German Democratic pronouncements on economic
policy.[40]

As the effects of the economic depression deepened, the DDP was
caught between its advocacy of government assistance to the lower classes

and the classic liberal distaste for high taxes. By 1929 the party had become a forceful advocate for cutting spending and reducing taxes.[41] The DDP joined other center and right parties in 1929 to block the SPD initiative to fund unemployment compensation and other social services.[42] Ironically, the DDP found itself frequently voicing support for the austerity legislation introduced by Chancellor Brüning in 1930.[43] In fact, Brüning appointed Hermann Dietrich, a prominent figure in the DDP, as his finance minister. Dietrich pushed for deflationary measures such as cuts in government spending and reduction of civil servant salaries. Not surprisingly, the DDP suffered an exodus of white- and blue-collar supporters.[44]

The erosion of DDP electoral support that had become obvious following the May 1928 Reichstag elections and the 1929 state and local elections became a primary concern of party leaders.[45] Hamilton sees the party as moving rightward in response to electoral losses.[46] DDP efforts in 1930 to join forces with the DVP and the Economic Party (Wirtschaftspartei) failed. Eventually, in July 1930, under the leadership of Koch-Weser, the DDP merged with the right-wing People's National Reich Association (*Volksnationale Reichsvereinigung*) and remnants of the Christian Trade Unionists to form the German State Party (*Deutsche Staatspartei*, or DStP).[47] The creation of the DStP alienated many Jewish supporters of the German Democratic movement because of the People's National Reich Association's reputation for anti-Semitism and defense of Christian culture.[48] In the 1930 Reichstag elections the DStP attempted to win back the middle class with promises of a comprehensive fiscal and administrative reform to reduce the tax burden and with their youthfully energetic style of political leadership. The reconstitution of the German Democrats into the DStP failed to halt the party's slide, and both the DStP and DVP emerged from the 1930 elections as big losers. In the aftermath of the 1930 Reichstag elections, the People's National Reich Association abandoned the DStP and Koch-Weser resigned his post as party chairman. Dietrich replaced Koch-Weser and began the process of shedding the left wing of the party. Under Dietrich's leadership the DStP took up the defense of Brüning's deflationary fiscal policies and devoted considerable effort to attacking the Nazi Party. The DStP leadership's refusal to part ways with Brüning's increasingly unpopular policies diminished prospects for a reversal of the party's sagging fortunes. In particular, the DStP's embrace of Brüning's government (notwithstanding the collapse of the Darmstadt National Bank in July 1931, the government's inability to restructure Germany's international debt, the introduction of salary cuts and freezes, and the steady erosion of Germany's economy) won the party few adherents. By early 1932 the DStP's following had almost completely eroded.[49]

The Catholic Center Party

In the aftermath of Germany's defeat in World War I the Catholic Center Party portrayed itself as the alternative to capitalism and socialism. To put it simply, the Catholic Center Party sought to be a Catholic Volkspartei. During most of the 1920s the Center Party had both progressive and conservative wings. The progressives followed the leadership of Joseph Wirth, whereas the conservatives were led by Wilhelm Marx.

The principal raison d'être of the Center Party was the defense of the Catholic religion in Germany. To this end the Center Party participated in government to ensure religious freedom, basic religious instruction in all schools, financial aid for parochial schools, and the preservation and strengthening of Christian culture and ideals in community life.[50] According to the Center Party's program, Christianity should be the basis for state, society, and culture, and German economic and social policy should moreover embody a Christian social spirit.[51] Throughout the Weimar era, the Center Party fought for the enactment of a national concordat between the German Reich and the Vatican and the passage of a National or Reichs School Law. Both proposals faced strong opposition from deputies of the DVP, DDP, and SPD, who argued that the enactment of the Center Party's bills would destroy the principle of state public education.[52] If passed, a Reichs school law would, according to its proponents, guarantee religious instruction and allocate funding for Catholic children who were unable to attend parochial schools. During the Weimar Republic the Center Party never succeeded in getting the Reichstag to approve a national school law; however, the party played an instrumental role in the ratification of the 1925 treaty between the Vatican and the state of Bavaria and the 1929 ratification of a concordat between the state of Prussia and the Catholic Church.[53]

Center Party leaders also found themselves embroiled in debates over divorce and pornography. The party marshaled its resources to halt all governmental efforts to facilitate divorce. The party's leadership equated laws facilitating divorce with the advent of bolshevism in Germany and the end of German Christianity and civilized culture. The Center Party threatened to quit the governing coalition if the government enacted a divorce reform law. In November 1926 the Center Party submitted a bill to the Reichstag for the protection of youth from pornographic literature (*Schund- und Schmutzgesetz*). The bill won Reichstag approval despite opposition from the Social Democratic and German Democratic deputies.[54]

The Center Party's political program also touched on economic concerns. The party sought to establish itself between the left and the right by defending the interests of employees and employers and owners and non-owners. For instance, in 1919 and 1920 party deputies advanced proposals for land reform, including a call for land redistribution, placing large tracts of inefficiently used land held by large farmers in the hands of new farmers. To clearly distinguish its programs from the programs of the political left, the Center Party asserted the sanctity of private property and included in its land reform proposal some remuneration for the large farmers.[55] Also, the Center Party remained active in the debates over the future of Germany's domestic economy and foreign trade. The party pushed for the creation of a greater-German economic region that would include Austria and would merge postal, customs, transportation, and currency systems.[56] Because of their desire to represent labor, urban-consumer, and agrarian constituencies, Center Party leaders appear to have been at different times proponents of free trade and advocates of protectionism. In 1926 party officials argued for the elimination of internal barriers to free trade.[57] According to an article in *Germania*, the official Center Party newspaper, a healthy export trade was seen as a major means of reducing Germany's debt.[58] But in 1929 Center Party leaders' concern with the growing agricultural crisis in Germany led them to reverse course and advocate a dramatic reduction in foreign agricultural imports, along with the implementation of a series of import duties.[59] But for the most part, Center Party officials came down on the side of fiscal conservatism. They promoted plans to restructure the German economy that emphasized debt reduction through reduced government spending and increased savings. The plans included proposals to renegotiate the reparations payment schedules and to restructure the republic's taxation policies. Party officials argued that failure to eliminate the German debt would result in domestic anarchy and the loss of foreign confidence in the German economy.[60]

Throughout the Weimar period, the Center Party participated in government as a fairly reliable and loyal partner. The party leadership realized that the party's direct involvement in government could significantly affect success of its social and religious programs. Also, underlying the Center Party's defense of the Weimar Republic was the extent to which the Catholic Church emerged as a beneficiary of the Weimar Constitution. According to Evans, the constitution fulfilled requests by the German Catholic Church for the dissolution of all ties between the individual German states and the Protestant churches and for the termination of the German state's participation in church appointments; at the same time the constitution granted that the German republic would continue to support the Catholic Church financially.[61]

During the 1920s the party was quick to come to the defense of the Weimar Constitution and democratic institutions and frequently scolded the parties of the left and right for their criticisms of the Weimar system.[62] With the resignation of the moderate party leader Marx, however, and the rise to power in late 1928 of Ludwig Kaas, the conservative Catholic prelate, the party began to move rightward.[63] Reversing its resolute support for parliamentary democracy, the party under Kaas's leadership announced its support for a constitutional state that would confer enhanced powers on the president of the Reich. In 1930, without the support of the Center Party, the Grand Coalition collapsed, an event that marked the end of interwar parliamentary democracy in Germany. The era of presidential rule commenced with the appointment of Brüning, head of the Center Party's parliamentary wing, as chancellor. With Brüning as chancellor, the Center Party occupied itself with defending the government's austerity measures and fending off the chancellor's leftist and rightist critics.[64] The Center Party vigorously opposed Brüning's forced resignation in 1932 and Hindenburg's decision to appoint Papen as the new chancellor. With Brüning's departure the Center Party leadership once again returned to a preoccupation with issues of Catholic culture and church politics.[65]

No examination of the Center Party would be sufficient without a brief mention of the party's Bavarian ally, the Bavarian People's Party (BVP), founded in November 1918. As the most popular political party in Bavaria, the BVP held between sixteen and twenty-two Reichstag seats throughout the entire Weimar period. The BVP advocated freedom of religious education, along with strong states' rights. Though the BVP was aligned with the Center Party, relations between the two parties were at times acrimonious.[66] The rift between the two Catholic parties can largely be attributed to their different constituencies. Whereas the Center Party strove to become a national Catholic Party representing all German states and all classes, the BVP, with its base in the primarily rural state of Bavaria, catered to the rural Bavarian Catholic population. The BVP refused to accept the Center Party's decision to participate in government with socialists and anticlerical liberals and disapproved of the Center Party's tepid support of states' rights; Center Party members meanwhile became extremely irritated when the BVP backed the Protestant Prussian Hindenburg for president in 1925 instead of Marx, the Catholic Party's candidate, and when the BVP denounced the Treaty of Locarno and Germany's entry into the League of Nations.[67] Between 1925 and 1929 the two Catholic parties shared common ground for the most part but disagreed again in 1929 over the Young Plan and taxes.[68] The rift between the two parties lasted throughout most of the Brüning chancellorship. The BVP initially welcomed the appointment of the Catholic Party's Brüning to head the government but soon voiced protest over Brüning's economic stabilization program, which included a 75 percent increase in the tax on beer making. Ultimately, the two Catholic parties patched up many of their differences and reached a compromise on Brüning's economic stabilization program. By mid-1932 the Center Party had become sufficiently antirepublican that there remained few obstacles to agreement on a common program with its conservative and quasi-antidemocratic Bavarian wing.[69]

The German Social Democratic Party

The German Social Democratic Party (SPD) unexpectedly emerged from World War I as Germany's leading political party. After decades of political opposition, largely by default, the SPD found itself in late 1918 governing a defeated nation and charged with the unenviable tasks of signing a peace settlement and framing a new constitution. Because of the SPD's significant role in the creation of the Weimar Republic, the fate of the SPD became inextricably interwoven with the successes and failures of the Weimar system. Despite a sizable SPD presence in the German Reichstag throughout the Weimar era, the party actually spent relatively little time as one of the coalition parties governing Germany. The SPD participated in most of the governing coalitions between 1919 and 1923 but then remained on the sidelines until the Social Democrat Müller became chancellor in 1928 of the Grand Coalition, which lasted until March 1930. From March 1930 until Hitler's accession to power in January 1933, the SPD was again out of power.

In the aftermath of World War I the SPD underwent a dramatic change in both its political ideology and its social constituency. The party committed itself completely to the principles of parliamentary democracy, calling for further democratization of local and state government, the civil service, and the professions. The SPD advocated the total elimination of legal discrimination based on race, religion, gender, and class.[70] The SPD also, in contrast to many Weimar political parties, favored greater legal measures to ensure complete equal rights for German women.[71] Retreating from its earlier Marxist positions, the SPD rejected a revolutionary path to socialism and opted instead for the democratic road, at the same time accepting shared governmental responsibility with bourgeois democratic forces in Germany.[72] The abandonment of the revolutionary path to power and the rejection of the notion of a dictatorship of the proletariat divested the SPD of its more radical elements. Those favoring the Leninist model of socialism left the party and eventually found a home in the Communist Party of Germany, the KPD. The decision to work within the parliamentary system did not mean that the SPD had abandoned hopes of transforming capitalist ownership of the means of production. According to the SPD's 1925 Heidelberg program, the transformation of the German economy from private ownership to social ownership remained the goal of the party but the emphasis had shifted from purely economic struggle to a political struggle. The program mentioned that the socialization of the means of production could occur only when the SPD achieved political power.[73]

The SPD set out to construct a welfare state in Germany that would gradually replace free-market capitalism. To build a welfare state, the party introduced legislation governing work. Included in this legislation were calls for an eight-hour workday, regulation and protection of child and female labor, enforced safety precautions in the workplace, yearly paid vacation, abolishment of cottage industry, expansion and revision of the social insurance system, curbs on monopolistic practices and speculation, and nationalization of key industries. The proposed social demands were to be funded through higher taxes on the highest incomes, a graduated tax on inheritance, the collection of back taxes, restrictions on the flight of capital, and lastly new taxes.[74]

Like the DDP and the DVP, the SPD advocated the separation of church and state. The party argued that religion was a private matter and that schools should promote secular education and instill in the young respect for the republic and a desire for world peace. Church meddling in politics particularly incensed SPD leaders. The *Volkswacht*, one of the leading SPD newspapers, made a habit of denouncing members of the clergy who attacked the republican state from the pulpit. A few examples of newspaper accounts of unacceptable church meddling in politics include one of a Protestant pastor who dedicated his Sunday sermon to the Nazis and referred to them as the liberators of Germany, a Protestant pastor who publicly blessed the Nazi party flag and then marched in a Nazi Party demonstration, a Catholic priest who, in a special service, consecrated the flag of the right-wing Stahlhelm, and a Protestant pastor who allowed a steel helmet, a sword, and a pistol to be laid upon the altar, hung a swastika flag above the pulpit, and according to the newspaper, was a leader of a Hitler Youth troop.[75]

Regarding trade issues and foreign policy, the Social Democrats favored the gradual elimination of protective tariffs through the establishment of long-term commercial treaties with Germany's trading partners. Given the party's interest in keeping food costs low for the urban working class, the SPD expended considerable effort to block moves by those representing German agrarian interests to introduce higher tariffs on agricultural imports. The Social Democrats approved of Germany's participation in the League of Nations but advocated a revision of the Versailles treaty by peaceful international cooperation based on the principles of national rights.[76]

During the 1920s the question of national defense dominated many Reichstag debates. The SPD often found itself at odds with other parties over the extent of autonomy for the armed service, the level of defense spending, and the political persuasions of members of the officer corps. Fresh in the minds of many SPD delegates was the abortive Kapp putsch; at the time the army leadership debated whether to support the coup or protect the government. Consequently, throughout Weimar the SPD remained sensitive to alleged efforts by rightist officials to recruit politically conservative youth into the armed services. Moreover, the Social Democrats strove to reduce military spending, preferring to spend governmental revenues on social programs than on a larger military. Party deputies also proposed legislation to reintroduce compulsory military service[77] and establish means to ensure that only those who were loyal to the republic be allowed in the military.[78]

From March 1930 to Hitler's appointment as chancellor on January 30, 1933, the SPD remained outside government in the role of an opposition party—one whose leaders believed that the party's goal of social democracy could still be achieved through democratic means.[79] For the Social Democrats, Hindenburg's decision to appoint Brüning as chancellor and to rule by Article 48 (presidential decree) signified the beginning of dictatorship, and the party, through its power in the Reichstag, tried to nullify Brüning's emergency decrees.[80] SPD party leaders sought to link the worldwide depression and the advent of presidential rule in Germany to the machinations of international capitalism. To end the depression, the party leadership called for state control of the banks and increased public control over the economy. The Social Democrats criticized the Brüning government's austerity program for attempting to balance the budget by imposing hardships on Germany's working class.[81] The Social Democrats chastised the Brüning government for cuts in wages and benefits and higher indirect taxes.[82] The replacement of Brüning with Papen in mid-1932 did not attenuate Social Democratic criticisms of the government. Papen was caricatured as a relic of the Wilhelmine past, whose goal was to restore the monarchy and who served the interests of big industry and the large landowners.[83]

The German Communist Party

The German Communist Party (KPD) broke with the SPD in the wake of Germany's defeat in World War I, over the issues of loyalty to the Soviet Union and allegiance to Lenin's Third International. The new KPD followed the Soviet line.[84]

A principal goal of the German Communist Party was the replacement of the capitalist economic system with communism. Party officials called for the elimination of private property and of the selfish pursuit of profit.[85] The KPD always retained the belief that a working-class seizure of power was necessary to eliminate capitalism, even though the party entered candidates in elections, ostensibly for the purpose of reaching a wider audience. After a number of futile attempts to seize power between 1919 and 1922, party leaders put the party's overt revolutionary strategy on the back burner and turned to broadening its appeal among the working class. Under the unimaginative leadership of Ernst Thälmann, the party, with approval from Moscow, pursued the strategy of a "united front from below" to prepare for the eventual working-class revolution in Germany. The party set out to win over the industrial working class by developing party cells within the factories. These party cells were responsible for organizing the struggle around bread-and-butter issues like the eight-hour workday and higher wages.[86] As economic conditions deteriorated rapidly in Germany after 1929, the KPD's strategy to recruit the working class increasingly included calls to protect unemployment benefits and implement new taxes on the rich (for example, a millionaire's tax, a 10 percent tax on dividends and on incomes over 50,000 marks, and a special tax on annual salaries of public employees earning in excess of 8,000 marks and on pensions above 6,000 marks).[87]

Throughout the Weimar period, the German Communists backed the foreign policy interests of the Soviet Union. Given the international isolation of the Soviet Union, Moscow instructed the KPD leadership to obstruct German efforts to reach a rapprochement with the West. Fischer notes that a Germany estranged from the West offered the Soviet Union a potentially important capitalist friend.[88] It is in this light that we can understand the logic of the KPD's sympathy for a brand of German nationalism. To many observers, the German Communist Party and the Nazi Party's common opposition to the Dawes and Young Plans for renegotiation of Germany's reparations and call for an annulment of the Versailles treaty may seem bewildering. Their similar policies had quite divergent objectives, however. The Communists' objective was to further the Soviet Union's interest in promoting hostile relations between Germany and the anti-Soviet capitalist West; the Nazis, by contrast, had no inclination to advance Soviet foreign policy interests.[89]

The KPD leadership gave considerable attention to the party's relations with the SPD throughout the Weimar era. The two parties competed for working-class support and had had a common history until 1918. Nevertheless, the German Communist Party engaged in a vitriolic campaign to discredit the SPD as a truly socialist party. The Communist attacks on the Social Democratic party increased in magnitude in response to political events in the Soviet Union (notably, Stalin's decision to pursue rapid industrialization and collectivization and his repudiation of the Soviet Communist Party's reformist wing). The German Communists followed the policy laid down by the Comintern that closed the door to any cooperation with reformist socialism. The effects of the Depression also contributed to the deteriorating relationship between German Socialists and Communists. The deteriorating economic conditions in Germany convinced the KPD leadership that the working class might now be more susceptible to the party's revolutionary strategy and that the party had nothing to gain from an alliance with reformist socialism. By 1928 the KPD party organs were referring to the German Socialists as social fascists and accusing them of being the henchmen of the German bourgeoisie and agents of French and Polish imperialism who were betraying the interests of the German working class.[90] The SPD made the likelihood of a rapprochement with the KPD virtually unimaginable by allowing the police in SPD-governed Prussia to violently suppress a Communist demonstration in 1929, killing more than thirty Communist demonstrators.[91] By 1929 the KPD had undergone a shift not only in its political orientation but also in the composition of its leadership cadres. The party's more moderate wing, which advocated a less hostile stance toward the German Social Democratic Party and greater independence from Moscow, had been vanquished by the Stalinist hard-liners led by Thälmann.[92] Any hopes of a KPD-SPD rapprochement that might block the ascendancy of the NSDAP were dashed after 1930. Under Thälmann's leadership and right up until Hitler's accession to power, the KPD continued to portray the German Social Democratic Party as a be-trayer of the German working class and a class enemy like the Nazi Party and the German middle-class political parties.

The German National Socialist Workers' Party

Out of the chaos surrounding Germany's collapse at the end of World War I sprang the German Workers' Party (*Deutsche Arbeiterpartei*). This party, which would eventually become the National Socialist German Workers' Party (NSDAP), was formed on January 5, 1919, in Munich under the leadership of Anton Drexler and Karl Harrer. Over the span of a few years the German Workers' Party grew in size, attracting a hetero-geneous following. One of the party's early recruits was Adolf Hitler. In short time, Hitler made his presence felt, becoming the party's most popular orator.[93] Between 1920 and 1921 Hitler established his complete au-thority over the party. He added the words *National Socialist* to the party's name and adopted the swastika as the party's symbol and flag, and in Feb-ruary 1920 the party issued its official twenty-five-point program. It called among other things for the union of all Germans within a greater Ger-many, repeal of the Treaties of Versailles and St. Germain, establishment of colonies for Germany's surplus population, exclusion of Jews from citi-zenship, appointment of only competent citizens to official posts (without regard to party affiliation), state promotion of the welfare and economic activities of its citizens, an end to non-German immigration, improvement of national health and fitness levels through obligatory physical activities, and promotion of the common interest above self-interest. With regard to economic issues, the party demanded abolition of the "thralldom of inter-est," confiscation of war profits, nationalization of syndicates and trusts, introduction of profit sharing in industry, improved old-age insurance, establishment and protection of a healthy middle class of artisans and merchants, implementation of land reform by means of "confiscation without compensation," abolition of interest on mortgages, and prohibition of land speculation. The twenty-fifth and final point of the program called for the establishment of a powerful central government, along with diets and vocational chambers to implement the laws proclaimed by the Reich and the various German states.[94]

Under Hitler's leadership the Nazi Party before 1923 became a rapidly growing Bavarian regional folk (*völkisch*) movement, although Hitler's initial attempt to seize power in Bavaria by means of a coup collapsed in November 1923. During Hitler's brief 1924 imprisonment in Landsberg prison for his part in the failed coup, the Nazi Party fell into disarray. Hitler refounded the Nazi Party in February 1925, two months after his release from prison. Later that year the Nazi Party replaced its "putschist" strategy with a strategy to gain power electorally, while establishing the foundations for a national organization. Between the reconstitution of the Nazi Party in 1925 and Hitler's appointment as chancellor in January 1933, Hitler would remain the undisputed leader of the Nazi Party.

The NSDAP electoral strategy hit a major roadblock in the general elections of 1928. The Nazi Party polled a meager 2.5 percent. In contrast to the disappointing showing at the polls, the party's recruitment of new members was extremely successful: membership grew from 27,000 members in 1925 to 108,000 in 1928.[95] In 1929 the Nazi Party gained substantial visibility as a result of the national campaign against the acceptance of the Young Plan in which the NSDAP and the DNVP worked together to gather more than four million signatures. Of particular significance for the Nazis was the opportunity, through the alliance with the DNVP, to make use of radio and print media put at the party's disposal by Hugenberg, the DNVP leader. As mentioned earlier, Hugenberg was the head of the Scherl publishing house. The electoral fortunes of the party rose in 1929, as evidenced by strong showings in state and local elections in Schleswig-Holstein, Lower Saxony, and Baden. The first major Nazi electoral breakthrough occurred in the general elections of September 1930. The NSDAP received 6,400,000 votes, or 18.3 percent of the total, and gained 107 seats in the Reichstag. As a result, the party was second only to the SPD in the size of its delegation. After the general elections of July 1932 the NSDAP replaced the SPD as the largest political faction in the Reichstag, with 230 seats. In the July 1932 election the NSDAP received 13,750,000 votes or nearly 38 per cent of the total. In the election of November 1932 (the last free Weimar general election) the NSDAP experienced a loss of 2,000,000 votes and 34 seats.

Given the NSDAP's strong electoral performance as early as 1930, one might have expected the NSDAP to have been called upon to participate in government. That the Nazis remained outside the Brüning, Papen, and Schleicher cabinets can be attributed largely to reluctance by the German power brokers to negotiate with the Nazis and to Hitler's intransigent refusal to accept anything but complete political authority. Whatever the reasons behind the NSDAP's extragovernmental position between 1930 and 1933, the popularity of the party had certainly not suffered from the exclusion. Unlike the DNVP, DVP, DDP, Center Party, and SPD, the NSDAP had never been saddled with governmental responsibility and hence had safely avoided the pitfall of close association with disappointing policies. Nor could the party be blamed for the effects in Germany of the worldwide depression. The NSDAP's exclusion from government ended on January 30, 1933. In light of the tremendous popular backing for the NSDAP, President Hindenburg changed his thinking about a Hitler-led government and appointed the Nazi leader chancellor of Germany.

Examinations of the ideology of the Nazi Party before 1933 have focused largely on Hitler's writings in *Mein Kampf.* Thus, it comes as no surprise that most treatments of Nazi ideology stress the primacy of nonmaterial themes such as racism, anti-Semitism, hypernationalism, and xenophobia. Gies mentions that the Nazis knew quite well that to build a party of the masses without writing a check on the future, they would do well to campaign on such general nonmaterialist themes as anti-Semitism, anticommunism, and antiliberalism and to steer clear of "hot potatoes" like economic promises.[96] Bullock in his recent book seconds Gies's assessment of Nazi themes: "Where other politicians were dismayed, Hitler was excited. Nothing could better suit his apocalyptic style of politics than the prospect of disaster, in which exaggerated fears and irrational beliefs easily gained ground. He grasped instinctively that, as the crisis deepened, an increasing number of people would be willing to listen to a leader who promised not a program of economic and social reform, but a spiritual transformation, a national renewal, drawing on Germans' pride in their nation's historic destiny, and his own passionate conviction that will and faith could overcome all difficulties."[97]

We must ask, however, whether millions of Germans would have supported a party that only offered vacuous promises and generalities. The party positions that were enumerated in the official Nazi Party programs have been too often ignored. Unlike the frequently vague and outlandish ramblings of *Mein Kampf* (which relatively few people read before 1933), the party programs taken together are characterized by a substantial degree of coherence and considerable emphasis on material themes. I do not wish to argue that racism, anti-Semitism, hypernationalism, and xenophobia played no role in Nazi ideology; nor do I deny that many people found the Nazi Party attractive because of its stance on these themes. I would argue rather that these nonmaterial leitmotifs have received disproportionate emphasis in explanations of the rise of Nazism.[98] By themselves, anti-Semitism and other racist and nationalist themes would not have made the Nazi Party into the most popular party in Germany before 1933, for obvious reasons. First, in the world of Weimar politics the Nazis did not have any ideological monopoly on anti-Semitism and xenophobia. Second, if themes like anti-Semitism and hypernationalism were so important to the rise of Nazism, why did the NSDAP fare so poorly in the elections before 1929? No one could argue either that the party discovered anti-Semitism and hypernationalism only after 1929 (the year that marked the beginning of the Nazis' spectacular rise in popularity), or that millions of Germans found these mindsets appealing only after 1929.

The Nazi Party leaders were savvy enough to realize that pure racial anti-Semitism would not set the party apart from the pack of racist, anti-Semitic, and ultranationalist movements that abounded in post-1918 Germany. Instead, I would suggest, the Nazi success can be attributed largely to the economic proposals found in the party's programs, which, in an uncanny fashion, integrated elements of eighteenth- and nineteenth-century nationalist-etatist philosophy with twentieth-century Keynesian economics. Nationalist etatism is an ideology that rejects economic liberalism and promotes the right of the state to intervene in all spheres of life, including the economy.

What, then, was the NSDAP economic philosophy? The Nazi Party, like other Weimar-era parties, had rival wings with competing philosophies. Before 1933 the NSDAP contained a right, a center, and a left. Gregor and Otto Strasser spoke for the party's left wing, advocating economic programs for the working class and curbs on private enterprise. Fritz Thyssen, Albert Pietzch, and Walther Funk spoke for the party's right wing, promoting the interests of the business community and extolling the importance of free enterprise, economic self-reliance, and private initiative. The center found a voice in the writings of Gottfried Feder, who advanced nominally leftist schemes like nationalization of the banks and job creation, as well as rightist demands for commercial autarky and an end to the credit shortage.[99] Despite philosophical differences within the NSDAP, by 1925 a particular economic direction emerged. In 1930 the party established a Department for Economic Policy, headed by Otto Wagener. Between 1930 and 1933 the NSDAP presented a series of important party programs laying out the party's general economic philosophy. Among these programs were the 1930 agrarian program, the 1930 NSDAP employment program, the 1931 WPA (*Wirtschaftspolitische Abteilung*) document, the 1932 Immediate Economic Program (*Wirtschaftliches Sofortprogramm*), and the 1932 Economic Reconstruction Plan (*Wirtschaftliches Aufbauprogramm*).

NSDAP economics sought to create "a third path" between Marxist centralized state planning and laissez-faire capitalism.[100] The Nazis were not the first in Germany to advocate or even to implement both nationalist-etatist and Keynesian economic principles, but they were the first to *merge* the principles of both schools in a seemingly coherent and innovative program.

In their nationalist-etatist thinking the Nazis drew upon the late eighteenth- and nineteenth-century contributions of the anti-laissez faire or anti-capitalist economists such as Adam Heinrich Müller, Wilhelm Roscher, Friedrich List, Georg Friedrich Knapp, Gustav Schmoller, and Adolf Wagner. Much of the impetus for nationalist-etatist thinking came from German philosophers who felt that English or Western economic theory had minimized the importance of national characteristics.[101] Among the ideas that the nationalist-etatist school contributed to Nazi economic planning were state socialism, autarkic economic development, and *Lebensraum*. The concept of state socialism was based on the principles that the economy should serve the interests of the state or Volk rather than the individual and that the state should oversee the direction of the economy. Proponents of nationalist-etatism argued that through a policy of autarky—that is, "a condition of economic self-sufficiency constructed on a network of production and exchange entirely encompassed within an integrated geographic area under a single overall authority,"[102] Germany could become economically self-sufficient and pursue an independent foreign policy.[103] The notion of autarky is based on the assumption that the needs of the national economy precede the needs of the international economy. Thus, proponents of autarky argued that the gold standard was unnecessary and that the state, through the implementation of an internal exchange rate, could control its monetary policy. Whereas the primary goal of German autarky with regard to monetary policy was to allow the state to create a state-controlled money and credit system, the geopolitical aims, stemming mainly from Germany's precarious geopolitical position, were to negate the detrimental consequences of a naval blockade by Germany's chief rivals (France, England, and Russia) of its world commerce.[104]

Nationalist-etatist thinking added that autarkic development could flourish only if Germany developed a continental economic zone (*Grossraumwirtschaft*, or *Lebensraum*). For Schmoller, Germany's establishment of a Grossraumwirtschaft or Lebensraum would be consistent with the behavior of other great powers like England, Russia, and China, which had all realized the importance, and taken advantage, of a continental economic zone for their economic survival.[105]

The nationalist-etatist thinkers saw eastern and southeastern Europe (*Mitteleuropa*) as the natural turf for Germany's economic survival and growth. They envisioned a German-dominated economic union in which middle Europe would serve as a prime market for products of German heavy industry, while at the same time German agriculture would no longer need to rely primarily on protective tariffs for its survival but would be protected by trade agreements with the members of the economic union.[106]

Nationalist-etatist thinking and in particular the idea of the need for Lebensraum gained in popularity after World War I, with the emergence of a new Poland and the growth of revolutionary socialism in Germany. Weimar academicians such as Max Sering saw Lebensraum as a strategy to populate East Prussia with German small farmers. According to Sering, not only were small farms more viable economically than large Junker-owned estates, but farmers could counter the growing influence of the Polish agricultural laborers employed by the owners of large German estates. Sering and others were also acutely aware of the nagging social tensions within German society and envisioned in Lebensraum a means to create new opportunities for those seeking a better life. To this end, Lebensraum could be to the frustrated German masses what the Western frontier represented to Americans during the nineteenth century—a new life.[107]

The Nazis were not the first political group in Germany to find value in the writings of the nationalist-etatist thinkers. Barkai asserts that the nationalist-etatist writings on state socialism appear to have had a pronounced influence on Bismarck's social insurance plans and Buchner's state socialism. He also notes that the prominent Weimar statesman and industrialist Walther Rathenau appeared to be championing the quest for Lebensraum when, during World War I, he stated that Germany needed to expand eastward because its territory was insufficient to provide for its large population. Nationalist-etatist ideas on anticapitalism, autarkic economic development, and Lebensraum also found a home among prominent German conservative thinkers of the early twentieth century, including Othmar Spann and Werner Sombart, and among followers of the Tatkreis movement (which was popular in the late 1920s).[108] The Nazis were not breaking new ground when they advanced the ideas of state socialism, autarkic development, and Lebensraum in the party's programs; the concepts had already become part of the German economic lexicon. The Nazi Party, however, was the first mass political party to make these nationalist-etatist concepts the core elements of its economic doctrine and to combine them with key notions from Keynesian economics.

There is some debate over whether Nazi economists had read John Maynard Keynes or whether they concluded independently of Keynes that direct state intervention in the marketplace could bring about full employment and an end to a recessionary business cycle. Whatever its origins, the Nazi economists found much to their liking in Keynesian economics. Keynes' *The Economic Consequences of the Peace,* which was critical of the Versailles treaty and the financial obligations it placed on Germany, brought Keynes to the attention of many members of the NSDAP leadership as early as 1920. Like Keynes, the NSDAP wanted to see the elimination of the gold standard. Most important, the Nazi Party agreed with Keynes that if governments and central banks hoped to maintain full employment and reduce the likelihood of economic recession, they should urge investment in new capital goods, ensure a cheap money policy, and initiate public investment. Much has been written about Franklin D. Roosevelt's adoption of the Keynesian notion of "pump priming" in the mid-1930s as a means to jolt the U.S. economy out of the Great Depression. What may be less well-known is that the NSDAP had urged the use of pump priming to start the German economy several years before Franklin D. Roosevelt.[109]

Nationalist-etatist principles and Keynesian economics made for a good match. Autarky was realizable, according to the thinking in the NSDAP, through government-initiated investment in the nation's infrastructure, including public works, residential reconstruction, resettlement, and reagrarianization.[110] In the end, the marriage of nationalist-etatist thinking and Keynesian economics allowed the Nazis to design some rather novel but nevertheless concrete economic policies. Barkai, in his provocative book, captures the uniqueness of Nazi economics when he writes: "The historical truth is that the Nazis and the economists attached to their movement were almost the only figures in the pre-1933 political arena to present genuine employment projects to be financed by unconventional measures and to realize these projects successfully after assuming power."[111]

As early as 1919 signs of nationalist-etatist and Keynesian thinking appeared in the German Workers' Party publications. Feder's 1919 "Manifesto for Breaking the Bondage of Interest" called for the creation of a new national socialist state that would play a major role in the management and ownership of public utilities, transportation systems, natural resources, and the German banking system. According to Feder, the state would in addition regulate interest, rent, and mortgage rates and would confiscate excess profits from private enterprise to fund social welfare programs.[112] Even in *Mein Kampf* we find some strong references to nationalist-etatist concepts. Hitler writes of the importance of building healthy industry and commerce, free of foreign influence and the vagaries of the world market, through reliance on protectionist measures, economic independence, and a continental economic zone in eastern and southeastern Europe. Germany, according to Hitler, if it were to invest its energies in the construction of its own autarky, should be able to prosper for the next hundred years.[113]

The NSDAP had begun to fuse nationalist-etatist concepts with Keynesian ideas by 1930. The clearest expression of the fusion is to be found in the contributions of Gregor Strasser. In many respects, Gregor Strasser was the foremost architect of Nazi economic policy before 1933. Strasser's contributions are evident in the 1930 NSDAP agrarian program, the 1930 employment program, and the 1932 Immediate Economic Program. He pleaded for economic self-reliance, believing that many of Germany's problems stemmed from its economic dependency. Since the early 1920s he had pushed for the adoption of autarky, to include reorientation of Germany's agricultural and industrial production toward the internal market, expansion of the nation's raw materials base, abandonment of the gold standard, and pursuit of agricultural and industrial rationalization (modernization and economic efficiency).[114] Strasser would present in addition the idea of a massive public works program for the construction of roads, housing, dams, and canals, financed through government spending and credit creation (*Kreditschöpfungstheorie*).[115]

I intend to highlight the role that the materialist elements of the Nazi Party program played in the party's successful mobilization efforts. This is by no means to suggest that economics dominated every aspect of Nazi

Party propagandizing. Other themes certainly helped the party to attract support. One that pervades many of the party writings was the establishment of a *Volksgemeinschaft,* or "people's community." This was seen as a means to overcome the historical divisiveness of class conflict. In a people's community, social classes would be abolished. Like most organizations, it was to be hierarchically arranged, with the leader at the top. Leadership was a function of accomplishment and was integral to the survival of the community. The people's community was to be racially pure, for racial homogeneity binds people to the community, whereas racial heterogeneity fosters disunity and leads to the deterioration of the native stock.[116] The people's community would also expurgate cultural bolshevism, while strengthening the traditional family way of life, or the three *K*s of *Kinder* (children), *Küche* (kitchen), and *Kirche* (church).[117] Whether the community was Protestant or Catholic did not matter in Nazi ideology, although the Nazis viewed the Catholic Church as a greater threat because of its institutional independence and supranational status. Ziegler suggests that in the Nazi trilogy of foreign conspiracy, Rome was, after Judah and Moscow, the greatest enemy in the Germanic Weltanschauung. The Protestant church, by contrast, was never recognized as an ideological enemy.[118]

The Nazis tried to depict National Socialism as a movement embodying the youth rebellion and combating Weimar foreign policy blunders and the "red scare." The party professed to represent the youth of Germany as opposed to the Weimar gerontocracy.[119] To appeal to young people, the Nazi Party emphasized its newness, antisystem politics, aversion to bourgeois formality, and dynamism. Colorful demonstrations and martial symbols and clothing were also intended to induce young males to join the movement.[120]

Kershaw observes that foreign policy issues were of only secondary importance in NSDAP campaigns before 1933.[121] Few Nazi gatherings devoted themselves to analyses of foreign policy. Although I agree with this assessment, I believe that the party used foreign policy as a means of highlighting its positions on issues more likely to attract mass support. Here are some examples: the "traitorous" character of Weimar politicians, exhibited in their failure to reverse the provisions of the Versailles treaty; the hemorrhage of German natural resources as linked to acceptance of the Dawes and Young Plans on reparations payments; the dependence of Germany's economy on the international marketplace; and the despair of German dairy and meat farmers over the signing of trade treaties with foreign dairy and meat exporters.

Nazi speeches and writings were frequently peppered with references to the threat of communism. The "Gefahr des Bolschewismus in Deutschland" theme was dramatized in conjunction with the growth of support in Germany for the Communist Party: 1.7 million votes in 1925, 4 million votes in September 1930, and 7 to 8 million votes in February and March 1932.[122] Much like the Italian Fascist Party, the NSDAP presented itself as a bulwark against the spread of communism.

A particularly dominant theme of NSDAP propaganda before 1933 was the failure of the Weimar system. Opposition to Weimar became the thread with which the Nazis linked communism, loss of national self-esteem, economic decline, foreign policy blunders, and Jewish influence. The NSDAP promised the total liquidation of the Weimar system, which, according to the party, was responsible for the host of evils that had befallen Germany.[123]

The Importance of Anti-Semitism in the Nazi Appeal

Finally, there is the issue of anti-Semitism as a principal theme of the Nazi Party before 1933. How important was anti-Semitism to the stunning rise of the Nazi Party in Weimar Germany? Dawidowicz claims that "racial imperialism and the fanatic plan to destroy the Jews were the dominant passions behind the drive for power." She adds that "Hitler's ideas about the Jews were at the center of his mental world. They shaped his world view and his political ambitions, forming the matrix of his ideology and the ineradicable core of Nationalist Socialist doctrine."[124] Anti-Semitism is indeed present in many early Nazi writings. Eckart, a major Nazi Party figure, was among the first to claim, in *Auf Gut Deutsch*, that Jewishness is not a racial but a spiritual condition. Conversely, Alfred Rosenberg, a rabid anti-Semite and editor-in-chief of the *Völkischer Beobachter*, the major Nazi Party newspaper, wrote in his widely read commentary on the *Protocols of the Elders of Zion* that Jewishness was unequivocally a racial condition.[125] Bracher suggests that in Nazi propaganda Jews were portrayed as the mainstays and chief beneficiaries of exploitative capitalism, the principal advocates of Marxist socialism and internationalism, and the major instigators of a worldwide conspiracy to destroy German and Aryan racial interests.[126] Gordon adds that "Jewish" became an adjective that the Nazis attached to the hypothetical evils they were combating.[127]

The centrality of anti-Semitism in Nazi propaganda has been overstated. By this I do not mean to argue that Hitler and his party faithful were not anti-Semitic but rather that by 1924–1925 they had concluded that for building a national party attractive to all German classes, the issue of anti-Semitism held insufficient appeal. Increasingly, anti-Semitic rhetoric was merged with economic and political issues and was used to preach to the already faithful.[128] Lane and Rupp note that as early as 1923 the Nazi Party began to give less space to anti-Semitic writings in its publications. They assert that Jew-baiting and conspiracy hysteria disappeared from the writings of most Nazi leaders, with the exception of Julius Streicher, between 1923 and 1933. Feder referred to anti-Semitism in a derogatory fashion and refrained from any systematic anti-Semitic writings until after the Nazi Party had achieved power. Even the rabid anti-Semite Rosenberg acceded to party wishes and shifted away from exclusive obsession with the Jewish conspiracy toward a more comprehensive political theory.[129] Gordon insists that few of the prominent Nazi leaders during the 1920s came to the party because of anti-Semitism. She includes among those who did not Goebbels, Himmler, Goering, Frank, the Strasser brothers, Schirach, Speer, Feder, and Eichmann.[130] But if Hitler did indeed hold unrivaled authority in the Nazi Party, why wasn't he able to enforce the ideological primacy of anti-Semitism? Hitler was astute enough as a politician to realize that his rabid anti-Semitism lacked drawing power among the German masses.[131] Indeed, it appears that increasingly the Nazi Party relegated anti-Semitism to a role as backdrop to other more materialist appeals.[132] Zitelmann's findings from his extensive survey of the content of Hitler's speeches and writings offer further evidence of the diminishing presence of public Nazi anti-Semitism between 1929 and 1933.[133]

Gordon notes that for many in the party anti-Semitism was simply part of the baggage of Nazism.[134] Koonz and Kershaw extend this characterization of the secondary importance of anti-Semitism, claiming that while the rank-and-file supporters of Nazism were obviously aware of the party's anti-Semitic stance, it was not a crucial motivating factor in their allegiance. Kershaw notes, however, that anti-Semitism may have been a prime motivating force for the early activist core that came to the Nazis via the numerous völkisch movements.[135]

Though the NSDAP de-emphasized its anti-Semitism between 1929 and 1933, the party did opportunistically employ the theme where it was thought that anti-Semitic rhetoric would work to attract support. In areas like Middle Franconia, parts of Hesse and Westphalia, and stretches of the Rhineland, where anti-Semitism had a long history, the party featured its anti-Semitic propaganda. Nevertheless, these instances stand as exceptions rather than the rule.[136] On numerous occasions the party realized that anti-

Semitism had potentially negative consequences for its strategy of building a mass following. Zofka's study of the party in Swabia illustrates how the Nazis excised anti-Semitic references from their campaigning, realizing that among the local farmers, economic concerns were primary and that negative references to Jews hurt party recruitment. Zofka claims that within the farming population of the Swabian district of Gunzburg, Jewish traders were held in high esteem and a popular expression was "Wenn kein Jude auf dem Markt ist, geht kein Handel" (If no Jew is at the market, there will be no trade).[137] Thus, the theme of anti-Semitism was suppressed in the NSDAP program in propagandizing in the Gunzburg region.[138]

We should not attribute the Nazi Party's success to its professed anti-Semitism, but that is not to argue that anti-Semitism was absent in Weimar Germany. Suggesting that propinquity may have bred contempt, Gordon claims that anti-Semitism prospered in Germany's larger cities, such as Berlin, where the highest concentration of Eastern European Jews resided. Having recently arrived in Germany, many of these Eastern European Jews had not yet become assimilated into German life.[139] It bears repeating that the Nazi Party did not possess a monopoly on anti-Semitism, which existed in both the Catholic and Protestant churches in Weimar Germany. As earlier illustrated, Protestant theologizing frequently included racist and anti-Semitic caricatures. Jews were depicted as corrupt and degenerate and eager to destroy German Christian morality. From their pulpits some Protestant clergy attacked the Jews for their alleged intellectualism and materialism. Conway observes that the Catholic Church was not immune from anti-Semitism, either. In those Catholic areas which had recently experienced an influx of Eastern European Jews, the Catholic Church had on occasion seen fit to target Jews.[140] And anti-Semitic utterances also found a home among other Weimar political parties other than the NSDAP. While it should come as no surprise that the more conservative parties, the DNVP and the DVP, frequently employed anti-Semitic rhetoric, the German left could also be counted on to opportunistically tap into anti-Semitism. In a speech to a student group in Berlin in July 1923, Ruth Fischer, a Jewish Communist Party leader, castigated the Jewish capitalists and proposed hanging them from lamp posts.[141] Not to be outdone, one month later in a speech in Stuttgart, Hermann Remmele, a Communist Party functionary, accused Jewish cattle dealers of extracting great profits from the Stuttgart cattle market while non-Jewish Stuttgart butchers had gone away empty-handed.[142]

Why has anti-Semitism received so much attention as a theme of the

Nazi Party before 1933? The Nazi regime's subsequent systematic policy of liquidating the Jewish people has irrevocably shaped our understanding of Nazism. It is only natural that our view of the Nazis' rise to power is colored by recognition of their profound anti-Semitism. Yet as difficult as it may be for many of us to believe, Nazi anti-Semitism, though a driving force in the foundation of the Nazi Party, hardly explains the NSDAP's spectacular rise to power. We have to distinguish between the pre-and post-1933 periods. Before 1933, while the Nazis were still competing for political power, they designed their strategy to increase their chances of attracting a large popular following. Many in the party were staunch anti-Semites, but anti-Semitism was perceived as lacking sufficient appeal to mobilize the masses because it was part of everyday Weimar political discourse. After installing themselves in power, the Nazis were at liberty to pursue themes regardless of their political popularity, and the party's anti-Semites were given freer rein.

Many examinations of Nazi Party principles fail to capture the party's uncanny skill at disseminating its positions and casting itself in the role of a winner. Both abilities played a crucial role in attracting support, for if people had been unaware of the party's programs or if they thought the Nazi Party had no chance of achieving power, they might not cast their votes for or join the NSDAP.

The NSDAP was one of the earliest parties to implement modern propaganda techniques, including whirlwind campaigns by airplane, highly coordinated press campaigns, films, slide shows, massive leafleting and postering, continual door-to-door campaigning, and direct mailings. The Nazis even established a speakers' school where party faithful who possessed knowledge of particularly useful subjects and good verbal skills were trained and then deployed throughout the country to speak at party gatherings.[143] A prime example of the care Nazis took in organizing meetings emerges from an article published in the July 1931 issue of the journal *Wille und Weg:*

> The first meeting in a village must be prepared in such a way that it is well attended. The prerequisite is that the speaker is fairly well-informed about specifically rural questions. Then, it is most advisable to go to a neighbouring village some time after but to advertise the meeting in the first village there as well, then many people will certainly come across. After this, one holds a big German Evening in a central hall for a number of villages with the cooperation of the SA and the SA band. . . . The German Evening,

provided it is skillfully and grandiosely geared to producing a big public impact, primarily has the task of making the audience enthusiastic for our cause, and secondly to raise the money necessary for the further build-up of propaganda. The preparation of the village meetings should best be carried out in the following way: most effectively through written personal invitations to every farmer or inhabitant. In the bigger villages by a circular, which is carried from farm to farm by party members.[144]

The NSDAP's strong electoral performance in 1930 dispelled any remaining notion that the NSDAP was a second-rate party. If before 1930 Germans had considered joining the NSDAP simply as a means of demonstrating their dissatisfaction with older parties, the results of the 1930 election convinced many people that the party was a potential winner and that a National Socialist Germany was now possible. Moreover, many Germans who before 1930 had adhered to regional parties and movements such as the Bauerbund and Landvolk movements, many of whose positions were similar to those of the NSDAP, switched their allegiance to the more nationally oriented Nazi Party.[145] Both Pridham and Noakes, in separate regional studies, mention how applications to join the NSDAP proliferated in the aftermath of the 1930 election. The party more than doubled its membership, increasing it from 389,000 to 806,294, during 1931.[146] The NSDAP was certainly aware of the importance of public perception of it as a major party. Zofka recounts that in the July 1932 general elections a Nazi slogan ran: "Now it comes down to Bolshevism or National Socialism. Now only major parties can help."[147] To sustain and further build its image as a potential winner, the NSDAP put to work its vast propaganda arsenal.

In this chapter I have presented an overview of the histories and principal ideologies of the major Weimar-era political parties. Beginning in 1928 the traditional parties of the right (DNVP and DVP), the center (DDP and Catholic Center Party), and the left (SPD and KPD) steered increasingly in the direction of exclusionary politics. The perception of hard economic times appears to have injected these parties with the fear that if they adopted a more inclusionary ideological orientation, they might lose their core constituency. The Nazi Party, on the other hand, skillfully developed an economic philosophy based on nationalist etatism and Keynesian economics that found increasing favor among millions of Germans as economic conditions deteriorated. To varying degrees, the competing parties also crafted specific political programs to win over members of the old and new middle classes and the working class. Among which social classes did the Nazis fare the best? Which specific Nazi programs appealed to the interests of small farmers, merchants, artisans, white-collar employees, or workers? In the next two chapters, I examine the constellation of material interests within these classes during the Weimar era, along with the particular class programs of the competing parties.

3

The Middle Class and
Weimar Political Parties

The consensus is that the middle class was a major constituency of the Nazi Party before 1933. But why did the German middle
class embrace Nazism? Did the various groups that constituted the middle
class uniformly support Nazism? (As mentioned at the beginning of Chapter 2, the middle class in fact comprised two separate groups, the old and
the new middle classes.) In contrast to the standard explanation that highlights the reactive character of middle-class adherence, I will stress its proactive nature; that is, I will seek to show that many middle-class Germans
joined the Nazi Party because they perceived the party's programs as the
ones that most nearly approximated their material interests. I also argue
in this chapter that German middle-class support for Nazism was corre-
spondingly uneven; the Nazi Party's programs appealed to some middle-
class groups more than to others.

In addition to examining the middle-class response to Weimar political parties, I undertake in this chapter to answer a number of intriguing
questions about the nature of agrarian fascism. For instance, Why did the
German state of Schleswig-Holstein become a Nazi stronghold? Why did
interwar agrarian fascist movements establish strongholds in Germany and
Italy but not in France?

Material Interests of the Old Middle Class

The old middle class in Germany, made up of self-employed farmers, shopkeepers, merchants, and artisans, experienced one economic blow after
another during the Weimar era. As a group, the old middle class constantly sought means of obtaining capital. The need for low-cost credit
from banks frequently forced these people to mortgage their shops or
farms, something that hardly endeared Germany's financial institutions to

them. Like its larger competitor, big business, the old middle class of proprietors suffered from market fluctuations. Unlike big business, however, the old middle class was seldom favored by governmental legislation, nor was it able to draw on a reserve of capital assets to stay afloat during economic downturns or expand in times of growth. Finally, the old middle class was frequently unable or unwilling to pursue strategies of economic rationalization and greater efficiency employed by both German business and agriculture after 1924.[1]

Material Interests of German Farmers

Agriculture and forestry accounted for 30.5 percent of Germany's employed population in 1925; German regions displayed significant variation in farm size, crop selection, and levels of revenues and indebtedness. To focus in this context on German farmers' interests makes particular sense, Kaschuba notes, because rural Germany was the fountainhead of Nazism.[2] In contrast to farmers in England, France, and Italy, German farmers were overwhelmingly property owners.[3] Nine-tenths of the agricultural surface and forests in Germany belonged to private citizens. Tenant farms made up the remaining farm- and woodland. Tenant farming was particularly concentrated near the Rhine River between Cologne and Aachen.[4] Medium farms of between five and a hundred hectares constituted nearly 62 percent of all German farms. Both small farms (of less than five hectares) and large farms (of greater than a hundred hectares) each accounted for one-fifth of all farms.[5]

Germany contained six major agricultural regions, which differed in their agricultural emphases. Typically, eastern German farmers cultivated grains, northwestern farmers raised livestock, and southern farmers raised livestock in conjunction with the cultivation of fodder crops, grapes, and tobacco.

The east, the territory comprising East Prussia, Pomerania, Grenzmark, Posen-West Prussia, Brandenburg, and Silesia, had a high proportion of large grain-producing farms owned by Junkers (former Prussian nobles) and worked by a large class of salaried agricultural laborers. Of all German regions, the east had the lowest per-hectare revenue and the highest agricultural indebtedness.[6]

Middle Germany included Saxony, the Free State of Saxony, Thuringia, and Anhalt. This region consisted predominantly of intensively cultivated, independently owned small- and medium-scale farms producing a variety of crops such as grains, vegetables, and root crops. Agricultural revenues varied greatly in Middle Germany but were consistently higher than in the east. Agricultural indebtedness was relatively moderate. The most prosperous agricultural area of Middle Germany was the fertile Löss triangle of Halle, Magdeburg, and Hildesheim.[7]

The northwest region of Germany consisted of the districts of Hannover, Schleswig-Holstein, Mecklenburg, and the Hanseatic states of Oldenburg, Braunschweig, and Schaumburg-Lippe. Here farms were generally independently owned and medium sized. The principal distinctive feature of the region's agriculture was its dependence on animal husbandry. Like Middle Germany, the northwest had a wide range of agricultural revenues and an intermediate level of agricultural indebtedness.[8]

The remaining regions, Rhineland-Westphalia, Hesse, and southern Germany (Bavaria, Württemberg, and Baden), shared numerous features. Farms were usually small and independently owned and produced cash crops such as grains, vegetables, tobacco, hops, and fruits. As in the northwest region, animal husbandry also played an important economic role in these three regions. The presence of a partible inheritance system (for division of the land among heirs) throughout much of these three regions distinguished them from other German regions. The practice of partible inheritance, in conjunction with the importance of cash crops, may have accounted for the preponderance of small farms in these regions. Rhineland-Westphalia, Hesse, and southern Germany had the country's lowest level of agricultural indebtedness and its highest agricultural revenues per hectare. However, among these three regions, Rhineland-Westphalia generally had the highest agricultural revenues per hectare and the lowest agricultural indebtedness, while Bavaria had the lowest agricultural revenues per hectare and the highest agricultural indebtedness.[9]

The halcyon days of German agriculture during Weimar were short-lived. The stabilization of the German currency in 1924 ended ten years of rising agricultural prices and set German agriculture on a path toward financial collapse. Certainly, some governmental changes in the mid-1920s benefited the farming community, but they brought farmers only temporary relief, like the legislation that both lightened property taxes and shifted their basis from assets to income; the granting of sales tax exemptions; and the elimination of inheritance taxes, in the case where property was transferred to the widow or children. German farmers' real income increased a meager 4.5 percent compared to the national average increase of 45 percent between 1913 and 1928. Although it constituted roughly 25 percent of the total population, the farming community earned only 8 percent of the national income.[10] Between 1925 and 1933 the cycle of crop failures, credit shortages, low prices for agricultural products, low tariffs, rising taxes, bankruptcies, and falling net profits increasingly ravaged Germany's farming community. As I will show, however, the impact of the crisis besetting German agriculture after 1925 was quite uneven.[11]

As long as agricultural prices rose during Weimar, there appeared to be no real debt problem.[12] By 1927, agricultural prices began a general decline. A fall in international agricultural prices hit German farmers particularly hard because of their unavoidably high production costs.[13] Dairy and meat production areas in Germany were the first to feel the impact of collapsing agricultural prices after 1924.[14] Wholesale cattle prices plunged from the 1930 rate (of 12 percent above the base level of 1913) to 17 percent below that level in 1931, and then to 36 percent below in 1932.[15] Between 1927 and 1932, while the market price fell 18 percent for rye and 10 percent for wheat, it dropped 33 percent for pork and 32 percent for dairy products.[16] Examining the course of agricultural prices in Germany between 1928 and 1933, Tracy finds that livestock and dairy farmers suffered the largest relative decline in prices for their products. He notes that while wheat prices fell from a base level of 100 (marks) in 1928–1929 to 91 in 1932–1933, and rye prices fell from 100 in 1928–1929 to 74 in 1932–1933, livestock prices declined from 100 in 1928–1929 to 59 in 1932–1933.[17] What made the fall in livestock prices particularly crippling for German livestock farmers was that in order to switch to capital-intensive livestock production they had borrowed heavily.[18]

Notably hurt by the price collapse were the hog farmers of Schleswig-Holstein and Lower Saxony.[19] Because the Nazis established one of their earliest rural breakthroughs in northwestern Germany, particularly in the states of Schleswig-Holstein and Lower Saxony, the agricultural crisis in these states has received considerable attention. Heberle, and Loomis and Beegle, cite the fluctuations in the extremely sensitive hog and cattle markets during the 1920s and 1930s as a principal cause of great financial hardship in the Geest and Heide areas of Schleswig-Holstein and Lower Saxony. The price fluctuations contributed to a high rate of bank foreclosures in these regions.[20] The fall in dairy and meat prices forced farmers to remortgage their farms in short-term, high-interest *Rentenmark* credits that ultimately wiped out the inflationary benefits they received on their previous mortgages.[21]

The decline in agricultural prices eventually reached German cereal producers, who had been sheltered until 1927 by German tariffs even though world wheat prices had been falling continually since 1925.[22] In 1930–1933, the grower received 23 percent less for rye than in the years 1925–1928; for barley the corresponding figure was 19 percent, for wheat 10 percent. Sales revenues in 1932–1933 amounted to only 62 percent of those in 1928–1929.[23]

Farmers who were able to diversify, like many of those in the Rhineland and Westphalia who raised livestock and also cultivated crops, were affected less by single-crop price declines. These farmers had room for adjustment to shifting prices; they could counter declining sales of livestock by increasing sales of rye.[24]

The decline in agricultural prices also affected German tenant farmers and agricultural laborers. Falling prices made it more difficult for tenant farmers to pay their rents; for agricultural laborers whose wages were paid "in kind," lower agricultural prices reduced their income, for they were obliged to sell their produce themselves or exchange their crops for other goods. In parts of eastern Germany agricultural laborers were paid between five- and six-sevenths of their wages in kind.[25]

Through subsidies and tariff and trade polices, the Weimar government had a significant impact on the livelihood of the German farming community. During the 1920s, in hopes of making German agriculture more efficient and competitive, the government set out to eliminate such obstacles to foreign trade as protective tariffs. Many German farmers felt that Weimar governmental policy favored industrial interests over agricultural ones. These farmers believed that higher tariffs on various crops were required to make German agriculture profitable, and they petitioned the government to help agriculture, as it had, they claimed, helped German industry earlier.[26]

The government ultimately implemented agricultural tariffs, but policy was uneven and frequently gave preferential treatment to grain growers at the expense of urban consumers and livestock farmers. Weimar tariff policy largely benefited German wheat, rye, and animal feed prices, which in 1930 were twice the world market prices, and did little for pork prices, which were below the English price.[27] An index of agricultural trade (1913 = 100) reveals that although grain imports were 87 percent of their prewar level in 1928, dairy imports had jumped by 116 percent and meat imports by 154 percent. Moreover, in 1930 the volume of grain imports stood at only 48 percent of pre-war levels, while the volume of meat and dairy imports rose to 188 percent and 158 percent of their 1913 volume, respectively.[28]

At the same time as the government acted to protect German grain producers, it concluded trade agreements with Denmark, the Netherlands, Sweden, and France that further increased the entry of foreign dairy and meat products into the German market.[29] Though the Tariff Act of August 1925 had reintroduced the pre-war tariff rates for imported products, commercial treaties had in many cases reduced protection for agricultural products. For example, the pork market was threatened by negotiations for a trade treaty with Poland. According to the treaty, Polish pigs would be imported into Germany in exchange for advantages for German industrial goods in Poland.[30] Domestic markets for Germany's meat and dairy goods shrank further in 1927 with the influx of cheaper foreign foodstuffs — Belgian dairy products, Danish beef and butter, and the Polish pork.[31] Also, cheaper frozen meats, lard, and bacon from Argentina and North America began to inundate the German market.[32]

This differential tariff policy was especially injurious to those farmers in northwest Germany who had during the last decades turned increasingly to intensive animal husbandry and who now confronted stiff international competition and higher prices for feed and other necessary grain products.[33] Moreover, the combination of lower agricultural prices and insufficient tariff protection resulted in plummeting agricultural incomes and soaring indebtedness and foreclosures. By 1928 farmers in Schleswig-Holstein demanded that the German government create a trade policy that included "independence from foreign sources of food" and the prohibition of all nonessential imports of agricultural products.[34] The inability of the government to resolve the growing anxieties of German livestock farmers after 1927 led many to blame the Weimar Republic for their economic problems.[35] Likewise, the government's preferential treatment of grain growers did not go unnoticed by other farmers. The years 1930–1932 had convinced many German farmers that their interests had been sacrificed in favor of antitariff export industry and subordinated in agricultural policy to the interests of eastern German grain farmers.[36] Many of these farmers had earlier supported the German National People's Party (DNVP) but now began to see the DNVP as unwilling or unable to redress their grievances and to cast about for a new political voice.[37]

Collapsing agricultural prices, insufficient tariff protection, and heavy borrowing resulted in a rising level of debt for many German farmers after 1924.[38] In fact, Germany's agricultural debt skyrocketed from zero marks in the 1923-1924 period to nearly twelve billion marks (three billion dollars) by the end of 1931.[39] High interest rates and reduced credit thwarted farmers' efforts to reduce this debt.[40] The currency stabilization that helped to end the German inflation of the early 1920s tightened credit and made the cost of borrowing more expensive. Particularly distasteful to farmers were the laws enacted after 1925 that restricted the reserves of the Deutsche Rentenbank, which had previously been a major source of credit for farmers.[41] Interest rates, which in 1925 were roughly twice their pre-war levels,[42] climbed steadily. James suggests that the credit difficulty was a consequence of a growing skepticism about agrarian loans in light of declining world market prices for agricultural goods. Major international financial markets were persuaded that German agriculture had a murky future.[43] Tightened credit and higher interest rates presented particular obstacles to enterprises that needed capital to expand or to upgrade.

High taxes also served to increase farmers' debts between 1925 and 1933. Farmers were obliged to pay income tax, property tax, land and building tax, a turnover tax, additional taxes to the village and village associations, road tax, vehicle tax, church tax, and social welfare contributions for their employees.[44]

By 1930 the growing debt burden in agriculture began to exact a toll in bankruptcies and enforced foreclosures. In 1931 an area of 177,000 hectares fell under compulsory sale.[45] As a result of the banking crises of July 1931 that sent interest rates higher, major banks tried to recall loans in order to maintain their own liquidity. But as agriculture prices collapsed, farmers had little hope of repaying their loans.[46] Consequently, when loans were called, the result was often bankruptcy and compulsory sale. In 1931, 5,765 farms were auctioned by receivers (.7 percent of Germany's farm land); in 1932, 7,060 (.6 percent).[47] Also, in 1932 alone a record 18,393 farms went into insolvency.[48] Bankruptcy and foreclosure hit the small- and medium-scale farms harder than the large estates.[49]

The rising incidence of farm foreclosures threatened the existence of inheritance—an institution that had for generations contributed to the basis of an organized community life.[50] The post-1925 agrarian crisis jeopardized the orderly transferal within families of farm property from one generation to the next which was carefully regulated by the Entailment Law and by custom, especially in areas of northwestern Germany where impartible inheritance was practiced, such as Schleswig-Holstein and Lower Saxony.[51] (In the Rhine area of southwest Germany partible inheritance predominated; in eastern Germany both impartible and partible inheritance were in use).[52]

Not all German farmers nor every region experienced indebtedness equally. Sering (who was an advocate for grain farmers) claims that the largest farms—grain farms—were hardest hit by debt. He observes that small and medium-sized farms had lower debts because they, unlike the larger farms, were not saddled with payment of wages and employee benefits.[53] And indeed though indebtedness for small farms rose by 15 percent between 1924 and 1928, indebtedness for large farms climbed by 33 percent.[54] Sering's findings tell only part of the debt story, however. His assessment of agricultural debt does not reveal that after 1925, German governments provided far more assistance to large-scale operations than to small family farms. By late 1927 the government had begun preparing emergency assistance programs for the large estates in eastern Germany, but similar assistance for Germany's small and medium-sized farms did not gain serious consideration until mid-1930. According to Abraham, from 1928 to mid-1930 thirteen separate policies were enacted by the government to assist eastern German farmers, whereas others had to wait until mid-1930 for the first general governmental assistance program.[55] The 1931 government assistance programs for large eastern German estates (*Osthilfe*) made available 1.5 billion marks to these farmers for debt conversion and lowered local taxes and freight rates.[56]

Increases in taxes and labor costs during the Weimar period did little to help alleviate the debt burden of the self-employed German farmer. German farmers subsidized new social welfare programs and higher wages for laborers because of programs introduced by the government between 1925 and 1930. The onset of the Depression produced a rapid rise in the amount of capital needed to fund unemployment insurance. Between 1929 and 1931 the bill for unemployment relief climbed from 1.8 billion marks to 3.2 billion marks.[57] To finance these new public expenditures, the government turned to employers. Contributions to social welfare pushed up farm costs. Between 1913 and 1927 the cost of social insurance for farmers who employed laborers climbed from 8.70 marks per hectare to 26.39 marks per hectare.[58] In addition to the higher costs for social insurance, farmers who employed laborers had to contend with the rise in wages for agricultural labor, which rose steadily until 1929, a year when they were 50 percent higher than their pre–World War I levels.[59] These additional financial burdens did nothing to enhance the government's standing among Germany's farmers. To many German farmers, like those in the labor-intensive regions of Westphalia and the Rhineland, the government appeared more interested in increasing wages for agricultural labor than in enhancing competition with foreign producers.[60]

Farmers also blamed the government for its acceptance of reparations payments. Even though the reparations burden had been lessened by the Dawes and Young Plans, in the eyes of many farmers, funds for reparations translated into higher taxes, tighter credit, and fewer funds for agriculture.

Seeking a vehicle for their grievances, German farmers turned initially to their formal agricultural organizations, which since the end of the nineteenth century had lobbied for favorable legislation. These organizations reflected Germany's denominational and regional boundaries: the Agrarian League or Farmers' League (the Reichslandbund—RLB—after 1920), tied to the DNVP, dominated in the Protestant east and north, the farmers' associations (*Bauernvereine*) associated with the Center Party held sway in the Catholic west and south.[61] Besides these two major agricultural organizations, other farmers' groups operated within individual states. For example, the Peasant League (*Bauernbund*), with its stronghold in Bavaria, had democratic, anticlerical leanings and subscribed to a narrow Bavarian particularism, and the *Bauernverein* (peasant association) located in Schleswig-Holstein was without religious ties and initially supported a liberal economic and political policy.[62]

Among the principal organizations representing German farmers during the Weimar era, the RLB was the largest and most influential. Although it comprised predominantly family farmers and landless laborers, the RLB largely reflected the interests of Germany's large estate owners. Much of the favorable governmental trade, tariff, and debt legislation for the large grain-growing estates of eastern Germany after 1927 can be attributed to the efforts of the RLB leadership to wangle concessions from the government.[63] Politically, the RLB took positions consistent with those of the DNVP. In particular, the RLB called for increased agricultural exports and decreased imports.[64] At the same time, the Farmers' League, dominated by the Catholic Center Party, issued a program calling for protection of Germany's economic independence through reforms in tariff policies.[65]

As the agrarian situation turned from bad to worse and many farmers concluded that their own advocacy organizations were unsuccessful in coaxing the government to help them, increasingly vociferous and radical agricultural movements sprouted throughout Germany. One of the best-known of the new movements was the *Landvolkbewegung* or *Landvolk* movement of Schleswig-Holstein, formed by farmers in the aftermath of a January 1928 demonstration that drew roughly 140,000 farmers. The Landvolk movement criticized the Weimar government for not doing enough for German agriculture. In particular, the Landvolk movement demanded governmental action to redress problems with taxes, interest rates, credit, debt payment, and foreign agricultural competition and to reject German blame for World War I and the reparations payments. The Landvolk movement spread rapidly throughout the farming areas of Schleswig-Holstein and Oldenburg and by 1929 had spread into neighboring Lower Saxony.[66]

Not only did the deepening agrarian crisis lead to the emergence of new movements like the Landvolk, it also led existing agrarian groups to pool their resources under the umbrella of the Green Front, which consisted of the *Landbund* (RLB), the *Deutsche Bauernschaft* (formerly *Bauernbund*), the *Vereinigung der christlichen-deutschen Bauernvereine* (Association of Christian-German Peasant Unions), and the *Deutsche Landwirtschaftsrat* (German Agricultural Council).[67] Among the many demands put forward by the Green Front were the halting of foreign food imports, institution of credit and tax-relief programs, creation of policies to enhance the viability and profitability of agriculture, and the establishment of a system of price indexing on all goods.[68] The majority of the Green Front's proposals were rejected by the government, however.[69]

The real power in the Green Front appears to have been the RLB, which placed its resources behind Junker interests (such as higher tariffs on grain and governmental passage of Osthilfe). In a move that won the Green Front few friends among the dairy and livestock farming community, the organization proposed that pig breeders of the northwest and southwest subsidize rye and wheat growers.[70] Eventually, many farmers became increasingly dissatisfied with the role their own agrarian organizations played in the Green Front's promotion of Junker economic interests and began to look elsewhere for a new standard-bearer for their grievances.[71]

In the face of the difficult conditions in German agriculture, few of the major Weimar parties showed much responsiveness: the parties of the center and right retained their faith in the market; the left had little interest in defending private property.[72] It is highly likely that in the eyes of many German farmers the Nazi Party's agrarian program offered fresh hopes for a better livelihood.

Material Interests of German Shopkeepers and Independent Artisans

Like the self-employed farmers, self-employed shopkeepers and artisans perceived an erosion of their economic and social standing. In 1932 German independent craftsmen attained only 33.5 percent of their 1928 profit levels.[73] Weimar's new emphasis on efficiency and economic rationalization, including the introduction of labor-saving techniques, made the occupations of the old middle class increasingly irrelevant. Artisan products lost ground to the cheap, mass-produced goods pouring from the new factories, and small shopkeepers increasingly suffered from competition from the chain and department stores and consumer cooperatives.[74] Lacking large reserves of capital, most independent artisans and shopkeepers were unable to renovate or modernize to compete successfully with the larger enterprises.

The Weimar Republic fostered the growth of both big labor and big business. As the economic importance of these two opposing giants grew, that of the old middle class declined.[75] Moreover, both big labor and big business appeared to have a greater capacity than before to shape governmental policy to their advantage, as demonstrated by a series of governmental compromises that included higher unemployment compensation for workers and new governmental subsidies and preferential tariffs for big business. The old middle class, among whom unemployment was not a major concern, benefited little from these governmental programs, and the subsidies and tariffs were not earmarked for them. To make matters worse, the old middle class had to foot a major part of the bill for governmental assistance to labor and big business. Brüning's 1930–1932 austerity program did little to ameliorate the economic plight of the old middle class. Instead, through the increase in unemployment insurance contributions, reduction in government tax transfers to state and local governments, and hike in interest rates, the program hurt many in the old middle class.[76]

After 1924, the fate of independent artisans and shopkeepers mirrored that of German farmers. Falling prices, shrinking markets, and expensive credit forced an increasing number of artisans and shopkeepers into heavy debt. Between 1925 and 1933, the average yearly income of the self-employed fell from 3,540 to 2,500 marks, while the income of people who were not self-employed dropped only from 1,710 to 1,520 marks. Almost 50,000 business firms went bankrupt between 1930 and 1932.[77] The livelihoods of farmers, artisans, and shopkeepers were often intertwined. Hard times for farmers frequently translated into hard times for artisans and shopkeepers. Thus, it comes as no surprise that the decline in pork prices in the northwestern German free state of Oldenburg in the late twenties and early thirties, for example, spurred protests from Oldenburg's farmers and shopkeepers.[78] Nor is it startling that in neighboring Schleswig-Holstein and Lower Saxony, the Landvolk protest movement of 1928 included a call for tax relief for craftsmen, shopkeepers, and farmers.[79]

Several scholars have noted the extent to which members of the old middle class adhered to a corporatist view of society as a *Volksgemeinschaft*.[80] Kater describes corporatism as the establishment of a "harmonious organic relationship between employers and employees" with a purpose of curing "the country of its socioeconomic ills."[81] He adds that corporatism did not appeal particularly to big business, whose economic philosophy favored the traditional vertical separation between capitalists and proletariat, but it did appeal to small-scale entrepreneurs whose economic interests encouraged them to favor forms of organization that guaranteed harmonious class relations and lessened risk.[82] We would expect the old middle class to favor a form of corporatism that included not only vertical relationships between employers and employees but horizontal relationships between farmers, merchants, and craftsmen.

The corporatist view of society held appeal among such old middle class groups as independent artisans, shopkeepers, and farmers, largely as a consequence of the strong social ties and the extensive economic interdependence among these groups. The vast majority of Germany's artisans, shopkeepers, and small farmers lived in small towns and villages and they shared multisided relationships. They frequently attended church together, participated in the same organizations, and sent their children to the same schools. Most important, they served as consumers for one another's goods; thus their economic fortunes were inextricably linked. A decline in profits for one group frequently meant hard times for the others. A poor harvest meant that farmers would have less disposable income to buy goods sold by artisans and shopkeepers, who, in turn, would have to pay higher prices for food. Because of their economic interdependence, all three groups had an interest in events and policies that affected the economic well-being of the others. We should expect that support for corporatism would depend on the groups' shared economic concerns and physical proximity and would rise in times of economic distress.

Like German farmers, many artisans and shopkeepers began to voice their grievances in organized protests after 1927, exemplified in the demands of the Schleswig-Holstein Landespartei in 1928, and in the 1932 program of the German crafts organization (*Deutsches Handwerk*). The Schleswig-Holstein Landespartei was composed of merchants, artisans, farmers, and intellectuals. In addition to expressing anti-Prussian sentiments and defending local culture, the Landespartei called for special protection for the old middle class against the encroachments of capitalism and industrialization.[83] In contrast to the Landespartei's rather vague demands, Zeleny, head of Deutsches Handwerk, outlined a specific set of demands to improve the position of the old middle class. His program called for the creation of a political chamber for the middle class, a plan for improved quality certification, restrictions on the business practices of the large department stores, and creation of an independent health insurance program for small business employees. In addition, it included measures to improve the earning capacity of artisans and shopkeepers, and efforts to increase credit facilities for businesses and ensure credit access at commercial banks.[84]

Eventually, members of groups like the Landespartei and Deutsches Handwerk would support the NSDAP because the NSDAP, more than any of the other political parties, combined an activist commitment to improving the lot of the old middle class with concrete proposals to redress its grievances. Furthermore, the NSDAP had never participated in Weimar government; thus, in the eyes of many farmers, artisans, and shopkeepers, the party had not forsaken them as had the DNVP, DVP, and DDP.

Material Interests of the New Middle Class

White-collar and civil service employees (*Angestellte* and *Beamte*) constituted the new German middle class, which owed its existence largely to industrialization and growth in government.[85] Since 1900 the new middle class had grown more than any other social class in Germany. Between 1907 and 1925, the total number of white-collar employees grew by 98 percent, compared with 22 percent for blue-collar workers.[86]

Blue-collar workers and employees from the new middle class shared roughly similar income levels; however, members of the new middle class usually drew a fixed weekly or monthly salary rather than an hourly wage. After 1925, representatives of both groups argued for legislation to improve welfare benefits and unemployment compensation. Until Brüning's austerity program of 1930–1932, however, blue-collar labor had more success than the new middle class in getting favorable legislation passed. Throughout the Weimar period, blue-collar labor lobbies were more organized and had greater access to government than did lobbies from the new middle class. One notable consequence was the passage of the 1927 unemployment insurance program, which ensured that jobless blue-collar laborers would receive disproportionately more income and social welfare benefits than white-collar employees.[87]

In many important respects the material interests of the new middle class differed from those of the old middle class. As salaried employees, those in the new middle class sought higher salaries and benefits and job security; by contrast, many in the old middle class, as employers, favored lower wages and employee benefits and a free hand in discharging employees. Additionally, the new middle class did not share the anxiety of the old middle class regarding economic modernization, because Germany's economic modernization was chiefly responsible for many jobs for the new middle class, for example in retail department stores.[88] The old middle class held the department store responsible for the loss of its business; for many in the new working class, the department store provided jobs and daily necessities. Another difference between the old and new middle classes was the extensive trade union organization that made the new working class more pro-union than the old middle class.

The period of growth in the sector comprising the new middle class began to wane in 1925, however, with efforts by German business to become more competitive through the introduction of more efficient business practices. For the new middle-class trades, streamlining took the form of replacing superfluous labor with capital-intensive technologies like typewriters, adding machines, and new bookkeeping devices. Thus, business efficiencies brought about a rise in unemployment among the new middle class.[89]

The worldwide economic depression, which reached Germany in 1930, took an additional toll on the new middle class. Numerous white-collar employees joined the growing ranks of the unemployed, and many of those who kept their jobs experienced a reduction in salary and benefits. The total number of unemployed workers climbed from 2,258,000 in March 1930 to 5,670,000 in December of 1931 and 6,128,000 in February 1932. Among them were not only blue-collar laborers but a sizable number of white-collar employees. Between 1930 and 1932 white-collar unemployment rose 150 percent and was disproportionately high among women. By 1932 an estimated 13.6 percent of the white-collar work force had lost their jobs.[90] Further, within white-collar occupations the ratio of applicants to jobs, which stood at 9 to 1 in May 1928, climbed to 26 to 1 by September 1930. Many white-collar employees who were fortunate to have a job experienced a noticeable decline in their earning power after 1928. For instance, the average Berlin bank employee who earned 166 marks in 1928 earned only 142 marks in 1930.[91]

The new middle class comprised salaried employees in both the private and public sectors. Unlike their counterparts in the private sector, public-sector employees had traditionally benefited from special legal privileges such as permanent job tenure. But many of the special privileges enjoyed by civil servants were eliminated during the Weimar period. Of utmost importance to civil service employees was job security. With the advent of the Weimar Republic in 1919–1920, however, many in government sought to sweep away vestiges of the Wilhelmine past, and political housecleaning meant that many civil servants perceived to be hostile to the new government were dismissed and sympathetic new civil servants hired. Furthermore, during the crisis of 1923–1924 the government was forced to institute major budget cuts that culminated in mass dismissals of public employees. Approximately 750,000 public officials and civil employees lost their jobs as a result of the government's stabilization policies of 1923–1924.[92] The post-1924 economic recovery did not restore the lost civil service positions.

For those civil servants fortunate enough to hold on to their jobs, the effects of the economic depression undermined their standard of living. As early as the second half of 1930, Chancellor Brüning cut civil service salaries between 12.5 and 16 percent as part of his deflationary program.[93] At about the same time, ignoring objections from the German Reichstag, Brüning incorporated into his first program for "Emergency Aid to the Reich by Persons in Public Service" an emergency surtax of 2.5 percent on civil service salaries.[94] In January and February 1931 he called for a 6 percent cut in salaries and wages that affected approximately 75 percent of Germany's salaried employees and industrial laborers. All told, between December 1930 and February 1932 civil servants experienced salary cuts of roughly 20 percent.[95] The Papen government instituted no new pay reductions for civil servants but did add a surtax on civil service salaries to help maintain the unemployment fund. Between 1930 and 1933 civil service salaries had been reduced by approximately 20 percent.[96] Though on one level, many public servants could appreciate the logic behind the government's austerity program as an attempt to restore Germany's financial credit in the world, on a more personal level, they favored measures that though stopgap and inflationary would bring back their jobs and halt salary cuts.[97]

As conditions deteriorated for the new middle class, its members searched for means to coax the government to act in their behalf. They initially turned to their trade union organizations. The principal organizations for white-collar employees were the *Allgemeiner freier Angestelltenbund* (AfA), affiliated with the SPD-dominated free trade unions; the *Gewerkschaftsbund der Angestellten* (GdA), a Hirsch-Duncker union; and the *Gewerkschaftsbund deutscher Angestelltenverbände* (Gedag), a front organization for the DHV (German Shop Clerks' Association).[98] In time, the new middle class realized that these traditional organizations did not know how to retrieve lost jobs or raise salaries, and many in the new middle class also realized that only the NSDAP was bold enough to come forward with creative Keynesian work schemes. At the same time, the Nazi Party's wooing of the old middle class and working class created formidable anxiety in the new middle class about Nazi Party adherence.

Weimar Political Parties and the Old Middle Class

What were the political choices for Germany's old and new middle classes during the Weimar era? What made the NSDAP such a popular party, particularly among farmers, shopkeepers, and artisans? Why did the NSDAP encounter roadblocks in its attempt to court particular segments of the white-collar population? Below I examine the contrasting political programs of the principal Weimar political parties aimed at the German middle classes.

The DNVP and the Old Middle Class

The leadership of the German National People's Party promoted the party as rural Germany's most consistent and reliable friend. Like its predecessor, the German Conservative Party, the DNVP had the backing of Germany's large estate owners, and many of the policies that party leaders advocated during the Weimar period reflected the interest of those farmers. Nonetheless, the DNVP sought to enlist a following among small and midsize farmers, as well as agricultural workers. To that end party officials stressed the common interests of all people engaged in agriculture.[99]

From the beginning of the Weimar Republic, the DNVP took the initiative in fighting so-called leftist governmental proposals to reform German agriculture. The DNVP accused the government of promoting legislation intended to break up large estates in eastern Germany and of planning to nationalize large holdings. Though the DNVP gave tacit approval to plans to resettle landless peasants in the eastern territories and to the creation of a larger group of small and median-scale farmers, it did not want these land reforms to come at the expense of the large estate owners.[100]

Above all, throughout the Weimar era the DNVP remained an advocate of protective tariffs for German handicrafts and agriculture. After 1924 German policy makers pushed for economic rationalization, endeavoring to finance reparations payments through greater German industrial and agricultural exports. As a consequence, the government generally opposed higher tariffs as harmful to free trade and encouraged more efficient agriculture as a means to competitive trade. On the grounds that this policy had been fashioned by the government's acceptance of the hated reparations plans and that Germany should achieve agricultural self-sufficiency (*Ernährungsautarkie*), the DNVP emerged as the principal critic of Weimar trade policy.[101] In opposition to Weimar trade policy, DNVP policy called for the creation of a strong national economy with a balance between industry and agriculture. To the critics of the DNVP's trade policy positions, who argued that high tariffs would bring foreign retaliation, party leaders replied that Germany could rely on its own domestic market to buy its goods. Furthermore, party leaders insisted that high tariffs would strengthen the bond between German agriculture and the domestic market and by limiting imports, would spur German agriculture to create more jobs, thereby lowering the unemployment rate among agricultural laborers.

The DNVP officials agreed on the need to make German agriculture more efficient and competitive but disagreed with other Weimar parties over how best to achieve greater efficiency. In lieu of a policy of free trade or foreign competition, DNVP leaders proposed that German agriculture could ultimately become more productive if it received government protection beforehand. To win backing for this proposal, they spouted the conservative refrain that during the Kaiserreich, agriculture had sacrificed itself for the sake of building German industry. Party officials proposed that in the spirit of fair play the government now pay agriculture back in the form of increased protection.[102]

With regard to specific legislation, DNVP policy in 1925 called for higher tariffs on barley, wheat, and oats. Between 1925 and 1927 the party opposed the government's decision to sign trade treaties with Belgium, Italy, the Netherlands, and Austria. DNVP leaders feared that these trade treaties would glut the German market with fruit, vegetable, and dairy products. In 1927 the DNVP deputies presented a plan to the Reichstag advocating, among other things, specific measures to enhance agricultural profitability; the establishment of an economy of self-sufficiency in nourishment (*Nahrungsfreiheit*); ceilings on imports; and protective tariffs.[103]

The DNVP achieved some notable legislative successes between 1924 and 1933. In early 1928 the party played an instrumental role in persuading the government to institute an emergency program for German agriculture that expanded credit availability for farmers and reduced certain taxes.[104] Nevertheless, DNVP leaders branded the government's assistance to the eastern German farmers as clearly insufficient. Thanks in large part to the appointment of the DNVP's Schiele to manage German agricultural policy, the party efforts on behalf of east German farmers culminated in 1930 in new aid programs. The new Osthilfe (eastern agricultural aid package) produced new import duties on grains, potatoes, and sugar beets, advantageous revisions in Polish-German trade agreements, increased credit availability for farmers, and liquidation or postponement of debt for farmers.[105]

The party's agricultural initiatives clearly benefited some farmers more than others. This was especially true after 1928, when Hugenberg, who was stridently pro-big business, replaced Westarp as head of the DNVP. Under Hugenberg's stewardship the DNVP intensified its efforts to promote the interests of the large farmers over those of the midsize and small farmers.[106] After 1928, many small farmers concluded that the DNVP had abandoned them. Consequently, as the DNVP solidified its hold on the constituency of large estate owners, it undermined its position among many small and midsize farmers.[107]

The DVP and the Old Middle Class

As a staunch defender of the free enterprise system, the German People's Party (DVP) for the most part advocated private initiative and a free trade policy. Throughout the Weimar period, representatives of the German People's Party rarely missed an opportunity to attack schemes aimed at the socialization of German industry and agriculture. Also, according to the leadership of the DVP, Germany needed to improve its trade balance with other nations if it hoped to finance the reparations payments. It had no choice but to trade with other nations to gain access to the goods it could not produce.[108] Under Stresemann's leadership the party fought against a protectionist economic philosophy (including economic autarky), referring to it as a veiled form of socialism.[109]

While Stresemann tried to influence the DVP to embrace free trade, which had broad support from the heads of German export industries, other voices emerged within the DVP calling for an economic policy more sympathetic toward handicrafts and agriculture. The DVP's vote in favor of protective tariffs for agriculture in 1924 was a sign of the party's ambivalence over governmental protection. Stoltenberg has pointed out that protectionist sentiment stemmed from one of the sad lessons of World War I:

that without economic self-sufficiency, Germany risked deprivation. Proponents of protectionism within the DVP feared that many farmers, independent artisans, and shopkeepers would have trouble supporting the party, given that Stresemann, as German foreign minister, had negotiated several trade treaties that afforded the German export industry preferential treatment.[110] The DVP never shed its image as the party of free trade, although protectionist attitudes surfaced within the party again during the Great Depression.[111]

The DDP and the Old Middle Class

The German Democratic Party (DDP) steered a steady course as an outspoken proponent of foreign trade and an equally fierce opponent of autarky and economic protectionism. From the beginning of the Weimar Republic, DDP leaders advocated a foreign policy based on the principle of international cooperation, which they saw as the means of restoring Germany's economic health. In contrast to the leaders of the DNVP and the NSDAP, who saw a link between Germany's economic health and closer ties with eastern Europe, DDP officials promoted stronger trade ties with the wealthier nations of western Europe and North America.[112]

In 1924 the DDP joined with the SPD to vote against protective tariffs for agriculture. German Democratic Party deputies argued that Germany's future lay in removing barriers between itself and Europe and that protective tariffs were an obstacle to that future. Paraphrasing the economic vision of Adam Smith, party officials also claimed that free trade provided the best prospects for improving the economic standing of the German nation and offered a means of alleviating Germany's chronic deficiency of key raw materials.[113] One year later, party members spoke out against efforts by the agricultural lobby to raise wheat tariffs, saying that the tariffs would undermine the buying power of urban consumers. These party members claimed that heavy industry was the real driving force behind higher wheat prices, which it was promoting as a means of garnering votes for its own programs.[114] Underlying the distrust that many farmers held for the DDP was the perception that DDP deputies had voted for bilateral trade treaties benefiting industry and commerce while they had opposed protective tariffs for agriculture, an indication to these farmers that the party placed the interests of industry and commerce over those of agriculture.[115]

Some of the best examples of the DDP's staunch promotion of free trade and international economic cooperation are found in the party's newspaper *Vossische Zeitung*. For instance, in an article on June 16, 1927, the *Vossische Zeitung* chided both foreign governments and German nationalists who endeavored to use the Geneva Conference to raise duties. According to the newspaper, for Germany to compete and profit in the world market, it would need to lower duties.[116] One week later, the *Vossische Zeitung* praised economics minister Julius Curtius for engaging in talks on a cooperative international economy. According to the newspaper, in contrast to the romantics and agitators whose "ideal" was a closed German economy, Minister Curtius proposed that Germany produce industrial machinery and manufactured goods as cheaply as possible for export. The *Vossische Zeitung* added that Curtius also had called for lowering duties on industrial goods and rejected calls to raise duties on agricultural products. Curtius had concluded by stressing that the fate of Europe was also Germany's fate.[117]

In addition to advocating expanded foreign trade and international economic cooperation, the DDP crusaded for tax reform and curbs on big business and big agriculture. As early as 1919, the party submitted a progressive tax program that included hikes in income, property, and inheritance taxes, along with a call for a war profits tax, the continuation of the wartime business turnover tax, and a capital levy.[118] Again in 1925 DDP delegates presented progressive tax proposals, including a special tax on all interest accrued since January 1, 1921, the introduction of higher taxes on large incomes, and a doubling of property and inheritance tax rates.[119]

At times, however, the DDP appeared to issue mixed messages regarding big business and agriculture. For instance, on the referendum to expropriate the former princely holdings, the DDP split: the left wing favored the referendum for its anti-elitist and progressive significance, whereas the right wing opposed the referendum as an attack on the right of private property. In the end the DDP took a neutral position on the referendum that earned the party few friends. That was one in a series of DDP political equivocations on issues that included Social Democratic socialization proposals, tax reform, and the Factory Council Law.[120] Though the DDP saw itself as a friend of the middle class, especially with regard to tax policy, many self-employed Germans probably disliked the party's advocacy of higher property and inheritance taxes.

The consensus in the literature is that the DDP's political strategy targeted the urban middle class. But by 1927, despite the opposition of the DDP's left wing, several party leaders seemed to have rediscovered the German farming community. The precipitous rise in farm foreclosures in

1927 alerted the party to its lack of an agricultural program. In early 1928, the DDP crafted and published an agricultural program and established a special agricultural committee. The program called for the elimination of the land tax for small and midsize farmers, increased protection of tenant farmers' rights, greater tariff protection for dairy and livestock producers, and the creation of small farms from the expropriation of large landed estates that were no longer economically viable. Unfortunately, the program and committee came too late to help the DDP, for the party's credibility among many farmers had suffered as a result of its prior voting record in the Reichstag and its failure to develop an economic program for the middle class.[121]

As the economic crisis deepened, the DDP (which had become the DStP in 1930) blamed the government's preferential treatment of big business and big agriculture. The DStP's 1930 "Manifesto of the German State Party" included calls for tax reduction through comprehensive fiscal and administrative reforms and greater protection of the middle class from the threat of extinction brought about by the concentration of economic power. Yet the party hedged on its criticism of government, finding fault with governmental policy but refusing to hold the *system* responsible for Germany's economic problems. Indeed, the DStP loyally backed Brüning's deflationary fiscal policies even though these policies did not seem to elicit much support from the old middle class.[122] For the remainder of the Weimar period, the DDP advanced no comprehensive program of its own for German agriculture and small business but rather concentrated on attacking the NSDAP's proposals on autarky and deficit-spending as unworkable and potentially damaging to Germany's economic health, while at the same time trying to convince the middle classes that they had benefited from Brüning's fiscal policies.[123]

The Center Party and the Old Middle Class

The Center Party encountered numerous roadblocks in its attempt to follow a consistent policy vis-à-vis the old middle class. Much of the difficulty lay with party members' hope of holding on to a relatively diverse Catholic constituency. Most urban Catholics favored lower agricultural prices, whereas most rural Catholics supported higher agricultural prices; most Catholic farmers, shopkeepers, and artisans engaged in the export sector favored free-trade policies, whereas most Catholic farmers, shopkeepers, and artisans involved in the domestic sector approved of higher protective tariffs. Consequently, Center Party social and economic positions lacked a consistent philosophical direction. At different times, for example, it promoted both free trade and economic protection. The party's oscillations on economic matters frequently led to conflicts between the national party organization and the party's Bavarian ally (the BVP); the national organization tried to represent both its urban and rural constituencies, but the BVP was mainly concerned with the interests of Bavaria's large agricultural population.

Throughout the Weimar era, the Center Party remained active in the debates over the future of Germany's domestic economy and foreign trade. In 1925 the Center Party's Reichstag faction joined with the DNVP in the quest for agricultural protection. Center Party members bemoaned the fact that while industry was protected by import duties on foreign goods, agriculture suffered from external controls. Party officials also lamented that the countryside was being sacrificed to the cities. Governmental tax and tariff policy benefited the urban areas to the detriment of the countryside, according to many in the party. Center Party deputies urged the government to implement a tariff to restore a balance between industrial and agricultural duties. The party's decision to support higher tariffs stirred considerable debate in the Center Party press, however, and drew criticism from many in the pro-labor wing of the party.[124]

But in 1926 party leaders called for the elimination of internal barriers to free trade. According to an article in *Germania*, the Center Party newspaper, a healthy export trade was necessary in order for Germany to reduce its debt.[125] One year later, representatives of the Center Party insisted that protective tariffs and lower taxes alone could not restore the health of German agriculture and handicrafts. Party leaders argued for the implementation of technical improvements to build up agriculture and manufacturing.[126] During the late 1920s the Center Party was reluctant to favor higher food prices, for fear of alienating the urban population.[127] The effects of the Great Depression, however, and growing pressure from the party's political ally, the BVP, produced a shift in the Center Party's position on tariffs. By late 1929 the Center Party was again advocating protective tariffs for German agriculture, albeit not very passionately. Having little faith that tariff walls could be dismantled worldwide, in November of 1929 Center Party deputies called for a dramatic reduction in foreign agricultural imports into Germany and the implementation of a series of import duties.[128] Tariffs again became a primary issue for the Center Party in June 1930. A writer for *Germania*, observing that Germany's agricultural crisis was due largely to the hemorrhaging of its capital through reparations payments, claimed that although tariffs by themselves could not restore the productivity of German agriculture, they were a necessary ingredient of any cure. The article concluded with a warning that if all other means failed to revive Germany's agriculture, the revocation of existing trade agreements was inevitable.[129]

As soon as Brüning took over as chancellor, the party began to downplay support for protective tariffs and governmental subsidies for agriculture. Brüning's administration imposed restraints on spending and looked with disfavor on economic protectionism, which, it asserted, would derail Germany's efforts to sell produce abroad.[130] Whereas the leadership of the Center Party felt obliged to back party leader Brüning, the allied BVP was under no such obligation. The BVP, which derived considerable electoral support from struggling Bavarian Catholic farmers, pressed Brüning to reverse his deflationary policies.[131] With Brüning's dismissal in mid-1932, Center Party representatives again supported protective tariffs and governmental assistance to agriculture. In 1932 the Center Party also broadened its appeal to the old middle class by advocating stable interest rates and the elimination of rural usury.[132]

The SPD and the Old Middle Class

The Social Democratic Party was an unlikely party of choice for Germany's old middle class. Among the strikes against it were its Marxist legacy of antagonism toward private property, its favoritism toward the industrial working class, and its consistent attacks on protective tariffs for agriculture.

The SPD had grappled with the issue of an agrarian program since the last half of the nineteenth century. In 1895 and again in 1920 and 1921, efforts by party moderates failed to get the SPD to abandon its opposition to private property and to support small-peasant agriculture. Instead, party leaders stuck to the traditional Marxist line on agriculture: independent small farmers, like the rest of the petty bourgeoisie, constituted a doomed social class; their holdings would eventually be gobbled up by the more efficient large-scale estates. Moreover, these same SPD leaders saw a positive value in the replacement of Germany's small independent farms with large capitalist estates. It would create a huge class of landless agricultural laborers, who like their urban counterparts could be easily mobilized by the party.[133]

Not until the 1927 Kiel party congress did the SPD develop a comprehensive agrarian program. The 1927 Kiel party program represented an important departure for the SPD with regard to the party's socialist plans for agriculture. For the first time, the party dropped its call for the appropriation of smallholdings. The Social Democrats proposed instead the confiscation of only large holdings (with compensation), which were to be redistributed to smallholders for intensive cultivation. The Kiel party program marked a victory for party revisionists, who had hoped that once the SPD no longer condemned small-scale possession of private property, the party could make inroads into an important and heretofore neglected constituency. The Kiel program also included an appeal for the creation of a governmental monopoly to regulate grain prices and imports; and promises of free legal aid to German peasants on credit and tax matters, along with free technical advice to help raise agricultural productivity.[134]

Notwithstanding the Kiel program, the SPD leadership's opposition to large farms was unabated. Indeed, large farmers remained a scapegoat for agrarian social ills. According to the Social Democratic newspaper *Volkswacht,* large landowners continued to benefit from a tax system that disproportionately burdened small and midsize farmers. In particular, the newspaper charged that large farmers' income tax was assessed according to the owners' own bookkeeping entries, whereas small farmers had to pay a flat rate. Consequently, in one county large farmers owned two-thirds of the land but paid significantly lower taxes than the small farmers, who collectively owned one-third of the land.[135]

At times the SPD actually undermined its own goal of curbing the influence of Germany's large farmers. In 1930, for instance, party deputies supported a bill to establish a state monopoly on grain that was meant to ensure a steady supply of grain to urban consumers. But by maintaining high grain prices, the monopoly had the unintended effect of bolstering the financial security of the large farmers.[136] That story was exploited by the German Communist Party press, much to the chagrin of the Social Democrats.[137]

It is debatable whether the Kiel program represented a significant shift within the SPD on agricultural matters and whether it actually improved the SPD's standing among German farmers. Abraham notes that the Kiel program, rather than marking a major departure for the SPD, furthered the party's goal of industrializing agriculture. By 1927 party officials concluded that the industrialization of agriculture and higher profitability required the elimination of large, inefficient estates and the encouragement of small, economically viable farms.[138] James and Stoltenberg claim that the Kiel party program resulted in electoral successes for the SPD among small farmers. Stoltenberg points specifically to the stronger electoral performance of the SPD among small farmers in Schleswig-Holstein in the 1928 elections.[139] By contrast, Schumacher, Linz, and Gessner contend that the Kiel program came too late to help the SPD among small farmers and that the party failed to follow up with specific legislation assisting farmers.[140]

If for German farmers a party's position on tariffs separated friend from foe, then the SPD faced an insurmountable obstacle to winning the farm vote. The party opposed protective agricultural tariffs for numerous reasons, including the desire to remove barriers to international cooperation and free trade, the wish to acquire less expensive raw materials from abroad, a traditional preference for industry over agriculture, and a pledge to lower food costs for urban workers.[141] In the debate between Germany's export and import sectors the SPD came down decisively on the side of the former. Hilferding, a prominent SPD financial expert, saw free trade as an essential means of achieving international peace and German economic recovery and cautioned that protectionism could lead to violent international conflict, imperial conquest, and social unrest in Germany.[142] Throughout the 1920s, the Social Democrats consistently rejected demands for higher agricultural tariffs. Party leaders and the party's unions agreed with industrialists who warned that higher tariffs would lead to retaliatory gestures on the part of Germany's best customers and that in the end, German living standards would fall as food prices rose. Even the framers of the SPD's Kiel program on agriculture, who were pro-agriculture, concurred that the SPD, as a party of the urban masses, could not advocate higher food prices.[143]

Unlike the DDP, the DVP, and the Center Party, which before 1929 had been allies in the struggle against higher agricultural tariffs, the SPD held firm on its opposition to protectionism until the end of the Weimar Republic. For instance, in February 1929 the SPD attacked plans to impose higher duties on ham and lard. *Volkswacht* claimed that these duties would burden the German masses directly, by forcing them to purchase more expensive domestic products. The newspaper cited Leberwurst, made up 80 percent of Danish liver, as an example of a product popular among Germans but not produced by German farmers.[144] The SPD kept up its attack on protective tariffs and the big estates during 1930-1932, lambasting the Brüning government for assisting the debt-ridden large eastern farmers at the expense of the urban poor: the cheapest frozen meats were now blocked from entering the German market. The party advocated a total overhaul of the state's agricultural policy. It favored public ownership of Germany's large farms, along with more efficient coordination among agricultural producers, distributors, and consumers, which was expected to result in lower food prices and the elimination of protective tariffs.[145]

The KPD and the Old Middle Class

Germany's independent proprietors did not need to familiarize themselves with the proceedings of the German Communist Party congresses to realize that they would not find in the goals of German Communism the recipe for their economic well-being—overthrow of the present order, smashing of the capitalistic state apparatus, and institution of soviet-based proletarian power. Throughout the Weimar era, the Communists made clear their opposition to private property and their unswerving support of the urban working class over the old middle class of independent farmers, shopkeepers, and artisans.

Consistent with its desire to improve conditions for urban workers was the KPD's steady opposition to higher protective tariffs. For instance, in December 1927 the major Communist party newspaper, *Die Rote Fahne*, stated that the trade pact with southern Slovakia being debated in the Reichstag would hurt the working classes: the agreement would restrict importation of meats and eggs, both major exports of Slovakia, and the proposed custom taxes would benefit only the rich. The article concluded by reiterating the Communist Party's rejection of any import duty on such necessary foodstuffs as bread, meat, lard, bacon, and potatoes.[146] Even when the Social Democrats backslid on the issue of protective tariffs for agriculture, as in the case of a bill to raise the price of corn from 3.20 to 5 marks, the Communists stood firmly opposed.

Though the Communist Party's attention centered on the industrial working class, the party did launch an effort, especially after 1929, to attract agricultural labor and small farmers to its ranks. Borrowing from Bolshevik strategy, the KPD appealed to urban workers to go out into the countryside and to form a common front with the enslaved farmworkers for the revolutionary liberation.[147] German Communists, seeking to attract peasants, promised that a Soviet Germany would be controlled by a government of both workers and peasants. Aware that many in the farming community opposed the KPD because of its outspoken disapproval of private property, KPD leaders attempted to convince farmers that the party would never force them to collectivize. Rather, the Communist Party would request (not demand) that farmers with small and midsized farms agree to combine their holdings into larger units more suitable for the use of modern agricultural equipment.[148]

After 1930 the KPD gave greater attention to the problem of growing rural unemployment. In July 1932 the party called for a halt in wage reductions for agricultural labor, and for state financial support of unemployed farmers, lower property taxes and indirect taxes, elimination of forced sales of farms, forgiveness of taxes and loans to farmers, and creation of a social security system for farmers.[149]

Like the NSDAP, the Communist Party had an activist commitment to farmers' struggles. Stoltenberg, in his detailed study of the rise of Nazism in the German state of Schleswig-Holstein, points to the KPD's active involvement in the 1932 campaign to win the release of a local hero who had been imprisoned for using violent tactics against the government's agricultural policy. Unlike the Nazis, however, the KPD failed to establish a substantial foothold in the farming communities of Schleswig-Holstein, because of the party's advocacy of land collectivization and its rejection of protective tariffs.[150]

The NSDAP and the Old Middle Class

There is obvious agreement among scholars that the German rural community was a mainstay of the Nazi constituency. But what did the old middle class find so appealing in Nazism? Scholarship on the rise of Nazism in rural Germany has focused largely on these themes: (1) Nazi Party success in garnering protest votes from the old middle class against the system and its political parties, (2) the attraction for the old middle class of such Nazi leitmotifs as a return to the good old days when independent farmers, shopkeepers, and artisans constituted the backbone of society, and (3) the NSDAP's skill at infiltrating and seizing control of agrarian organizations. Although these factors help to explain the popularity of Nazism in rural Germany, they tend to deflect attention from the elements of the Nazi Party's old middle class policies that appealed to the material interests of these groups. Also, these interpretations of the party's rural success fail to explain why the NSDAP appealed more to some old middle class groups than others. Why, for example, did livestock farmers more often join the Nazi Party than those involved in grain cultivation or fruit and vegetable farming? There is evidence that the specifics of the

NSDAP's rural programs significantly affected both the size and the complexion of the Nazis' rural constituency.

The conventional interpretation of the Nazi Party's relations with the old middle class emphasizes the disjuncture between the pre-1928 and post-1928 periods. Before 1928 the NSDAP appeared to people in Germany as a party hostile to private property and largely preoccupied with its urban strategy. Consequently, the Nazis failed to make significant inroads among the old middle class.[151] Hitler realized the impact of the agrarian crisis and hoped to win a sizable rural vote in the May 1928 general elections. He therefore decided to reinterpret point 17 of the Nazi Party's official 1920 platform, which had called for the "unremunerative expropriation of land for the common weal." Hitler explained that point 17 referred only to land wrongfully acquired (obtained illegitimately or administered without regard for the good of the people) and primarily owned by "Jewish property speculation companies" (*jüdische Grundspekulationsgesellschaften*). Thus, by 1928 the Nazi Party became a strong proponent of private property, according to the traditional explanation.[152]

That explanation, however, has exaggerated the degree to which 1928 signaled a shift or a reversal in the NSDAP's strategy to win over the German old middle class. The NSDAP had been preoccupied since its inception in 1920 with the old middle class and its issues, and the party's pronouncements on these matters after 1928 were generally consistent with its earlier positions. Let us examine some of the major Nazi Party initiatives for Germany's old middle class before 1933.

In the aftermath of World War I, the Nazi Party, like many other Weimar parties, favored land reform. The 1920 official party platform urged the adoption of a land reform policy that would offer Germany's land-hungry peasantry and urban wage workers an opportunity to farm. In *Mein Kampf* Hitler underscored the importance of a large and thriving farming community and emphasized that a strong stock of small and mid-size farmers constituted the best protection against social problems.[153] The party's land reform program envisioned the establishment of new farming communities in eastern Germany. For many in the NSDAP, a resettlement program in eastern Germany offered at least two important benefits: it would satisfy the land appetite of the landless population and would serve as a bulwark against Polish immigration into Germany's eastern regions. Unlike the SPD and KPD plans, the Nazi plan did not include a call for the expropriation of large estates but rather a demand that vacant land, idle estates, and state-owned land be distributed to the landless.[154]

From its origins in 1920 the Nazi Party had been a consistent defender of private property; however, the party opposed private property that resulted from land speculation. Nazi Party publications referred to this form of private property as unnatural and unhealthy because (according to Nazi philosophy) it destroyed the social purpose of farming—namely, the cultivator's direct involvement in agriculture. Hitler instructed his Reichstag delegates in 1926 to vote against the leftist-sponsored bill on the expropriation of properties of former royal households, but that had more to do with a defense of private property than a desire to curry favor with the class of large landowners. Hitler excoriated his party's left wing for advocating the Marxist position and reminded Strasser and Goebbels that a defense of private property was necessary if the party hoped to attract those who feared communism.[155]

Nor was the NSDAP opposed to capitalism. The NSDAP in its early years distinguished between productive and unproductive capitalism. The party favored productive capitalism (*bodenständigen Kapitalismus*), which embodied profit from one's own labor; but it disapproved of unproductive capitalism or loan capitalism, which derived profit from speculation or "the greatest possible income with the least amount of work" and which pitted the interests of the worker against those of the employer. For many in the party, Henry Ford, the American carmaker, was the epitome of the productive capitalist.[156] Also, Nazi propaganda targeted the capitalistic practices of big business, banks, the stock market, department stores, and consumer cooperatives, which the Nazis claimed hurt small businesses. By distinguishing between good capitalists and bad capitalists, the Nazis successfully staked out their own space between the Left (the SPD and KPD), which was critical of all forms of capitalism, and the Right (the DNVP and DVP), which was a staunch proponent of big business. I suggest that the NSDAP's preference for one form of capitalism over others struck a chord with many in the old middle class.[157]

As the farming crisis deepened after 1927, the NSDAP heightened its efforts to mobilize the support of farmers, shopkeepers, and artisans. Party leaders convened local meetings of groups from the old middle class to familiarize them with the NSDAP's positions on the issues, and it called for the creation of *Berufskammern* (professional organizations) to represent the interests of the old middle class.[158] Among the issues the NSDAP highlighted were the unavailability of affordable credit, the deficiency of insurance and welfare programs for the old middle class, and the lack of decisive governmental action to protect the old middle class from both foreign competitors and big business. Central to the Nazi campaign to win over the old middle class was the party's vitriolic attack on the practices of department stores and consumer cooperatives. The Nazis accused these organizations of undermining the economic foundations of mercantile and artisanal groups. The NSDAP urged the government to enact legislation to curb the marketing practices of the large department stores and consumer cooperatives and after 1931 devoted a section of the party's chief newspaper, the *Völkischer Beobachter*, to promotion of the struggle against the power of department stores and monopolies.[159]

Many of the principal themes of the 1930 NSDAP agrarian program were already in evidence as early as 1924. In line with its general advocacy of nationalist etatism, the NSDAP called for the establishment of an autarkic economic system in which the importation of foreign agricultural commodities was to be sharply reduced. In addition to economic autarky the NSDAP consistently advocated a program to open up lands for new farming communities; it also called for reductions in taxes, interest rates, and social expenditures. Party leaders insisted that all of these measures were necessary in order to restore economic security and social honor to the German farming community.[160]

Throughout the 1920s the NSDAP gave considerable attention to the issues of agricultural prices, tariffs, credit, and taxes. Heinrich Himmler's well-known 1926 essay, "Farmer, Wake Up!" offers an example of NSDAP leaders' concern over falling agricultural prices.[161] In the essay, Himmler skillfully linked the fall in agricultural prices to Jewish capitalists' control over the fertilizer and grain markets and the Weimar government's cowardice about reparations payments. According to Himmler, the end result of Jewish capitalist practices and governmental policy was that German farmers received less money for their produce and paid higher taxes.[162] In 1927 the Nazis blamed governmental insensitivity to farmers' concerns and Jewish oligopolistic control for the flood of foreign agricultural commodities.

The NSDAP's pronouncements included more than scathing attacks on the alleged enemies of agriculture, for the Nazis realized that potential adherents want more than a target for their frustrations; they want a road map for a better future. The party's policies between 1928 and 1930 largely echoed the program of the emerging *Landvolk* movement. In particular, the NSDAP called for raising agricultural productivity through reductions in the cost of credit, production costs, trade margins, taxes, and land prices. Furthermore, party officials argued that only a National Socialist state, not specifically regional or class movements, would be capable of saving German agriculture from international capitalism.[163]

The 1930 NSDAP agrarian program stands as the party's major statement on agricultural matters before 1933. The agrarian program (*Partei-amtliche Kundgebung über die Stellung der NSDAP zum Landvolk und zur Landwirtschaft*) appeared in the *Völkischer Beobachter* on March 6, 1930. Though many credit Walther Darré with authorship of the program, it appears that Darré had considerable assistance from Gregor Strasser, Himmler, and Feder.[164] The program embodied both specific proposals for improving the agricultural situation in Germany and an ideological encomium of the Nordic or Aryan race.[165] Many of the proposals contained in the agrarian program were not new; the NSDAP, the DNVP, and various regional agricultural groups had voiced them earlier.[166] The NSDAP displayed innovation, however, in the way it combined these proposals into what appeared to many Germans a single coherent program linked to the party's general economic and social strategy.[167] The program also contained some novel and politically opportunistic proposals on inheritance.

Inheritance and resettlement figured significantly in the 1930 agrarian program. The Nazis had claimed that Germany's impartible inheritance system had been eroded by the introduction of Roman law in Germany, the Napoleonic occupation, and the state's acceptance of laissez-faire economic policies. In Germany's predominantly Catholic Rhineland and southwest, partible inheritance was in more common use than elsewhere in Germany. The reintroduction of a compulsory system of impartible inheritance would be necessary to restore vitality to the German family farm and protect the farmer from the world market and capitalistic speculation, the Nazis maintained. The NSDAP urged the enactment of a law of hereditary entailment to ensure that Germany's farmland remained in the hands of pure Germans (persons of German origin) and to guarantee that farms specified as hereditary (*Erbhöfe*) remained with the same family in perpetuity. According to the Nazi proposal, only the eldest child should inherit, to prevent fragmentation of the farms among the various heirs. Also, the property could not be sold or held as collateral for a loan. According to the Nazis, their inheritance proposal would among other things eliminate the farm fragmentation, land speculation, and bank foreclosures that had driven thousands of farmers from their hearths.[168]

Closely linked to the NSDAP's inheritance proposals were its pronouncements on resettlement. Realizing that the elimination of partible inheritance would produce a sea of disinherited, party leaders sought to entice those people with new land in the east. The NSDAP resettlement policy called for the establishment of large-scale settlements along the eastern frontier, peopled mainly by disinherited farmers' sons and aspiring landworkers. The Nazis suggested that besides unused land, underutilized or poorly used lands from large eastern German estates be made available for the new settlements. The state had the obligation, the Nazis claimed, to seize land that large estate owners failed to farm and make this land available, in the form of hereditary leaseholds, to Germans who were landless but willing to farm. The creation of farms alone, though, would not ensure their economic viability; the Nazis envisioned the establishment of cities alongside the new farms to provide farmers with local markets for their produce as well as easy access to required nonagricultural commodities.[169]

From this summons for resettlement, the agrarian program easily established a logical basis for greater autarkic development. The building of new farming communities in the east would ease Germany's transition to total self-sufficiency in food. Under a Nazi regime, two chief ends of foreign policy would be internal colonization and the securing of a larger domestic food supply. For the immediate future, party leaders demanded greater protection for domestic agricultural production through higher tariffs and state regulation of imports. Rather than posing agricultural protection as a potential setback for industrial interests, NSDAP leaders shrewdly connected agricultural and industrial interests, claiming that agricultural protection would give farmers greater purchasing power, which would result in higher demand for industrial goods.[170]

Because higher tariffs and restrictions on imports alone would not restore German agricultural productivity, the agrarian program urged the establishment of government-backed agricultural cooperatives. These cooperatives would provide farmers with inexpensive fertilizers, electricity, seeds, agricultural machinery, and advice on soil enrichment, pest control, and animal breeding. The cooperatives would also manage wholesale trade in agricultural commodities and thereby eliminate the role of the stock exchange in setting agricultural prices.[171]

The 1930 agrarian program reiterated Nazi support for the availability of cheaper credit, the restoration of prewar interest rates, lower taxes, and an end to usury. The agrarian program proposed that farm size and productivity serve as determinants of farmers' taxes, in lieu of the tax regulations then in effect. Regarding usury, the NSDAP appealed for governmental regulation to end land speculation, stating in the program that land should no longer furnish owners with unearned income and that one who purchased a farm should be obligated to farm it.[172]

The 1930 agrarian program constantly underscored the promise of a better economic future. The program discussed the need to improve the lot of the agricultural laborers by raising them to the status of farmer. This could occur largely through the party's resettlement program. Transforming German agricultural laborers into farmers fit the party's strategy to stem the flight of the laborers from the land and reduce the demand for imported agricultural labor.[173] In addition, the resettlement program offered the hope of a brighter future to noninheriting sons of farmers.[174]

Shortly after the publication of the NSDAP agrarian program in 1930, Hitler announced the establishment of an NSDAP agricultural department, headed by Walther Plesch, to provide farmers with agricultural information.[175] A year later, in an article in the *Völkischer Beobachter*, Darré reemphasized the NSDAP's belief that a resolution of the agricultural crisis required a commitment to autarkic economic development and the expansion of farming:

> No other kind of dependency so centrally damages a state with a will to live as dependency in foodstuffs: this can paralyze it completely. A people is only guaranteed an independent supply of foodstuffs if it has space available to nourish itself through its own energies. From the standpoint of the organic idea of state the question of food supply is probably the most essential task to be faced by the government. The government will therefore direct its main attention to those who above all have the responsibility for providing foodstuffs, the farmers. It will make the farmers the cornerstone of the state.[176]

Hitler followed in May 1931 with a speech to farmers stressing the need for German economic self-reliance. In a speech in the town of Eutin (Schleswig-Holstein) on May 8, 1931, Hitler blamed the deteriorating situation in German farming and manufacturing on the government's continuing policy of importing cheap agricultural produce and finished products. In a National Socialist Germany the interests of the German producers would come first and the economy would be completely controlled by Germans, Hitler stated.[177] Autarkic development remained a theme in early 1932. In the northern free state of Oldenburg, the NSDAP criticized the government's policy of importing fruit, meats, vegetables, cars, and finished products at a time when German agriculture and industry produced these same commodities. The party asserted that money must go to German producers and jobs to German workers ("Erst kommt mein Volk und dann die andern alle, erst meine Heimat, dann die Welt"). The Nazis called for the rebirth of the Hanseatic league of former days and proposed to lower unemployment through a resettlement program in eastern Germany. Every young German should be guaranteed a profession, they proclaimed.[178] During 1931 and 1932 Nazi propaganda continued to highlight the proposals contained in the 1930 agrarian program. Moreover, the Nazis increased their efforts to attract agricultural laborers through promises of higher wages in money and kind and a plan to furnish them with small-scale homesteads along the eastern frontier. Party members also campaigned against the DNVP and the Osthilfe program, which the Nazis described as grossly inadequate to remedy the agricultural crisis; Osthilfe, they claimed, was largely a gimmick to help Junker farmers while doing little for small farmers.[179]

Both the NSDAP's May 1932 Immediate Economic Program and its November 1932 Economic Reconstruction Plan addressed the concerns of the old middle class. Each program included measures to enable small businesses to acquire less costly raw materials more easily and gain access to the newest manufacturing technologies.[180] Both programs further emphasized the need to furnish small businesses with low-cost credit.

The NSDAP differed from most other parties in its level of commitment to the interests of the old middle class. Unlike most other political parties, the NSDAP displayed a readiness to act on its principles. The literature on the rise of Nazism abounds with examples of Nazis actively engaging in popular causes. Throughout the farming districts of Franconia, East Prussia, Pomerania, and Schleswig-Holstein, Nazi activists organized and participated in farmers' protests (some violent). In Franconia, East Prussia, and Pomerania, the NSDAP joined with farmers to obstruct the forced auctions of farms.[181] In Pomerania and Schleswig-Holstein the NSDAP joined demonstrations protesting governmental litigation against local farmers.[182] In Oldenburg the NSDAP participated in large-scale demonstrations demanding agricultural price stability.[183] And, in Bavaria, the NSDAP organized a protest against a bank whose directors had allegedly placed excessively high interest rates on loans to farmers.[184] Active Nazi participation had the effect of convincing many members of the old middle class that the Nazis' commitment to their causes was real.

If acting on conviction helped the NSDAP win support among the old middle class, failure to do so hurt the party. Schaap's and Stokes' studies of Oldenburg offer an excellent illustration of how a lack of commitment hurt the NSDAP. Both Schaap and Stokes show how the NSDAP's dominant electoral position in Oldenburg in the late spring and early summer of 1932 began to unravel by November 1932.[185] Both authors point to the NSDAP's inability, as Oldenburg's governing party, to enact legislation for tax relief. During the May 1932 Oldenburg state election campaign, the party had pledged that a National Socialist government would lower taxes. Nevertheless, during the autumn of 1932, with the Nazis in control of state government, state taxes increased. In Oldenburg the overall vote for the NSDAP fell between 10 and 15 percentage points between the elections of July and November 1932, though it fell less than 5 percentage points nationwide. Stokes' data corroborate Schaap's findings, demonstrating that in the district of Eutin the NSDAP vote fell from 56.48 percent in the May 1932 state election to 43.65 percent in the November general elections.[186]

An examination of the interests of the old middle class in Germany and the political programs of the various Weimar parties raises a question that should have tremendous relevance for the study of the rise of interwar European fascism. Given the aversion of many farmers, artisans, and small shopkeepers toward big business, and the essential antipathy on the Left to big business, could the German Left have mounted a viable challenge to the NSDAP in the German countryside and possibly thwarted the Nazi rise to power? We should not forget that the Nazi Party's initial electoral breakthrough—which may have contributed substantially to the party's ultimate electoral successes in 1932—occurred in the countryside. The NSDAP's ability to establish a foothold among German farmers was greatly enhanced by the ideological dogmatism of the Left. A brief examination of the differences in leftist ideology in Germany, Italy, and France during the interwar period should make this point clearer.

Among these three countries, only in France did the Left successfully counter fascist efforts to build a popular movement among independent farmers. The Left in Germany and Italy failed to fashion a program that appealed to the material interests of the farming community. In particular, whereas the French Left supported land redistribution and private property, leftists in Germany and Italy never abandoned their call for collectivization of land and public ownership of the means of production. As a result, millions of farmers in Germany and Italy who might have been attracted by pleas for greater social equality and denunciation of large farmers were repelled by the leftist rejection of private property.

A leftist policy that supports private property may seem paradoxical, but it has done so in France. French Marxists have frequently advocated one policy for industry—nationalization of the means of production—and another policy for agriculture—championship of small private property.[187] Since the French Revolution, when the Montagnards implemented the *Code rural,* the French Left has unfailingly supported the rights of small peasant cultivators.[188] More than one hundred years ago, Ledru Rollin, a notable Democrat-Socialist, eloquently stated the French Left's position on property: "Property is liberty. We will therefore respect property, but on condition that it will be infinitely multiplied. We do not want it for some; we want it for all."[189]

The French Left continued to hold to its defense of small private property throughout the nineteenth century and into the twentieth century. In 1921 the new French Communist party joined the Socialist Party in making the defense of small property part of its own agrarian program.[190] Small independent farmers in Mediterranean and central France found their economic prosperity whittled away by the capitalistic practices of the large farmers and by the French government's decision to allow importation of cheaper foreign agricultural products. Not surprisingly, many of these French farmers voted for the Socialists and Communists in the general elections of 1924, 1928, 1932, and 1936.[191] The same kinds of farmers, I suggest, rejected the Left in Italy and Germany and eventually aligned themselves with the Italian Fascist Party and the German Nazi Party.

Italian Fascism could hardly have succeeded if it had not first secured a foothold in the farming regions of north-central Italy.[192] Though the Italian Left had amassed a considerable following among poor agricultural laborers and sharecroppers by advocating wage increases, a program to alleviate rural unemployment, and a program of agrarian collectivization intended to eliminate private property, it alienated potential adherents who aspired to own property or expand their holdings.[193] The Italian Socialist Party argued forcefully against the cultivation of land for personal profit or advancement.[194] The Italian Socialists considered the creation of small private properties through land redistribution reactionary.[195] At the 17th Party Congress in January 1921, Nino Mazzoni, a Socialist Party leader, argued that Italian Socialists should not repeat the mistake of Robespierre, who created a class of smallholders during the French Revolution. Land should be given to the peasant collective, not to individual peasants.[196] The Italian Socialist Party aimed to transform tenants and owners into proletarian members of an agricultural cooperative.[197] The party opposed individual ownership and strongly advocated land collectivization, a policy that cost it the support of many sharecroppers and agricultural laborers who had backed the party in 1919–1920, when it forced landlords to provide higher wages and better contracts. By 1921, the Italian sharecroppers and laborers wanted to climb the social ladder, and they began to search for a political party that would allow them to achieve their goal of land ownership. The Italian Fascist Party, meanwhile, had made clear its opposition to agrarian socialism and land collectivization. The Italian Fascists proposed to transform agricultural laborers into sharecroppers, sharecroppers into tenant farmers, and all three eventually into landowners.[198] Unlike the Socialists, the Italian Fascists addressed the aspirations of those who wanted land—both those who had never had any and those who wanted more.

In much the same way, the German Left forfeited the potential backing of many farmers who could never feel comfortable in a party that attacked private property and thereby rejected the farmer's dream of social advancement. Like the Italian Fascist Party, the NSDAP crafted an agrarian program that included a defense of private property and offered farmers the promise of a better future. Their success might suggest that French leftists' advocacy of land redistribution and peasant smallholdings may have blocked fascism's easy access to a rural constituency in France during the 1920s and 1930s.

My explanation of the rise of interwar fascism in the European countryside would seem to conflict with the provocative thesis advanced by Gregory Luebbert. For Luebbert, the composition of class coalitions rather than ideological intransigence determined the fate of fascism in rural Europe. Luebbert asserts that in countries such as Denmark, Sweden, and Norway where socialist parties were able to build coalitions embracing both the family peasantry (self-employed farmers) and the urban working class, fascism failed to establish a foundation in agrarian communities. By contrast, Luebbert says, fascism gained a rural constituency in countries (Spain, Italy, and Germany) where socialist parties failed to build a coalition between the family peasants and the urban working class. The critical factor, in Luebbert's view, is who organized the agrarian proletariat. In Germany, Spain, and Italy the socialists took the lead in organizing the rural population, whereas in Sweden, Norway, and Denmark the socialists made no inroads in that constituency, which had already been organized by other parties. Luebbert believes that where the socialists took the initiative to organize the agrarian proletariat, they invariably made commit-

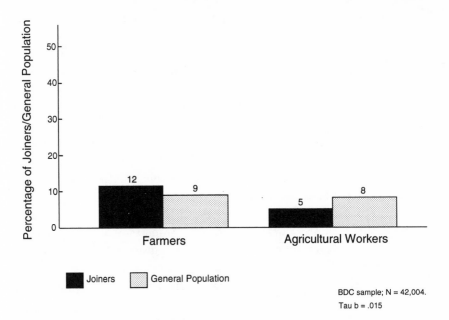

3.1 Nazi Party Joiners Who Were Self-Employed Farmers or Agricultural Workers, 1925–1932

ments to that class that alienated them from the family peasants. A fascist social order, according to Luebbert, depended on a coalition between the urban middle classes and the family peasantry.[199]

The empirical evidence for Germany appears to support Luebbert's claim that the family peasantry rather than the agrarian proletariat formed the backbone of the Nazi Party's rural constituency. See figure 3.1 for comparative percentages of Nazi Party joiners who were self-employed farmers and agricultural workers. We find that compared with the general population, self-employed farmers were overrepresented in the party, whereas agricultural workers were underrepresented. But Luebbert never convincingly explains why the family peasantry turned to the Nazi Party rather than to another political party or why a fascist social order requires a coalition between the urban middle classes and the family peasantry. Luebbert claims that the family peasantry was the sole agrarian group with the capacity to destabilize the polity—by virtue of its numbers, its rate of political participation, and its distinct political agenda; this claim, however, is insufficient to explain the rise of Nazism in Germany.[200] What is missing from Luebbert's explanation of the rise of fascism is an examination of the programs of the competing political parties. Why did so many family farmers support the Nazi Party rather than some other political party? Between 1925 and 1933 German farmers had several political choices. In this chapter, I have tried to demonstrate that the Nazi Party attracted a great number of farmers by offering concrete proposals to improve their material situation. Luebbert appears to accept Lipset's thesis that fascism is a form of middle-class political extremism. As demonstrated by the data on Nazi Party joiners presented in Chapter 1, it is inaccurate to depict the Nazi Party as a class party and in particular as a middle- or lower-middle-class party. A movement that established such strong roots in the blue-collar working class can hardly be called a lower-middle-class party.

Again, I start with the assumption that people join the political parties that most nearly reflect their interests. This reasoning leads me to argue that because of the heterogeneity of interests in the German old middle class, not every group within that class was equally inclined to join the Nazi Party. For instance, livestock farmers should have been more inclined to do so than large grain growers or the export-oriented vegetable and fruit farmers; and Protestant livestock farmers should have been likelier to join than Catholic livestock farmers. Through both their championing and their rejection of certain policies, Nazis appealed more to the interests of Protestant German livestock farmers: through their forceful advocacy of economic protectionism, resettlement, impartible inheritance, and tax relief and through their attack on Weimar policies regarding reparations and subsidies to large eastern German grain growers. That Protestant livestock farmers should have been more predisposed than grain, fruit, or vegetable producers to adhere to the Nazi Party before 1933 should help explain another interesting puzzle about the rise of Nazism: the degree of regional variation in Nazi Party membership.

On the one hand, the areas of Schleswig-Holstein, Lower Saxony, and Danzig manifested exceptionally high numbers of NSDAP votes and members; on the other hand, Westphalia, Württemberg, Cologne-Aachen, and Koblenz-Trier exhibited relatively weak attraction for the NSDAP. In fact, the ratio of Nazi Party members to total population was more than five times greater in Schleswig-Holstein than in northern Westphalia.[201] Why did the NSDAP fare better in some German regions than in others?

We know that Protestant regions of Germany were more attracted than Catholic regions to the Nazi Party, but confessional differences are an insufficient explanation, given that within predominantly Protestant and Catholic regions, Nazi support varied significantly. The political geography of Nazism is largely attributable to divergent regional constellations of material interests. The following examples should illuminate this thesis.

In the states of Schleswig-Holstein and Lower Saxony, the typical farmer was a smallholder engaged in highly precarious dairy farming and hog fattening.[202] During the final years of the Weimar Republic, many of the farmers of Schleswig-Holstein and Lower Saxony protested against what they perceived as the government's insensitivity to their economic plight. They demanded a German trade policy that would eliminate foreign sources of food; an immediate state takeover of mortgage interest payments; a law lowering the rate of interest; governmental financial assistance; lower taxes; and less-expensive fertilizer and electricity.[203] It was exactly these concerns that the Nazi agrarian program addressed and for which it proffered solutions.

Farmers in Germany's more prosperous regions — many of whom were less affected than those in Schleswig-Holstein and Lower Saxony by price changes in the international market for dairy and beef — were also less susceptible to Nazi promises and to the Nazi appeal for autarky.[204] For example, in parts of Rhineland-Westphalia, Baden, Bavaria, and Württemberg, many farmers specializing in the production of highly exportable cash crops such as tobacco, beer, wine, and fruits favored free-trade policies and worried about having to face foreign retaliation if Germany imposed agricultural tariff barriers.

Large eastern German grain producers were not won over by the Nazi agrarian program, either. Although the government seemed insensitive to the plight of the Geest dairy and meat farmers, it enacted a series of policies between 1928 and 1930 that largely benefited the large grain producers in eastern Germany. The grain producers also became the beneficiaries of massive state aid in 1931 under the Eastern Assistance Program. These farmers continued to cast their lot with the conservative DNVP.

Many farmers in Germany's more prosperous regions had an additional reason to look unfavorably on the Nazi agrarian program. The Nazi promise to halt the sale of farms outside the family line meant that owners could not sell their property or offer it as collateral against loans.[205] The theory of interest-based political choice predicts that this policy should have received support in the economically depressed northwest, where farmers were fighting to prevent foreclosure on their properties; the policy should not have been well received by farmers in the relatively prosperous zones of North Rhineland-Westphalia, Baden, and Bavaria. There the sale of land was still a source of profit, and using property as collateral against a loan was seen as a suitable means of obtaining capital to expand one's holdings.

Also, in many Catholic parts of southern Germany, Hesse, and North Rhineland-Westphalia, farmers had particular difficulties with the Nazi proposal for a compulsory system of impartible inheritance. If implemented, it would have terminated the practice of partible inheritance (dividing land holdings among all heirs) that was in effect in much of the region and guaranteed by regional laws.[206]

Many farmers in Schleswig-Holstein and Lower Saxony, by contrast, had no problem with the Nazi position on inheritance—impartible inheritance was already in practice there. Moreover, many of these farmers enthusiastically welcomed the concomitant Nazi promise of a settlement program through which disinherited farmers' sons would receive land parcels in eastern Germany.[207] In the economically depressed farming areas, older farmers did not have sufficient cash to pay monetary compensation for the inheritance to their younger sons, as custom in northwestern Germany dictated.[208] The Nazi program offered both parents and children an appealing way out of their dilemma.[209]

I would maintain that attachment to Nazism in Schleswig-Holstein was based on self-interest. This explanation shares with both Rudolf Heberle's and Gerhard Stoltenberg's exemplary and detailed studies (which focus on the rise of Nazism in Schleswig-Holstein) an emphasis on the economic foundation of Nazism's appeal. The principal difference between the theory of interest-based adherence and Heberle's and Stoltenberg's studies is that those authors ascribe support for the Nazi Party to a protest vote or anti-Weimar vote and thus ignore the degree to which people voted *for* the Nazi Party, which offered concrete proposals to improve the material conditions of Schleswig-Holstein's farming community. The theory of interest-based attachment to Nazism in Schleswig-Holstein between 1925 and 1933 diverges significantly from Rietzler's interpretation, by contrast. Rietzler attributes Schleswig-Holstein's affinity for Nazism to the region's particular mentality or consciousness (*einem schleswig-holsteinischen Sonderbewusstsein*). Constituent elements of this mentality were anticapitalism, anti-Marxism, racism, hypernationalism, and anti-Semitism. Rietzler contends that hypernationalism became significant after World War I with the loss of northern Schleswig to Denmark. Anti-

Semitism plays a central role in Rietzler's interpretation. In particular, the works of such leading nineteenth-century and early twentieth-century anti-Semitic and racist figures as Langbehn, Gobineau, Chamberlain, and Bartels held a special allure for the region's populace. Moreover, regional folklore held Jews responsible for the cholera and plague epidemics.[210] For Rietzler, the Nazi Party's irrationalist themes found an exceptionally hospitable climate in Schleswig-Holstein. Rietzler's study, however, takes issue with Stoltenberg and Heberle's contention that Schleswig-Holstein's affinity for Nazism marks a political discontinuity. In Heberle and Stoltenberg's view, Schleswig-Holstein made a political about-face after 1928, changing from a bastion of German liberalism to a Nazi stronghold. Heberle and Stoltenberg cite the region's electoral support for the two liberal parties before 1928. Rietzler claims that the two authors have misinterpreted the region's affinity for German liberalism. According to Rietzler, the National Liberal Party before 1914 had two major components: the left liberals and the right or conservative liberals. In Schleswig-Holstein, Rietzler claims, it was the right liberals rather than the left liberals who espoused nationalistic, expansionistic, and antisocial democratic themes. But even if Rietzler's claim is correct, that the right wing of the National Liberal Party prevailed in Schleswig-Holstein before 1914, it does not validate his thesis that the predisposition in the region toward anti-Semitism, racism, hypernationalism, and authoritarianism is the key to the region's political behavior. Rather, voters there may have favored conservative liberals before 1914 simply because conservative liberal programs responded to Schleswig-Holstein's dominant economic interests. The dairy farmers of Schleswig-Holstein favored protective tariffs and autarky, which the conservative liberals advocated, and opposed free trade, which the left-wing liberals promoted.[211]

If self-interest indeed accounted for the sociology of the Nazi Party, as I suggest, the party should have done well among Germany's old middle class. And indeed, figures 3.2 and 3.3 show that Nazi Party joiners from the old middle class were overrepresented in comparison with the percentage from the old middle class among the general population.[212] The old middle class constituted between 30 and 35 percent of the Nazi Party joiners in each year from 1925 through 1932, with the exception of 1926 and 1927, when the old middle class joiners represented 29 percent. Figure 3.3 indicates also that males from the old middle class were overrepresented in the Nazi Party by comparison with females from the same class.[213]

The theory of interest-based political adherence further leads us to

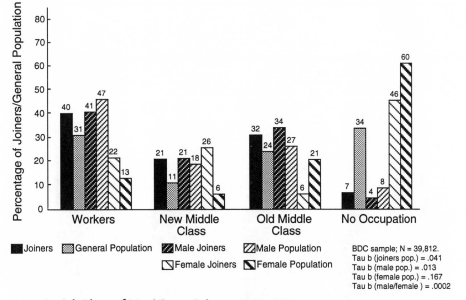

BDC sample; N = 39,812.
Tau b (joiners pop.) = .041
Tau b (male pop.) = .013
Tau b (female pop.) = .167
Tau b (male/female) = .0002

3.2 Social Class of Nazi Party Joiners, 1925–1932

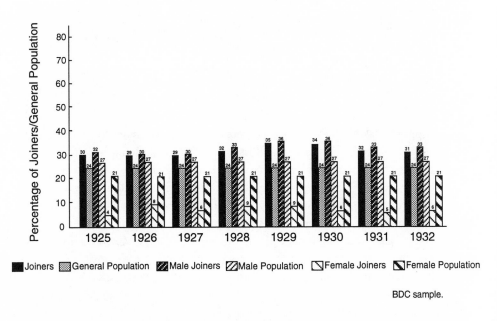

BDC sample.

3.3 Nazi Party Joiners from the Old Middle Class, 1925–1932

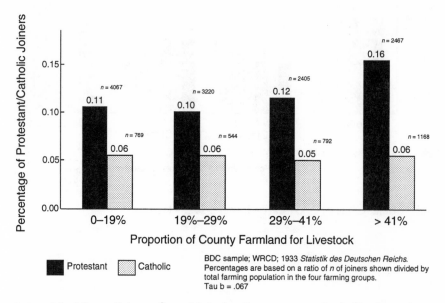

3.4a   Nazi Party Joiners from Majority Protestant or Catholic Counties, by County's Farming Mix

suppose that Nazi Party joiners were more likely to have come from agricultural regions that specialized in livestock rather than grain or fruit. We would not expect, however, that inhabitants of all livestock-raising areas embraced the Nazi Party with equal fervor. In particular, we would expect residents of Protestant livestock-farming areas to have been likelier than residents of Catholic livestock-farming areas to join the Nazi Party. As we have seen, members of the old middle class in Catholic livestock-raising communities, though they found the Nazi Party's positions on tariffs, credit, foreclosures, and governmental subsidies consistent with their own interests, objected to the party's inheritance proposals, which would have forced them to abandon the practice of partible inheritance. Moreover, the old middle class residing in Catholic livestock communities had a viable alternative to the Nazi Party. The positions of the Bavarian People's Party mirrored the NSDAP's positions on agriculture, and, what is more,

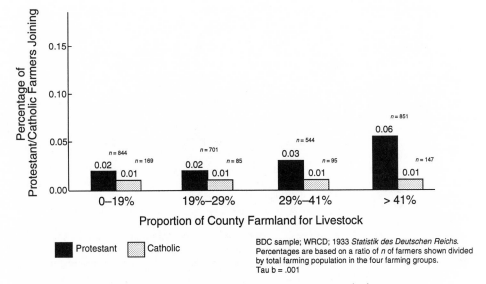

3.4b   Nazi Party Farmers from Majority Protestant or Catholic Counties, by County's Farming Mix

the BVP promotion of the interests of the Catholic Church made it a better choice than the Nazi Party for many Catholic Germans. Figure 3.4a demonstrates that, in general, the greater the proportion of farmland devoted to livestock farming in Protestant German counties, the higher the percentage of the population that joined the Nazi Party. (The percentages are quite small because party joiners constitute a relatively minor proportion of total eligible voters.) In majority Protestant counties with less than 20 percent of the farmland devoted to livestock use, only .11 percent of the total eligible voting population joined the NSDAP, compared with .16 percent in majority Protestant counties with more than 41 percent of the farmland devoted to livestock use. In counties with a Catholic majority, an increase in the proportion of farmland devoted to livestock farming did not correspond to a rise in the proportion of Nazi Party joiners. The results of figure 3.4b corroborate the findings of figure 3.4a. Figure 3.4b

Table 3.1 Regression Analysis of Nazi Membership Rates for German Counties, 1925–1932

Variables	Unstandardized	t-values	Standardized
PROPROT	1.01+++	12.50	.46
SELF33	4.43+++	4.53	.24
PROAGRIC	0.88+++	4.71	.18
LIVESTOCK	0.81+++	4.49	.17
UNEMP	1.45ns	1.83	.10
POPDEN33	−0.00ns	−0.12	−.00
INDEBTED	0.00ns	0.52	.02
Constant	−1.41+++	−4.10	

$R^2 = .23$

Note: N = 638; +++p<.001; ns = not significant at .05.
Source: Brustein-Falter BDC sample; Falter's WRCD file; 1933 Statistik des Deutschen Reichs.
Variable Descriptions:
   PROPROT: proportion of county's population who were Protestant in 1933
   SELF33: proportion of county's gainfully employed county population who were categorized as self-employed in 1933
   PROAGRIC: proportion of county's gainfully employed population who were employed in agriculture in 1933
   LIVESTOCK: proportion of a county's farmland devoted to dairy and livestock farming in 1933
   UNEMP: crude unemployment rate for county in 1933, dividing unemployed persons by county population
   POPDEN33: crude measure of density, dividing county's population in 1933 by total German population figure
   INDEBTED: average level of farm indebtedness across all farms in the county in 1931

focuses exclusively on Nazi joiners who classified themselves as farmers. Again, we see a positive relation between residence in Protestant livestock-farming counties and Nazi Party membership. In counties with a Protestant majority, the proportion of NSDAP farmer joiners (as a ratio of NSDAP joiners to total eligible voting population in those counties) rises from a low of .02 percent in counties with the lowest concentration of livestock farming to .06 percent in counties with the highest concentration. The proportion of farmer joiners in the predominantly Catholic counties remains at .01 percent regardless of the change from livestock to nonlivestock farming. A regression analysis of Nazi Party membership on several independent variables represents a final test of the importance of livestock farming as a determinant of Nazi Party joining. Table 3.1 presents the results of the analysis. After controlling for the effects of alternative variables—religious confession, self-employment, agricultural population, unemployment, population density, and agricultural indebtedness — we find that livestock farming is still a significant predictor of Nazi Party joining.

Weimar Political Parties and the New Middle Class

In contrast to the relatively prolific pronouncements from the principal Weimar parties on issues concerning the old middle class, party declarations on behalf of the new middle class were conspicuously few. This seems surprising, given that the service and clerical occupations, whose employees came from the new middle class, constituted Germany's fastest growing sector. It may be that the Weimar parties' inability to classify these employees as part of either the working class or the (old) middle class explains the dearth of remarks directed to the new middle class.

The DNVP and the New Middle Class

Though the German Nationalist People's Party wooed primarily big business and big agriculture, it did attempt to court the new middle class through its links with the conservative white-collar unions, the Deutschnationaler Handlungsgehilfenverband (DHV), the Reichsbund Deutscher Angestellten-Berufsverbände (RDA), the Gewerkschaftsbund deutscher Angestelltenverbände (Gedag) and the conservative civil service union, the Gesamtverband Deutscher Beamtengewerkschaften (GDB). The DNVP's promises to the new middle class contained little in the way of concrete proposals to increase employee's salaries or social benefits. Rather, DNVP propaganda highlighted the importance of the work performed by the new middle class and trumpeted the party's anti-Marxism and fervent nationalism. The DNVP's staunch promotion of higher tariffs and import restrictions for agriculture should have undermined the party's standing in the new middle class: higher food costs ran counter to the desire for less-expensive food among the generally urban members of the new middle class. After Hugenberg took the helm of the DNVP in 1928, the party began to abandon its claim to represent the entire pronationalist, anti-Left constituency. Hugenberg, who sought to reconstitute the DNVP along ideologically purer lines, began to break the party's ties with groups such as the employees from the new middle class who objected to his monarchical and big-business sympathies and his distaste for democracy. In response to Hugenberg's actions, support for the party declined within the Deutschnationaler Handlungsgehilfenverband.[214] If DNVP policy was ambivalent toward many professions in the new middle class, it lent unequivocal support to civil servants. In the view of many in the DNVP as well as outside, civil servants, by virtue of their education and their access to governmental resources, constituted a distinct entity within the new middle class. Throughout the Weimar era, the DNVP fought to protect civil servant salaries and the civil service seniority system. For instance, in 1932 the DNVP joined with the NSDAP to attack Brüning's surtax on civil service salaries. Childers cautions us, however, that the DNVP was more interested in protecting the privilege of the civil service elite rather than the livelihood of the civil service rank and file.[215] Childers' claim seems plausible, for the elite, by virtue of its economic standing, aligned itself more readily than the lower-level civil servants with the big-business sympathies of Hugenberg's DNVP.

The DVP, the DDP, and the New Middle Class

The two liberal parties, the DVP (German People's Party) and the DDP (German Democratic Party), hoped to win over the new middle class on the basis of their advocacy of secular education, economic growth, free trade, and anti-Marxism. Neither party offered much in the way of concrete proposals to improve the material conditions of the new middle class. Both parties should have won some adherents within the new middle class because they tried to hold the line against higher tariffs on agricultural commodities. Moreover, the liberal parties had succeeded in developing links with the white-collar Gewerkschaftsbund deutscher Angestelltenverbände (GdA) and the Deutschnationaler Handlungsgehilfenverband (DHV).

The two liberal parties took contrasting positions on restructuring the German civil service. As early as 1919, the DVP called for a German civil service free from partisan political meddling and for a restructuring of the civil service salary schedules that would enable civil servants to regain lost income. Again in 1927 the DVP came out in favor of a civil service salary reform. In 1924 DVP leaders spoke out against the SPD's plan to "democratize" the German civil service—a plan that the DVP suggested would eliminate the special privileges accorded to public officials. By contrast, the DDP joined the SPD in pushing for a purge of the civil service; the hope was to root out public officials who held antidemocratic and promonarchist sympathies.[216]

In 1931 and 1932 neither the DVP or the DDP (DStP) won friends among civil servants when both parties voted in favor of Brüning's cut in civil servant salaries and surtax on civil service salaries.[217] Since Stresemann's death in late 1929 the big-business wing had increasingly steered the German People's Party away from promoting the concerns of the new middle class when those concerns conflicted with the interests of the big-business wing. Cuts in civil servant salaries would enhance Germany's capital formation. Hoping to hold on to some civil service support, DDP spokespersons explained that the party's vote was best for the economic health of Germany and asked the civil service to rise above its particular class interests.[218]

Under Stresemann's guidance the DVP sought to attract the support of white-collar employees through the creation of white-collar professional committees within the party and, more important, through party efforts to establish a white-collar insurance program in 1927.[219] In its efforts to woo white-collar employees, the DVP should have benefited from its opposition to organized labor. Many white-collar employees felt threatened by the growth of organized labor and in particular saw the gains achieved by organized labor in the mid-1920s as another sign that the system had cheated them. But by 1931 many of the gains the DVP had made among white-collar employees began to evaporate as the big-business wing within the DVP gained the ascendancy. For instance, relations between the DVP and the leadership of the Deutschnationaler Handlungsgehilfenverband (DHV), a long-time ally of the DVP, deteriorated after DVP party chairman Dingeldey failed to support the principle of compulsory arbitration between management and labor in wage and salary disputes.[220]

The German Democrats forged few specific programs aimed directly at the material interests of members of the new middle class. The party hoped to win their support by emphasizing the party's opposition to big business, its support of tax relief, its advocacy of free trade, and its defense of the Weimar Republic. The DStP's embrace of Brüning's deflationary fiscal policies damaged the party's fortunes among many white-collar employees. The DDP (DStP) hoped to attract female support within the new middle class because, of the major Weimar parties, the DDP and SPD were the principal advocates of women's rights. Women made up a relatively sizable proportion of the new middle class (nearly one-third of all white-collar employees).[221]

The Center Party and the New Middle Class

The basis of the Catholic Center Party's appeal to the new middle class was the party's defense of the Catholic religion and its anti-Marxism. During the mid-1920s, because of its vote for free-trade legislation, the Center Party maintained credibility among groups seeking lower food costs. During the 1920s the party should have obtained further support from the new middle class thanks to the legislation it introduced to raise the salaries of civil servants. In 1928, claiming that their salaries had fallen behind those of other groups, the chancellor, Wilhelm Marx of the Center Party, presented a bill to increase civil servant salaries by 10 percent (Interestingly, the Reichstag voted to raise salaries of public servants by 21 to 25 percent).[222] After 1930, however, the popularity of the Center Party waned in the new middle class, as a result chiefly of the party leaders' acceptance of Brüning's austerity program, which among other things pushed for wage and price controls and cuts in the salaries of public employees. Moreover, unlike the German Democrats and Social Democrats, who encouraged female participation in middle class professions for the new middle class, the Center Party endorsed policies to keep women at home. For example, in 1931 a female Reichstag deputy from the Center Party proposed that as a step to reduce German unemployment the government should remove married women from their jobs in government service.[223] Thus, it is unlikely that married women holding government jobs would have found the Center Party's position on female employment acceptable.

The SPD, the KPD, and the New Middle Class

By promulgating a pro-labor program, the German Left (the SPD and KPD) drastically undermined its ability to construct a solid base in the new middle class. The Left may have erred in attempting to attract the support of the new middle class by stressing the commonalities and shared interests of wage earners and salaried employees. The Social Democratic Party made every effort to highlight the similarities between manual and mental labor.[224] I suggest that the Left's strategy of focusing on the similarities between the two classes may have backfired: the German Left failed to appreciate sufficiently that integral to the identity of the new middle class was the perception that mental labor is superior to manual labor and middle-class employees are socially superior to working-class employees.

The Left thus conveyed the impression to many in the new working class that it favored lowering the status of the new working class.

As for specific policies of the leftist parties, the Reichstag faction of the SPD pushed for the passage of a modernized civil service code.[225] In the early years of Weimar both the SPD and KPD worked to dismantle the career civil service and launched efforts to diminish the power of high-ranking civil servants. Both parties hoped to win over low-ranking public employees, who had little sympathy for their entrenched and relatively well-to-do colleagues.[226] The leaders of the SPD realized as well that their efforts to build a foundation for social democracy required the removal of the old class of governmental bureaucrats, whose sympathy for social democracy was questionable.

If the SPD had, through its policies, alienated many civil servants, it may have attracted some white-collar support: party deputies frequently presented and voted for measures to raise this group's salaries, establish a social benefits program for them, improve their working conditions, provide them with union representation, and, very important, promote the rights of women. The SPD succeeded in establishing a socialist-oriented civil servants' league, the Allgemeiner Deutscher Beamtenbund (ADB), and an association of white-collar unions, the Zentralverband der Angestellten (ZdA). But ultimately, the Left's ability to attract a significant constituency from among the new middle class suffered from miscalculation of the aspirations of the new middle class for social mobility.

The NSDAP and the New Middle Class

The Nazi Party's efforts to develop a constituency in the new middle class had mixed results. On the positive side of the ledger, the Nazis successfully courted civil service employees. The Nazis often reminded civil service groups that one of the party's original planks in its 1920 program had been the preservation of a professional civil service. During the early 1920s, party officials took exception to legislation introduced by the DDP and SPD to democratize the civil service, which the Nazis argued opened the door to the advancement of unqualified personnel. In 1924, party members campaigned forcefully for the dismissal of the newly hired pro-Republic civil servants (referred to by the Nazis as the "revolution officials") and the reappointment of the professionally trained civil servants who had been removed from their positions through the efforts of

the SPD and DDP. The Nazis hoped to woo many civil servants by appealing to their threatened elitist tradition, which after 1920 became the target
of "the democratic excesses of the Weimar system." The Nazis blamed the
government for an economic policy that continually eroded the economic
standing of members of the civil service. In 1924, the NSDAP demanded
that the civil servants receive higher salaries, shorter working hours, and
longer vacations.[227]

In their 1929 campaign against the Young Plan, the Nazis claimed that
cuts in domestic spending would result in economic sacrifices for the civil
service. Shortly thereafter, the NSDAP rallied again to the side of the
civil service, attacking Brüning's austerity program of 1930–1931, which
included a reduction in civil service salaries and pensions. In response to
the Brüning administration's imposition of a 2.5 percent surtax on civil
service salaries, NSDAP leaders blamed the cut on the government's acceptance of reparations payments and claimed that the civil service was
bearing the brunt of unjust reparations payments. When both the Prussian
state government and the Brüning administration declared that membership in extremist political movements such as the NSDAP and the KPD
was incompatible with public service, the Nazi Party also came out ener-
getically in defense of the political freedom of the civil service.[228]

Throughout the general election campaigns of 1930–1932 the Nazis
stressed that an NSDAP government would restore to German civil servants the honor and prestige they had enjoyed before the November revolution and their economic standing, which had suffered from Brüning's
and Papen's austerity programs. In many respects, the NSDAP demands
for the civil service mirrored those advanced by the German Civil Servants' League (DBB). The NSDAP strategy to win over civil servants included an aggressive, unambiguous appeal to their material interests. This
strategy contrasts sharply with the party's confused and lukewarm support of white-collar employees.[229]

One might think that the Nazi Party would have done well among
white-collar employees, who had been neglected by the other Weimar
parties. But the NSDAP's quite detailed programs for the working class
and the old middle class and its antifeminist stance should have seriously
hindered the party's efforts to attract a white-collar constituency. As the
party negotiated its way between the conflicting interests of manual and
mental labor, it frequently fell into the trap of minimizing the differences
between the two groups. In its literature the NSDAP treated the two forms
of labor as two components of the *Arbeitnehmerschaft* (work force) or as

"Arbeiter der Faust und der Stirn" (manual and mental workers). In the eyes of many employees from the new middle class, the Nazi view of the two forms of labor reduced them to proletarians—a not too flattering identity.[230] The NSDAP's verbal assault against the large department stores and consumer cooperatives—institutions central to the economic survival of many white-collar employees—ensnared the party: the elimination of large department stores and consumer cooperatives was sure to appeal to the shopkeepers and merchants of the old middle class, but to white-collar employees it meant job cuts and the elimination of sources of inexpensive food and other necessities.[231]

In their appeals to the working class and the new middle class, and in an attempt to present themselves as advocates of traditional German values, the Nazis stressed that married women belonged at home caring for their families rather than in factories and offices. For many male workers and employees, notably those unemployed or threatened by unemployment, the removal of married women from the workplace had a particular appeal. But again, a promise that held allure for one group carried negative implications for another. Many women saw the Nazi pledge to return married women to the hearth as a threat to their career aspirations.[232] The Nazis were aware of their objections to the policy and in 1932 attempted to placate women by suggesting that although they firmly believed that the proper place for married women was in the home, those who wanted to work should be able to do so.[233]

Not every NSDAP maneuver before 1933 diminished the party's prospects for gathering white-collar support. For example, one would imagine that the Nazis won over many white-collar employees with their campaign against Brüning's freeze on white-collar salaries. The party may have also benefited from its ties with the Deutschnationaler Handlungsgehilfenverband, the conservative white-collar union.[234] Even more important, as unemployment climbed precipitously in the white-collar trades, the Nazi Party's stance on job creation should have appealed to many white-collar employees, especially those who had lost jobs or feared unemployment. Innovative proposals for creating new jobs were included in the 1930 NSDAP Employment Program, the 1931 NSDAP Public Works/Inflation Program, the 1932 Immediate Economic Program, and the 1932 Economic Reconstruction Plan.

If the hypothesis is correct that party affiliation was largely based on self-interest, civil servants should have been overrepresented among NSDAP joiners between 1925 and 1932, whereas the white-collar employ-

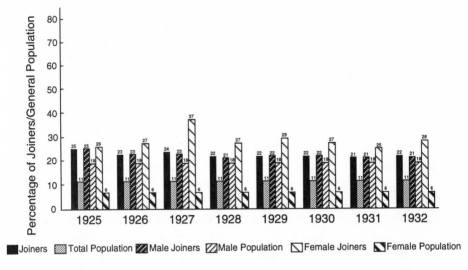

3.5   Nazi Party Joiners from the New Middle Class, 1925–1932

ees, especially female white-collar employees, should have been underrepresented in comparison with the general population. Furthermore, according to this theory, employees from the new middle class should have been less reluctant to join the party after 1930, in light of the NSDAP policies on job creation. In figure 3.5 the proportion of NSDAP joiners from the new middle class is shown by year in comparison with the proportion of employees from the new middle class in the eligible population. The results of figure 3.5 do not support the theory that people joined the Nazi Party out of self-interest as regards either the proposition that the new middle class was underrepresented in the Nazi Party between 1925 and 1932 or the claim that the proportion of joiners from the new middle class increased after 1930. NSDAP joining remained fairly consistent within the new middle class throughout the period from 1925 to 1932.

The findings from figure 3.5 moreover fail to confirm that female em-

Table 3.2   Marital Status of Nazi Party Joiners, by Class and Gender, 1925–1932

| | Married | | Not Married | |
	Male (%)	*Female (%)*	*Male (%)*	*Female (%)*
Old Middle Class	58.5	25.3	41.5	74.7
	(*n* = 2689)	(*n* = 15)	(*n* = 1907)	(*n* = 44)
New Middle Class	53.6	4.3	46.4	95.7
	(*n* = 1644)	(*n* = 11)	(*n* = 1424)	(*n* = 242)
Workers	34.6	7.9	65.4	92.1
	(*n* = 1796)	(*n* = 13)	(*n* = 3396)	(*n* = 151)

Source: Brustein-Falter BDC sample.
Note: These represent only the joiners providing a marital status—"married," "single," "divorced," or "widowed."

ployees from the new middle class were reluctant to join the NSDAP. Indeed, such workers were significantly overrepresented in the Nazi Party.[235] But before we dismiss the prediction of the interest-based model about female joiners from the new middle class, we should delve deeper into which of these women joined the Nazi Party before 1933. If sheer self-interest is the predictor of who joined the party, married women should have been less likely to join the Nazi Party than unmarried women, given the Nazi Party's stated preference to keep married women at home. If the theory holds true, we should find few *married* female Nazi Party joiners from the new middle class. The data in table 3.2 show dramatically that the NSDAP female employees from the new middle class were unmarried. Nearly 96 percent of such women were unmarried, compared with 46.4 percent unmarried male NSDAP joiners from the new middle class. In fact, the proportion of unmarried female joiners is consistently higher than the proportion of unmarried male joiners in the old middle class, new middle class, and working class.[236] We would moreover expect, if people joined the party out of self-interest, that single female employees from the new middle class, particularly those concerned about losing their jobs, should have welcomed the Nazi Party call for married employed women to relinquish their jobs and become full-time mothers and wives. For many such single women, the potential benefits to be derived from the removal of married women from the labor force were obvious: new job opportunities and less competition for existing jobs. The results of the cross-tabulations presented in table 3.3 reveal that more than 70 percent of single female

Table 3.3   Single Female Nazi Party Joiners, by Class and
Unemployment Level, 1925–1932

Unemployment level in community (%)	Class			
	Old Middle Class (%)	New Middle Class (%)	Workers (%)	Without Occupation (%)
0–9	8.6	6.2	19.2	20.1
	(4)	(12)	(25)	(10)
10–19	29.0	23.4	36.9	28.7
	(6)	(48)	(47)	(18)
20–29	49.4	52.3	32.6	34.6
	(11)	(120)	(51)	(22)
30+	13.0	18.1	11.4	16.6
	(4)	(42)	(20)	(6)
N	25	222	143	56

Source: Brustein-Falter BDC sample; WRCD.
Note: Chi Square (cases weighted) = 662.14 (p < .001) Phi = .27
Chi Square (cases unweighted) = 28.53 (p < .001) Phi = .25
The individual column percentages are based on weighted cases because of the disproportionate sampling scheme (by year of entry into the party). Beneath each percentage is the actual number of single female Nazi Party members.

Nazi Party joiners from the new middle class resided in communities with an unemployment level of 20 percent or more.

Figure 3.6 presents the results of a comparison of both white-collar NSDAP joiners and civil servant NSDAP joiners with white-collar employees and civil servants in the general population for the period of 1925 to 1932. The results of figure 3.6 regarding the proportion of NSDAP civil servant joiners do not support the theory that because their interests clearly lay with the NSDAP, civil servants should be overrepresented in the Nazi Party. There is no difference between the proportion of NSDAP joiners in the civil service and the proportion of civil servants in the general population.

All in all, for the new middle class, the results shown here do not convincingly confirm the propositions about adherence to the NSDAP on the basis of material self-interest.[237] In Chapter 5, however, we shall see that once we expand the model to include the role of selective incentives and disincentives in shaping people's decisions about joining the Nazi Party, we understand why the Nazi Party succeeded in attracting large numbers of white-collar employees, why civil servants were reluctant to

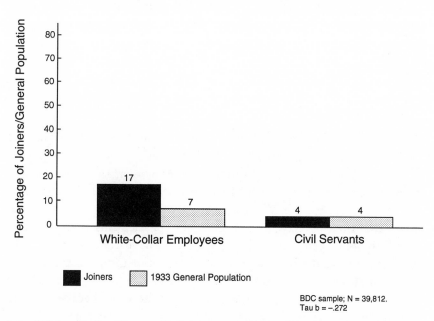

3.6   White-Collar Versus Civil Servant Joiners of the Nazi Party, 1925–1932

join the NSDAP before 1933, and why so few married women joined the Nazi Party. But that is getting ahead of the story. Some of the most intriguing findings from this research concern the relationship between the Nazi Party and German blue-collar workers. Did the NSDAP fashion a working-class program, or did it give up on weaning the working class away from the political Left? In the next chapter we turn to an examination of working-class interests and Weimar party programs.[238]

4 The Working Class and Weimar Political Parties

German labor was a pillar of the Nazi Party from 1925 to 1933, contrary to generally accepted ideas about the social origins of Nazism. What did Nazi Party programs offer workers that other Weimar political parties did not? To what kinds of workers did the Nazi Party programs especially appeal? We shall see below that the Nazi Party crafted innovative working-class programs combining elements of nationalist-etatist thinking and Keynesian economics. The party's working class programs attracted wide support from the nationalistic, nonunionized, import-industrial sector and from skilled workers.

The fortunes of German blue-collar labor alternated between growth and decline during the Weimar era. Workers briefly enjoyed social and economic gains after World War I. The Weimar constitution accorded German labor the right to organize, recognition of collective bargaining, state commitment to expanding social welfare, and constitutionally guaranteed parity between labor and capital in the formulation of economic policy.[1] German labor experienced a major shock between 1923 and 1924, when the reparations payment controversy and the French occupation of the Ruhr exacerbated Germany's financial situation and contributed to hyperinflation. By December 1923 more than one-half of Germany's labor force was either unemployed or underemployed. For those who had jobs, the high inflation eroded their income so that real wages fell to nearly half their 1921 level. Workers also saw many of their hard-won gains of the previous years evaporate as the government extended the work week from forty hours to

Note: A preliminary version of parts of Chapter 4 was published in William Brustein and Jürgen Falter, "Sociology of Nazism: An Interest-Based Account," *Rationality and Society* (1994) 6: 369–99, and William Brustein and Jürgen Falter, "Who Joined the Nazi Party? Assessing Theories of the Social Origins of Nazism," *Zeitgeschichte* (1995) 22: 83–108.

forty-eight and in some cases to fifty-four, in an attempt to stabilize the economy and to enhance production.[2]

With the revival of the German economy in 1924, due in large part to the influx of foreign capital, conditions improved dramatically for many of Germany's blue-collar workers. Unemployment among unionized workers had dropped to 9 percent by May 1924 from a level of 27 percent during the previous January, and wages for both skilled and unskilled labor rose gradually.[3]

Between 1924 and 1930, Germany's blue-collar labor force benefited enormously from social and economic legislation. A large part of labor's success resulted from the extraordinary rebound of German industry between 1924 and 1929. Overall, industrial productivity grew 40 percent between 1924 and 1927. In 1923 German industrial production made up 8 percent of world production, compared with 16 percent in 1913. But by 1928, German industry had surpassed the prewar level and represented a healthy 19 percent of world production. Industry could thus afford to act generously toward labor. During these years, various Weimar governments enacted substantial social legislation to protect and improve the livelihood of blue-collar workers. Among labor's gains were the implementation of compulsory and binding arbitration of contract disputes, introduction of relatively high wages industrywide, restoration of the eight-hour workday in most large enterprises, expansion of occupational health and safety standards, and the crown jewel, the enactment of a major unemployment insurance program.[4] In July 1927 legislators passed the Employment Facilitation and Unemployment Insurance Law, which put into place a comprehensive unemployment insurance program to be funded by contributions from employers, employees, and, indirectly, the state. The new law unburdened union treasuries of a huge expense.[5] The law raised the eligibility requirement for unemployment insurance from thirteen weeks of employment to twenty-six but guaranteed that workers who were ineligible would be supported by emergency welfare payments.[6]

Yet declining rates of unemployment and rising wages masked a major structural change that was under way within German industry after 1924. Many in government and industry felt that if Germany were to meet its international financial obligations and rebuild its economy, German industry would have to become much more competitive on the world market. Between 1924 and 1929 German industry underwent a major technological, financial, and economic reorganization, commonly referred to as industrial rationalization. One of the principal results of German industrial rationalization was that semiskilled and unskilled labor increasingly replaced skilled labor. By 1933 there were roughly half as many skilled industrial workers as there had been in 1925.[7]

The deleterious effects of the Great Depression on Germany's working class are well known. Beginning in 1930, unemployment among blue-collar workers skyrocketed, while wages declined precipitously. In September 1929, 17 percent of organized metalworkers were either unemployed or working part-time. One year later that figure jumped to nearly 45 percent. Metalworkers were not the only laborers to suffer a decline in their economic livelihood. Blue-collar laborers in the woodworking, clothing, leather, linoleum, and construction industries experienced a similar fate.[8] Between 1928 and 1930 average real wages for blue-collar labor fell roughly 11 percent.[9] Germany's unemployment situation was further exacerbated by demographic factors. World War I had lowered the number of potential male job seekers. By 1930, however, the males born shortly before 1914 began to enter the labor market in large numbers, in search of a diminishing number of jobs.

Blue-collar labor turned to government for assistance. Considerable debate emerged within government around the issue of expanding unemployment relief. One outcome of that debate was the collapse of the Grand Coalition. On March 27, 1930, the government fell when the left wing of the SPD refused to accept the recommendation of the DVP to cut the rate of unemployment benefits and the DVP rejected a proposal to increase the employers' contribution to the fund. The costs of unemployment compensation had climbed from 1.2 billion marks in 1928 to 2.7 billion in 1930. Unemployed workers were entitled to draw upwards of 70 marks in unemployment compensation for thirteen weeks, after which period the amount was reduced.

Blue-collar workers' efforts to persuade the government to expand relief facilities encountered a stone wall with Brüning's introduction of austerity measures. His deflationary policies won few friends among labor. Brüning sought to stimulate business investment by making capital available, to stabilize prices and wages, and to limit government spending for public works and unemployment compensation. In July 1931 and again in the summer of 1932 Brüning reduced the amount and duration of unemployment compensation. At intervals during 1931, he also introduced cuts in wages, and in December 1931, by virtue of a presidential order under the extraparliamentary Article 48 of the constitution, Brüning decreased wages to their January 1, 1927, level, regardless of existing collective agreements.

Thus, within a period of two years the administration had eroded many of the gains that German labor had achieved between 1924 and 1930 and at the same time had undermined the binding nature of labor-management wage negotiations.[10]

The year 1932 brought no relief for the economic woes of blue-collar labor. Unemployment continued to climb. By summer, more than 40 percent of Germany's unionized workers were either unemployed or forced to work part-time. In a number of major industries unemployment affected between two-fifths and three-quarters of the labor force. Particularly hard hit were metallurgy, construction, clothing, and woodworking. In January 1932, for example, unemployment reached 41.4 percent in metallurgy, 77.3 percent in construction, 42.7 percent in the garment industry, and 66.1 percent in woodworking.[11] Pay for both skilled and unskilled labor continued to fall in 1932. By the fall of 1932, wages for skilled labor had sunk to 84 percent of their 1928 level, compared with 89 percent in the United States and 96 percent in England.[12] Overall, real net wages had declined by 1932 to 64 percent of their prewar level.[13] With Papen's appointment as chancellor in 1932 the government cut further into workers' benefits. In the hope of facilitating circulation and accumulation of capital, Papen announced a set of wage cuts ranging from 20 to 50 percent, a 23 percent reduction in unemployment insurance benefits, a 10 percent cut in "crisis" support, a 15 percent drop in welfare payments, and a 7.5 to 15 percent decline in disability benefits. Furthermore, Papen lowered the maximum benefit period for unemployment insurance to six weeks.[14]

Emergency decrees enacted by the government ostensibly to assist workers did more for the employers than the employees. For example, in September 1932 the government enacted legislation on the forty-hour work week and job creation. But it was not clear that this legislation actually improved the lot of workers. Employers received a tax break of a hundred marks per worker per year. Workers were to receive full wages up to thirty hours per week, but with the new legislation, hours thirty-one through forty could be paid at the minimum wage of 40 percent of full wage if the firm introduced 20 percent more jobs. Any hours beyond forty were to be paid at full wage, a measure intended to ensure the forty-hour work week.[15] Similarly, the Papen government's winter subsidy welfare package in the autumn of 1932 was not available to younger workers without dependents. According to this legislation, only unemployed workers in certain wage classes who had dependents were entitled to receive a weekly benefit of thirty-six marks.[16]

But the impact of the worldwide depression on German labor was uneven. Moreover, the groups that made up the German blue-collar labor force held contrasting views on remedies to improve their material situation. Like the old and new middle classes, the blue-collar class included groups with divergent interests. Though all workers undoubtedly wanted higher wages, a shorter workday, and improved health and retirement plans, workers frequently disagreed over the benefits accruing from free trade or protectionism, unionization, and the ownership of private property. Much of the divergence in workers' attitudes stemmed from differences in their skill level and factors related to their particular industrial context—for example, whether the workers were skilled, semiskilled, or unskilled, whether they worked in large or small plants, and whether they worked in export-oriented or domestic-oriented, dynamic or stagnant industries.

The skill level of German workers varied. In 1925, for instance, 83 percent of the laborers employed in the mining industry, as compared with only 15 percent of laborers in the rubber and asbestos industries, were classified as skilled. Moreover, by 1933 many industries that had employed a high proportion of skilled laborers shifted significantly from skilled to semiskilled and unskilled labor, principally as a result of German industrial rationalization. In particular, between 1925 and 1933 the proportion of all industrial jobs classified as skilled fell from 83 percent to 46 percent in mining, 70 percent to 54 percent in woodworking, 44 percent to 17 percent in textiles, 54 percent to 30 percent in iron and steel, and 55 percent to 35 percent in leather and linoleum. By contrast, industrial rationalization hardly affected the proportion of jobs for skilled labor in other industries. Indeed, the proportion of all industrial jobs classified as skilled between 1925 and 1933 remained at 59 percent in the electrotechnical, precision, and optical industries, and the proportion actually rose from 23 percent to 25 percent in the chemical industry.[17] Consequently, many skilled workers employed in industries that had witnessed the erosion of skilled jobs may have looked quite favorably on the promises of job creation and economic autarky as a means to save their skilled jobs.

The level of unionization constituted a further distinction within the ranks of labor. Although I have no direct information on individual-level union membership during Weimar or even information by industrial branch, I assume that unionization was greatest in industrial branches dominated by large plants—that is, where the ratio of employees (blue-collar and white-collar) to entrepreneurs was highest—and that unionization was lowest in industrial branches dominated by small plants—that is, where the ratio of employees to entrepreneurs was lowest.[18] In his examination of 1925 census data on industrial branches, Childers shows that the highest ratios of employees to entrepreneurs were in metal production, utilities, and rubber production and the lowest ratios were in food, leather, and clothing production. Given that most German labor unions had strong affiliations with either the Social Democratic Party or the Catholic Center Party, unionized workers should have had an interest in defending their unions' political patrons as long as those workers continued to receive valuable resources from their unions.

In addition to skill level and unionization, the market orientation and level of industry-specific profitability shaped workers' material interests. Abraham, though he is primarily interested in the views of industrial elites, focuses on the division within German industry between an import/domestic and an export/dynamic sector. The import/domestic sector was characterized by older, cartelized, more labor-intensive heavy industrial branches. Among the branches that Abraham places in the import/domestic sector are mining, steel, iron, and coal.[19] This sector suffered from relatively low profits and relatively high expenditures for wages, salaries, and social insurance. Unlike the newer, more capital-intensive industries of the export/dynamic sector, the older industries of the import/domestic sector tended to be more labor-intensive.

The import/domestic sector pushed for higher prices for its goods, lower employee costs, expansion into central and eastern Europe, and a larger share of the domestic market. For instance, quotas enacted by the international iron cartel in 1925 closed the door to further international expansion for Germany's iron makers. These iron makers, consequently, turned their sights inward and saw promise in an expanded domestic market. As a group, industries in the import/domestic sector favored limiting imports, introducing protective tariffs, lowering taxes, establishing autarky, reducing social welfare expenditures, and terminating reparations payments.[20]

Abraham describes the export/dynamic sector as decentralized and capital-intensive. The machine, metal-finishing, electrotechnical, optics, and chemical industries belonged to this sector. The export/dynamic sector enjoyed relatively higher profits and relatively lower employment costs. Its industries favored reduced prices on imports, free trade, expanded markets, economic modernization and rationalization, and fulfillment of Germany's reparations payments. This sector's support for measures to improve exports made sense in light of its international competitive advantage. For instance, Germany's chemical industry held 43 percent of the world market in chemical exports in 1928, and Germany's coal industry (import/domestic) maintained a 10 percent share of the world market.[21] By agreeing to the allies' reparations demands, proponents of the export/dynamic sector believed that Germany would obtain much-needed foreign credits and that German industry would benefit from a most-favored-nation status that would open doors to the world's richest markets, such as the United States, Britain, the Netherlands, Belgium, and France, the major markets for many of the high-quality, high-cost goods manufactured for export. Dynamic German industries depended on these nations for vital imports.[22]

During the first two years of the Depression the gap between the two sectors grew. As the situation for import/domestic industries deteriorated between 1929 and 1931, Germany climbed from the world's number three exporter in 1929 to number one in 1931.[23]

Abraham provides an informative glimpse into the rivalry between competing sectors of German industry. Abraham's dichotomous separation of industrial branches assumes incorrectly, however, that domestic industrial branches are inherently stagnant and export industrial branches are inherently dynamic. If we measure the export value of an industrial branch by the value of its exports divided by the ratio of German workers in that branch to all German workers, and then we measure the dynamic value by the profits-to-earnings ratios for the branch, we find that though some export industrial branches were dynamic, others were stagnant. In particular, while the chemical industry achieved both export value and a high profit ratio, the machine industry scored high on export value but had a negative profits-to-earnings ratio. Conversely, not all import/domestic branches were stagnant. The coal and the food and food processing industries ranked low on export value (29 and 45.6 respectively) but had positive profits-to-earnings ratios (2.22 and 2.84 in 1932 respectively). A more accurate separation of German industrial branches would situate branches along a two-dimensional continuum: one ranging from production for export to production for import and the other ranging from positive profits-to-earnings ratios to negative profits-to-earnings ratios.[24]

Abraham's examination of industrial sectors in Weimar Germany has an additional limitation. It focuses exclusively on the role played by elites: on industrial and political leaders rather than on the implications of industrial policy for blue-collar workers. Regarding labor's interests, Abraham implies that they were inherently at odds with those of management. His claim is misleading. On the one hand, labor and management should have held dissimilar positions on wage levels, unionization, collective bargaining, and unemployment compensation. On the other hand, labor and management should have had a shared stake in the economic health of their industry, for workers were more likely to lose jobs in an unprofitable industry than in a profitable one, and a profitable industry was more likely than an unprofitable one to accede to demands by labor for higher wages and improved benefits.[25] Consequently, if, on the one hand, free-trade policies were favored within a particular industrial branch, then we should expect both workers and management in that branch to support free trade; if, on the other hand, protectionist policies were favored within a particular industrial branch, then we should expect that workers and managers within that branch should support protectionism.

What becomes amply clear from a cursory examination of blue-collar labor during Weimar is that workers did not constitute a homogeneous class. Thus, their views on key issues such as protective tariffs, free trade, unionization, socialism, and reparations payments should have varied.

The DNVP and the Working Class

In the hope of appealing to the nationalist aspirations of German workers, the DNVP presented itself as a Volksgemeinschaft or non-class party. As early as 1920 at the party's conference in Hannover, the leadership of the DNVP described the party as a defender of the working class, charged that the Versailles treaty was enslaving the German working class, and called on employers and workers to join hands to promote German national interests.[26] During the early 1920s the DNVP and its auxiliary organizations fashioned policies and built an institutional framework aimed directly at attracting workers. The party established a blue-collar labor organization, *Deutschnationaler Arbeiterbund* (DNAB), and a white-collar labor organization, the *Deutschnationaler Angestelltenbund* (DNAgB). In December 1924 the DNVP's paramilitary organization, the Stahlhelm, opened an Office for Social Policy through which financial help and food were offered to the unemployed. The Stahlhelm also organized a housing program and an employment service for its unemployed working-class members.[27] The DNVP set out to win over farmworkers as well with promises of a new settlement program in eastern Germany and a program of reduced lease rates to encourage farmworkers to become tenants.[28]

Under the leadership of the more moderate wing of the DNVP, the party platform called for protection for workers from the excesses and inequities of the capitalist economy. The rise within the party of the pro-big business Hugenberg wing in 1928, however, terminated the party's appeals on behalf of the working class. Hugenberg left little doubt that he preferred the interests of big agriculture and big business over those of labor. In response to the DNVP's changing of the guard, working-class support eroded.[29]

The Liberal Parties and the Working Class

Of the two German liberal parties, the DVP and the DDP, only the DDP made serious efforts to attract blue-collar support. The more conservative DVP held firmly to the principle that what was good for big business was good for German labor. Under Stresemann's leadership, however, the DVP agreed to work along with the SPD, the Center Party, and the DDP to pass legislation beneficial to Germany's working class. Yet the party steadfastly opposed schemes for the socialization of labor, such as the proposed nationalization of the coal industry. After Stresemann's death, the DVP played a decisive part in defeating the SPD's efforts in 1929 and 1930 to defend and improve the unemployment compensation program and other social services.[30] Between 1930 and 1933 the DVP continued to be a forceful proponent of big business and an outspoken critic of labor. In 1931 the DVP proposed that management be given a completely free hand in determining labor contracts.[31]

Until 1930 the DDP had consistently followed a pro-labor policy. A sample of articles from the *Vossische Zeitung* and the *Volkswacht* offers support to this claim. The February 18, 1926, edition of the *Vossische Zeitung* deplored the low weekly wages that miners received. According to the newspaper many miners suffered from malnutrition and terrible living conditions and earned less than they would have received through unemployment benefits.[32] In the January 15, 1927, edition of the *Volkswacht*, German Democratic Party officials urged the reestablishment of the eight-hour workday and the institution of a system of overtime pay that would include progressive hourly wage increments to be paid by the employer for each hour worked after eight hours.[33] Also, in June 1927 in a *Volkswacht* article party leaders publicly chastised a Reichstag deputy who had stated before the legislature that Germany did not need a social welfare program because workers should take the responsibility of saving for their own illness and retirement. According to the newspaper, the deputy had added that by providing social benefits to the workers the state encouraged them to slack off. The newspaper reported that DDP representatives had cautioned this deputy that without the social welfare program, 50,000 Germans would perish.[34]

With its failure to support the Social Democratic chancellor Müller's plan to fund unemployment compensation and other social services in 1930, however, the DDP appeared to abandon its prior commitment to labor.[35] Despite the DDP's turn to the political right in 1930, party positions continued to call for programs to benefit unemployed workers. In late 1931 the DStP published a list of measures to help Germany's unemployed. Among these were a program that would have farmers offer potatoes, flour, butter, and margarine at wholesale prices to the unemployed, who would pay for them out of welfare payments; a measure to make discounted train tickets available to the unemployed; a proposal to provide the free use of heated public buildings such as schools and gyms for the unemployed in the late afternoon and evening; and a program offering free athletic and foreign language classes to the unemployed, taught by unemployed athletic teachers and foreign language teachers.[36] These measures fell far short of a comprehensive program to solve the economic crisis of workers. Nevertheless, they do indicate the party's sensitivity to the plight of the working-class unemployed.

The Center Party and the Working Class

With its strong ties to the Christian trade unions, the Center Party's leadership felt well positioned to elicit the backing of the sizable Catholic working-class population located in the Ruhr and Rhine areas as well as in the industrial pockets of eastern Germany. Along with the DDP and SPD the Catholic Center Party had ensured that Weimar governments until 1930 passed legislation beneficial to the working class. The party's record of promoting social legislation for the working class was impressive. In 1925 the Center Party called for the expansion of social insurance and the implementation of laws governing labor arbitration. These calls were accompanied by a petition to the International Labor Exchange in Geneva to extend Germany's labor policies to workers in the predominantly Catholic Saar region.[37] In early 1927 Catholic Party deputies proposed a series of labor initiatives that included a job security law, limits on the length of the work week, restrictions on work over the Sabbath, restructuring of the government's social insurance program, expansion of illness insurance to other industries, and international agreements on labor issues.[38] As early as April 1927, Center Party representatives called for extended unemployment relief, a comprehensive job creation program, and an affordable housing policy.[39]

Between 1924 and 1929, when Germany was experiencing significant economic growth, the Center Party encountered relatively few obstacles in juggling the interests of its farming and working-class constituencies. In 1928, however, Center Party advocacy of working-class issues began to wane. That the Center Party selected as its head the conservative Kaas rather than the pro-labor Stegerwald may have played a role in this evolution. Moreover, with the onset of the Depression, the rivalry between the party's working-class and farming constituencies grew. First, the Bavarian wing of the Catholic movement (the BVP) claimed that increased expenditures aimed at improving the lot of the working class meant that less aid was available for Germany's Catholic farming community. BVP delegates were incensed that their Catholic Party colleagues refused to join them in condemning the Grand Coalition's passage on December 9, 1929, of an emergency finance program that included a tax on beer and tobacco to help fund increased allocations to the unemployment fund. In response, the BVP broke ranks with the Center Party and withdrew its support from the government.[40] Second, as the Depression worsened, the Center Party also became increasingly skeptical of governmental spending initiatives, many of which funded programs for the working class. No doubt the rise of Brüning (a strong proponent of fiscal conservatism) to head of the party's parliamentary delegation influenced the Center Party's position on governmental spending.

Throughout Brüning's administration, the party press defended the chancellor and called on Catholic workers to accept temporary cuts in programs and benefits, a sacrifice that would, the press declared, in the short term produce lower unemployment and in the long term economic stabilization.[41] This is not to say that the party totally wrote off efforts to improve short-term conditions for the working class. The party press took special note of Brüning's bill on emergency victims that earmarked 322 million marks to assist the unemployed during the winter months of 1930–1931. The bill went down to defeat in the Reichstag, however, and Center Party dignitaries blamed the bill's opponents for forsaking the unemployed. The Brüning cabinet in its last months also devised a plan to resettle unemployed workers on new farms formed from unprofitable estates in eastern Germany.[42] All told, between 1930 and 1932 the Center Party's record clearly demonstrated unwillingness to support schemes advanced by other parties to raise the premiums for unemployment insurance. The party steadfastly maintained that deviation from the austerity program would create higher unemployment in the future.[43]

The SPD and the Working Class

It cannot be disputed that throughout the Weimar period the German Social Democratic Party consistently championed such working-class issues as a shorter workday, compulsory arbitration, and unemployment insurance. Nonetheless, because of the party's goal to act as a responsible coalition partner, the SPD occasionally pulled back from its commitment to remake German society. The party's political vacillation eventually undermined its standing in the eyes of many workers.

Among some of the early SPD proposals were the establishment of the eight-hour workday, reduction of night-shift hours for men, elimination of night work for women and children, introduction of new child labor laws, protection of the rights of women in the workplace, establishment of an uninterrupted weekend break of at least forty-two hours, restrictions on cottage industries, conversion of the social insurance system into a comprehensive public assistance program, creation of special assistance programs for large working-class families, and defense of labor's right to organize.

The class of agricultural workers was a major beneficiary of Social Democratic working-class policy. Beginning in 1919 the SPD pushed for and won increases in agricultural laborers' wages, the right to unionize, compulsory arbitration in wage disputes, and access to health, disability, pension, and unemployment plans. The SPD successfully organized large numbers of agricultural laborers into the party's German Agricultural Labor Union (*Deutscher Landarbeiterverband*). The party also called for the nationalization of large land holdings in Germany's eastern regions.[44]

The SPD's 1925 Heidelberg Program represents one of the party's clearest strategic statements regarding the establishment of social democracy in Germany. The Heidelberg Program called for the transformation of the capitalist system of private ownership of the means of production to social ownership. The program justified the SPD's involvement in government, stressing that the struggle against the capitalist system was not only an economic struggle but also a political one. The party noted that the socialization of the means of production cannot fully develop unless the working class has political rights. The program further called for the liberation of the international working class. The program also ruled out the violent overthrow of the capitalist system to ensure the liberation of the proletariat. Instead the SPD proposed that the social, economic, and political success of the working class would ultimately lead to the gradual elimination of capitalism.[45]

A major political force in the Reichstag during the 1920s, the SPD introduced legislation promoting unionization, elimination of child labor, annual paid vacations, steeper progressive income and inheritance taxes, and elimination of all tuition fees for students.[46] In 1925 the Social Democrats introduced legislation to raise workers' disability and retirement pensions from 16 marks to 26 marks per month and increase child support payments from 3 marks to 7.5 marks per month.[47] In the same year, Social Democrats put forward a revised unemployment insurance bill that included farmhands, domestic help, and temporary workers in its definition of the unemployed. The bill also called for an extension of unemployment benefits beyond the maximum of twenty-six weeks and for an increase in unemployment benefits of 50 percent.[48]

The SPD carried the fight for changes in the unemployment insurance program into 1927. In that year Social Democratic deputies insisted that agricultural workers be allowed access to unemployment insurance protection and that payments be set at a rate of 50 to 60 percent of the wages earned during the last period of employment.[49] To fund these social programs the Social Democrats proposed higher taxes on the wealthy and redirection of government expenditures away from nonessential programs such as the one to construct "pocket battleships." Social Democrats campaigned in 1928 with the motto: "Oppose the building of battleships! For the feeding of children."[50] The party's hard work to pass pro-labor legislation and the willingness of many representatives of industry's export-oriented sector to compromise with organized labor produced some notable successes. German labor obtained the right of collective bargaining, a system of shop councils, a national economic council comprising representatives of management and labor, the eight-hour workday, the 1923 Old Age Pension Act, and the 1927 Comprehensive Unemployment Insurance Act, largely owing to the efforts of the SPD.

The economic prosperity of the mid- to late 1920s created a receptive environment for many SPD-sponsored labor measures. During these years the export-oriented industrial sector guided German foreign and labor policies and saw fit to accede to many of labor's demands. The SPD offered its parliamentary support to the export sector in exchange for this sector's acquiescence on labor matters. Caution began to replace receptiveness after 1929, however, as industry's profit margin declined. The issue of unemployment insurance broke the back of the socialist-led Grand Coalition. In light of the worsening economic situation that German labor faced, the left wing of the Social Democratic Party urged that unemployment insurance be extended to fifty-two weeks of benefits and that it be available to all professions.[51] These Social Democrats reminded the other parties that the Weimar Constitution obliged the state to provide for the unemployed.[52] In early 1930 the Grand Coalition collapsed when the left wing of the SPD refused to accept proposed reductions in unemployment benefits and many members of the Grand Coalition, who had earlier favored expanded social welfare benefits, voted against additional expenditures.[53] The Social Democrats claimed that an increase in the fund had become necessary because the number of unemployed had exceeded 800,000, the maximum number the fund could support.

After the fall of the SPD-led Grand Coalition in early 1930, the SPD became part of the parliamentary opposition. The Social Democrats criticized Brüning's economic policies as harmful to the working class and accused the chancellor of dismantling the hard-earned social reforms of the late 1920s.[54] As measures to revitalize the German economy and lower unemployment, the SPD leadership called for the establishment of a forty-hour work week, a standard wage accompanied by state-imposed price controls, a monopoly office to scrutinize business practices, a central planning office to coordinate the activities of commerce, agriculture, and industry, cuts in the highest salaries in the public and private sectors, and greater emphasis on a *collective economy*, or public ownership of large farms, utilities, and transportation enterprises.[55]

Kele claims that these Social Democratic proposals contained few fresh ideas on how to restart the German economy and suggests that by sticking to the motto "Neither inflation nor deflation," the SPD handcuffed itself and failed to produce a comprehensive or innovative program to redress the economic slide. For instance, at the same time as the party called for a rise in unemployment compensation, it defended a balanced budget.[56] The SPD, in seeking to act as a responsible party, too often compromised its positions on the issues.[57] As examples of SPD concessions, Hamilton points to the decision by many SPD deputies to vote with the majority in the Reichstag to overturn the eight-hour workday, the SPD's decision in 1928 to disallow unemployment benefits to striking steelworkers, and the party's tacit toleration of many of Brüning's deflationary policies.[58] As a further indication of the SPD's concessionary stance, the party backed Brüning's 10 percent across-the-board wage cut in June 1930 and voted in favor of many of Brüning's procapital tax programs.[59] In the eyes of many of the party faithful such concessions indicated a lack of commitment on the part of the SPD. In defense of the SPD's strategy of compromise, Mommsen and Childers observe that the SPD, albeit greatly disillusioned with Brüning's administration, feared that the collapse of the government could open the door to Communist or Nazi rule.[60]

More than any other issue, the debate within the SPD over deficit spending and job creation exemplified the party's lack of political boldness in a period of economic crisis. Within the Social Democratic organization the initial impetus for public works programs, including housing and road construction, came in early 1932 from the unions, the Socialist Federation of Trade Unions, and the Free Trade Union Federation.[61] Shortly thereafter, in March 1932, the SPD newspaper *Vorwärts* called on the Labor Ministry to employ funds allocated to the Reichsbahn and Reichspost for road construction.[62] A month later the Extraordinary Congress of the Free (Socialist) Trade Union Federation convened to discuss the Woytinsky-Tarnow-Baade (WTB) plan to create one million new jobs, principally through greater public spending. The WTB plan elicited criticism, however, from some in the labor movement, who perceived it as unworkable.[63] In May 1932 the SPD newspaper *Volkswacht* called on the Reichsbank to provide more accessible credit to finance road construction projects. The *Volkswacht* further contended that by spending 650 million marks on these projects, the government would reduce unemployment insurance payments by 42 percent.[64]

Throughout the spring of 1932 the SPD flirted with the ideas of deficit spending and a job creation program. Ultimately, party leaders rejected these notions for fear of fueling inflation and continued to emphasize the themes of anticapitalism and antiradicalism.[65] Hamilton, Breitman, and Barkai all attribute the Social Democratic decision to reject deficit spending and job creation programs to the influential role played by Rudolf Hilferding. Hilferding, a leading financial expert in the party, argued that deflationary measures had a better chance of solving the economic crisis than inflationary ones.[66] The SPD's reputation as the vanguard of the working class was tarnished in the eyes of many workers by the party's failure to take radical measures to remedy Germany's economic woes, a failure exemplified by its rejection of the massive government-financed public works program called for by the unions.

The KPD and the Working Class

The German Communist Party strategy to woo the working class consisted of a total rejection of the capitalist system and the promise of an idyllic future based on the construction of a Soviet Germany.[67] The KPD never abandoned its strategy to overthrow capitalist rule and construct a Soviet Germany; by 1924, however, it did append to its strategic plan a list of nonrevolutionary methods to build up its organization while awaiting a more propitious climate for a revolutionary seizure of power. In 1924 the party thus embraced a strategy of building a revolutionary base through political indoctrination, accompanied by constant efforts to mobilize the working class. The party urged workers to fight for reforms, for example, by pressuring the government to improve the material situation of the unemployed.[68]

Members of the KPD, unlike members of many other political parties, frequently took to the streets to publicize their agenda. In January 1926 the party organized a massive march to bring attention to the plight of the unemployed and to the poor working conditions in German industry. The Communists demanded that the government act immediately to raise wages and unemployment benefits, reinstitute the eight-hour workday, and terminate illegal overtime.[69] In a move that angered many in organized labor, the KPD joined with the conservatives to fight against measures to institute compulsory, binding arbitration in labor-management disputes.[70]

The KPD consistently made the unemployment issue its central theme. The improvements in the unemployment insurance program resulting from government legislation in the mid- to late 1920s did not deprive the KPD of an issue. The Communists pushed for additional measures to help the unemployed. In late 1929 the party published a set of specific recommendations addressing unemployment in Berlin. These recommendations included calls for significant increases in unemployment compensation, with payments to begin from the very first day of unemployment, and for the introduction of a seven-hour workday with full pay. In addition, the Communists urged that the unemployed be provided with financial assistance to enable them to pay their rent and utilities, free travel on transit lines, exemption from property taxes, free teaching materials, free milk for their children, and work preparing construction materials for houses, apartments, and schools.[71]

The mention as early as 1929 of job creation in KPD position statements might suggest that the NSDAP was not the first German political party to present a comprehensive public works program. Unlike the NSDAP proposal, however, the KPD proposal failed to set forth specific details on the public works program. The Communists were perfectly clear about one thing: the funds for public works should derive principally from the expropriation of capitalist wealth. In particular, the party proposed the introduction of new taxes on the wealthy, cancellation of indemnities to the former royal families, reduction of salaries and pensions of the highest-paid civil servants and white-collar employees, annulment of obligations to foreign creditors, and curtailment of military appropriations.[72] Yet other evidence appeared to indicate that the leadership of the KPD actually disapproved of public works programs. In the spring of 1932 German Communist Party leaders chastised the socialist unions' call for a massive public works program as a desire "to experiment with autarky and inflation."[73]

Although the KPD's attention centered on attracting the industrial working class, the party did try to lure agricultural laborers to its ranks. After 1930 the KPD paid greater heed to the problem of growing rural unemployment and called on the state to assist unemployed wage laborers financially.[74]

The defense of the working class and assistance to the unemployed served as central elements of the KPD's short-term working-class program. The Communists also immersed themselves, albeit with less zeal, in other Weimar political debates. The party called for opposition to higher tariffs on food staples such as wheat and corn because higher prices translated into larger financial outlays by workers. The Communists also attacked the implementation of the Dawes and Young Plans. According to the party leaders, the implementation of these plans would result in severe cutbacks in programs to help the poor and sick and would place the burden of payments on the working class.

During the last few years of the Weimar Republic the Communist Party competed for working-class votes and membership with the German Social Democratic Party and the Nazi Party. In many ways the political playing field was uneven: the KPD carried distinct liabilities. Foremost among these was the party's failure to discard its image as a foreign party. Many in the labor movement were quite aware of the influence that Moscow, through the Comintern, had on German Communist Party policy.

KPD leaders constantly reinforced its image as a pawn of the Soviet Union by proclaiming the party's goal of building a Soviet Germany and by constantly alluding to international proletarian solidarity. As Fischer so aptly notes, the party's incessant appeal to internationalism conflicted with the strong nationalist feelings of many in the German working class. Fischer adds that if the German Communists had pursued a national communist program, they very likely would have attracted a larger German working-class following before 1933.[75] I agree fully with Fischer's assessment and submit that given a choice between a working-class party advocating the interests of the international proletariat and a working-class party promoting the interests of the German proletariat, the average German worker would have selected the latter. As we shall see below, the Nazis, in striking contrast to the German Communists, spoke only of the German working class.

A second major liability of KPD strategy was its intransigence on reformism.[76] As appealing as the communist utopia appeared to many German workers, daily improvements in their lives probably concerned them more. Though the party presented some proposals to bring about improvements in workers' daily lives, KPD leaders generally viewed reforms as detrimental to the ultimate objective of bringing about a revolutionary collapse of the capitalist system, for according to many German Communists, programs that created temporary relief had the potential to delay that collapse. KPD leaders' advocacy of general strikes between 1929 and 1933, at a time of high unemployment, and the official policy that party members must belong to a Communist trade union were prime examples of the ideological intransigence that hindered the Communists' ability to attract workers. Economists, including Karl Marx, have convincingly argued that when unemployment is high, workers are at a disadvantage in bargaining with management. During the Depression, many German workers probably viewed the Communist calls for the general strike as harmful to their immediate preoccupation—keeping their jobs.[77] The Communist Party's policy requiring party members to maintain trade union affiliation proved impossible to carry out and conflicted with other aspects of German working-class life.[78] Communist leaders' unwillingness to accept the legitimacy of the non-Communist labor movement was an additional example of inflexibility and no doubt hindered the party's chances to compete successfully with the SPD and the NSDAP for working-class support. German Communists divided the world of Weimar politics into two camps: the good guys and the bad guys. The KPD and the downtrodden working class constituted the good guys, while all other Weimar political parties, along with the capitalist thugs who ruled Germany, represented the bad guys. The major Communist Party newspaper, *Die Rote Fahne,* suggested on May Day 1928 that in view of the control over Germany's parliament and principal political parties (excepting the KPD) exercised by the captains of industry, the inscription on the Reichstag building in Berlin should no longer read "Dem deutschen Volk" but, more appropriately, "Dem deutschen Kapital."[79] The leaders of the KPD refused to acknowledge the legitimacy of the Social Democratic movement during the entire Weimar period, referring to the Social Democrats as Social Fascists and accusing them of betraying the working class by acting as the henchmen of the German bourgeoisie and as volunteer agents of French and Polish imperialism.[80] In sum, because the party portrayed itself as an outsider, and one unwilling to compromise, many potential supporters probably decided to affiliate themselves with another working-class party.

The NSDAP and the Working Class

Numerous scholars hold that the NSDAP was a working-class party in name only. They claim that the party failed to attract a sizable working-class following and after the 1928 general elections redirected its campaign almost exclusively toward the middle-class electorate. Kele dates the party's initial detour from a working-class orientation to 1920, with the publication of the official party program that included (allegedly) bourgeois statements, such as that the most capable ought to have the greatest opportunity to earn money and that skilled workers should view themselves as belonging to the middle class rather than to the proletariat. For Kele a further sign of the party's drift away from a pro-labor orientation was the ascendancy of Hitler, rather than the more socialist-inclined Anton Drexler, within the party. Kele sees additional signs of the NSDAP's pre-1925 abandonment of the working class in the party's affiliation with the Deutschnationaler Handlungsgehilfenverband (DHV) and its front organization, the Gewerkschaftsbund deutscher Angestelltenverbände—unions that disapproved of strikes and the class struggle—and in the NSDAP leadership's decision to support management in the March 1922 Munich railway strike, its reluctance to support the eight-hour workday, and its position to tolerate only strikes aimed at fighting high prices or taxes.[81]

Though Kele underscores the NSDAP's lack of commitment to a

working-class political agenda, he does acknowledge that some painstakingly endeavored to steer the party in a pro-labor direction. He claims that when the party was reconstituted in February 1925, it began to attract measurable working-class support in northwestern Germany, especially in the Ruhrgebiet, thanks primarily to the innovative efforts of Strasser and Goebbels. According to Kele, they successfully recruited workers to the party by highlighting the anticapitalist and pro-socialist leitmotifs of the NSDAP. In October 1925 Strasser launched the *Nationalsozialistische Briefe* (National Socialist letters), a pro-labor publication edited by Joseph Goebbels. Kele asserts that the left-wing program of Strasser and Goebbels quickly ran into a roadblock chiefly because the program backed a national plebiscite on expropriation of royal land holdings and espoused a pro-Russian foreign policy—two positions that clearly struck a discordant note with the party's Munich leadership, which was pro–middle class.[82] Strasser and Goebbels tried to convince Hitler and staff at the Munich party headquarters that given that the NSDAP stood for socialism and against capitalism, the party was obliged to favor the expropriation of German royal land holdings without compensation, as well as alliance with the Soviet Union (a proletarian state that was being victimized by a gang of capitalist nations).[83] In the end, under pressure from Hitler, Strasser and Goebbels moderated their position.[84]

Kele further reports that with Strasser and Goebbels towing the line, the party steered a course more favorable to the middle class while still attempting to woo the working class through token gestures. After 1926, efforts to attract a working-class following were seriously hampered by the party's ambiguous language and its inconsistencies toward the major bread-and-butter issues of interest to labor. The case of the 1928 metalworkers' strike is illustrative, according to Kele. By November 1928, nearly 250,000 metalworkers had been locked out by management. Strasser and Goebbels urged the party to give unqualified support to the strikers, but many in Munich party headquarters insisted that the party consider the interests of the employers. After five weeks of intense debate the NSDAP finally adopted Strasser and Goebbels' recommendation to support the strikers. By contrast, the KPD backed the strikers from the outset. Kele claims that workers took notice of Nazi hesitancy regarding the defense of working-class interests. Kele states also that Hitler's decision to ally with the conservative DNVP in 1929 in support of the plebiscite against the Young Plan further damaged the party's hopes of gaining working-class backing.[85]

Whereas Kele insists that the party began to change its working-class orientation as early as 1920–1921, other scholars date the break as coming between 1925 and 1928. Böhnke suggests that the NSDAP's shift away from a pro-labor orientation occurred in 1925. According to him, the pro-labor philosophy of Esser and Feder held sway in the party between 1919 and 1925. After 1925 Esser and Feder lost influence within the Munich wing, as evidenced by the party's positions on labor issues such as wage hikes, strikes, the eight-hour workday, and working-class conditions.[86] Spielvogel and Kater date the NSDAP decision in 1928 to discard the party's working-class mantle to the leaders' realization that their "urban strategy" had failed, except in the highly industrialized Ruhr region and Berlin. Spielvogel points to Hitler's defense of private property and his pro-business outlook as detrimental to the party's chances of gaining a working-class following, and Kater concludes that the party's positions on strikes, lockouts, and unions impaired NSDAP hopes of weaning the working class away from the German Communist Party, which had pledged its resources to these issues.[87] Stachura does not assign a date to the NSDAP leadership's decision to forsake the working class; rather, he stresses that the philosophies of National Socialism and German labor were inherently contradictory. In particular, the Nazi emphases on dictatorship, racism, hypernationalism, and Volksgemeinschaft clashed with workers' deeply ingrained beliefs about the democratic ideals of parliamentary government, class solidarity, and class consciousness and what Stachura terms the instinctive dislike among workers of racist chauvinism.[88]

A number of scholars argue that although the NSDAP relinquished its goal of winning over the working class by 1928, some workers continued to adhere to the Nazi Party. Indeed, Kater suggests that though the NSDAP failed to win over industrial workers living in the principal urban agglomerations, the party attracted a significant following among industrial workers who resided in rural areas but commuted to work in major urban areas. What was decisive, according to Kater, was the pull of the rural environment that bound the worker to the soil through property ownership or the aspiration of ownership.[89] Childers and Noakes and Pridham state that many workers in handicrafts and small-scale manufacturing found a home in the Nazi Party. Forgotten by big business and big labor, these workers found in the Nazi Party a means to express their bitter social resentment.[90] Although he claims that workers as a group were underrepresented in the NSDAP, Winkler, like Childers and Noakes and Pridham, subscribes to the claim that the Nazi Party successfully recruited workers in occupations with a low degree of trade union organization—farmworkers, railway workers, postal and service workers. Winkler moreover views female textile workers and unemployed youth as more likely adherents of Nazism.[91] And finally, Stachura notes that workers most susceptible to the appeal of Nazism were those with few ties to their own class (lumpen element of the industrial working class), those in enterprises where the owner had a direct and strong presence (auxiliary workers and workers employed in small businesses), those influenced by the Nazi themes of ultranationalism, pseudo-egalitarianism, and the folk community, or those lured by the Nazi attributes of dynamism and activism (young workers).[92]

In contrast to those who argued that the NSDAP abandoned a working-class program sometime between 1920 and 1928, I subscribe to the minority view that the NSDAP never diverged from its strategy to woo the working class to its ranks. The majority has overlooked the substantive content of the Nazi Party's labor program and has erred in assuming that an economic program that was anti-Marxist and favorably disposed toward private property did not appeal to many workers. It seems a serious misreading of German working-class interests to assume that all workers lacked the aspirations to climb the social ladder and enter the middle class. By combining nationalist-etatist thinking with creative Keynesian economics, the NSDAP, more than any other party, fashioned a program that addressed the material concerns of many German workers.

In the Nazi Party's official program drafted in February 1920, ten of the twenty-five points were clearly pro-labor. The program championed the right to employment and called for the institution of profit-sharing, confiscation of war profits, prosecution of usurers and profiteers, nationalization of trusts, communalization of department stores, extension of the old-age pension system, creation of a national education program for all classes, prohibition of child labor, and an end to the dominance of investment capital. Moreover, Anton Drexler's observations that "the greatest opportunity to earn money should be given to the most capable" and that "the skilled worker ought not to consider himself a proletarian but as one of the middle class, an equal citizen of the state," are for me a convincing manifestation of a working-class orientation that addresses the workers aspirations for social mobility and not, as Kele writes, evidence that the NSDAP had, as early as 1920, begun to abandon its working-class orientation.[93]

From the outset Hitler emphasized that the Nazi Party would not be a working-class party like the Social Democratic Party or the Communist Party. The NSDAP was above all a German nationalist workers' party, that is, a party that put the interests of German labor above those of the international labor community. The Nazis would continually underscore this theme to gain working-class support throughout the Weimar period. Nazi Party leaders asserted that both the Social Democratic and the Communist Parties had betrayed the German working class and that the Communist Party in particular placed the interests of international bolshevism before the national interests of the German working class. The Nazis cautioned workers that the Communist Party sought to remold them in the image of Russian workers, who toiled twelve hours a day and had lost the right to strike.[94]

Before the Depression the issues of reparations and the betrayal of labor by the SPD and KPD dominated much of the NSDAP campaign to attract workers. The party attempted to convince labor that Germany's acceptance of the reparations plan would aggravate inflation and destroy German industry and agriculture. The NSDAP warned that the end result of the Dawes and Young Plans would be the enslavement of German workers. Reparations provided the party with a departure point for attacks on international high finance, international Jewry, and Weimar traitors, in addition to what many writers have misconstrued as antilabor stands on strikes and the eight-hour workday.[95] After the signing of the Dawes Plan in August 1924, the NSDAP used the reparations issue to justify its opposition to both issues; strikes and the eight-hour workday, which the Left advocated, forestalled German economic growth while at the same time benefiting Germany's foreign enemies, the Nazis assured the workers.[96]

Beginning in 1929 the Nazi Party increasingly blamed the reparations payment plans for the nagging problem of German unemployment. In large part because of the national exposure the NSDAP received in 1929 as an ally of the DNVP in organizing a national plebiscite against the Young Plan, many more German workers became aware of the NSDAP's position on reparations payments. To educate the working class about the Nazi positions on labor affairs in general, the party established a series of special labor newspapers like *Der Angriff*, *Der Erwerbslose*, and *Arbeitertum* and included a special labor section entitled "Deutsche Arbeiterpolitik" in the *Völkischer Beobachter*, the party's major daily.[97]

NSDAP leaders lambasted the Social Democratic Party for its alleged treachery, as they described its role in government. According to Nazi propaganda, the SPD represented a clique of workers who by accepting the Versailles treaty, the Locarno pact, and the Dawes and Young Plans, showed their indifference to improving conditions for the working class and their intention of carrying out the allies' policy of enslaving the German working class. The Nazis portrayed the German Communist Party as equally treacherous, highlighting the KPD's "slavish dependence" on Moscow and espousal of proletarian internationalism.[98] The Nazis also reproved the Social Democratic and Communist Parties for their supposed refusal to represent the interests of those engaged in mental labor. The NSDAP claimed for itself the title of the working-class party that advanced the cause of both manual and mental labor ("Arbeitertum der Faust und der Stirn").[99] The leaders of the NSDAP described the party as a non-class party, with the intent, I argue, to mitigate the effects that lower-class status had on the self-image of workers.[100] By substituting the notion of a nationalist folk community for that of a class-based society, the Nazis offered workers a view of society that differed from that offered by the traditional leftist parties but, more important, made them feel better about themselves and instilled in them the desire for social advancement.

As the effects of the Depression hit Germany, the Nazis shifted their focus increasingly to the merits of autarkic economic development and job creation. Party positions emphasized the need to put the interests of German industry ahead of those of foreign industry. To this end, NSDAP officials denounced government and those in big business who had allowed foreign laborers into Germany to take jobs from German workers. For instance, the Nazis blasted the government for admitting more than 200,000 foreign workers into Germany between 1929 and 1930. Given the high level of unemployment among German farmworkers, the Nazis accused the government of further exacerbating the deteriorating situation of German agricultural workers. NSDAP propaganda criticized the government for failing to resolve the problem of growing unemployment. The party linked acceptance of the Young Plan for reparations payments to unemployment, claiming that these payments to Germany's enemies had the effect of reducing job opportunities in Germany while creating jobs abroad. Moreover, the Nazis indicted as substantially deficient Brüning's 1930 plan calling for the construction of 40,000 units of public housing and the establishment of a labor service for unemployed youth and agricultural workers. Brüning's austerity program was the focus of numerous NSDAP denunciations. The party accused Brüning of cutting wages while failing to lower prices and of undermining the livelihood of the unemployed by reducing unemployment relief.[101]

The NSDAP emerged as a viable choice for many German workers not only because of Nazi attacks on unpopular government programs but by virtue of the party's ability to generate a set of innovative ideas to redress the economic problems confronting workers. After 1930, German workers clamored for action and the Nazi Party, unlike so many other Weimar parties, promised action. Beyond proposing the restoration of the eight-hour workday, a structure to allow workers to help formulate company policy, the establishment of profit-sharing schemes, a ban on the hiring of women and juveniles in large plants, and the creation of affordable small-scale homesteads for agricultural laborers, the NSDAP laid "great emphasis on job creation and commitment to a major scheme of public and related works to soak up the unemployed."[102]

In the NSDAP employment program announced in Strasser's October 7, 1930, Reichstag speech, the Nazis called for the introduction of a one-year compulsory labor service to help overcome unemployment. According to the program the state would constitutionally guarantee employment opportunities. The 1930 employment program also called for the creation of a public works program. To finance the works program, the Nazis proposed the establishment of a state building and loan association.[103] The NSDAP developed further its idea of job creation in its Public Works/Inflation Program in 1931. While Brüning and the parties supporting him continued to subordinate economic recovery measures to reparations payments, the NSDAP argued for inflationary spending and job creation to fight the effects of the economic crisis.[104] The Nazi proposals were subjected to vitriolic attacks by parties of all ideologies. In particular, the Nazis' suggestions about stimulating economic activity and employment through expanding credit and priming the pump were generally viewed as irresponsible and inflationary by the major political parties. Even the right-wing DNVP and the left-wing KPD joined in warning that the implementation of the NSDAP program would lead to a new, harmful inflation.[105]

Job creation served as the theme for a series of speeches that Hitler delivered during 1931 and 1932 to groups of traders and artisans. Many center and right-wing political parties proposed deflationary measures to enhance the profitability of business during the economic crisis, but Hitler argued for inflationary measures such as job creation and linked the economic well-being of the middle class to the elimination of unemployment.[106] At the same time that he was trumpeting the need for job creation, Hitler was stressing the need for German economic self-reliance. In a speech in the town of Eutin (Schleswig-Holstein) on May 8, 1931, Hitler blamed the deteriorating situation in German farming and manufacturing on the government's continuing policy of importing cheap agricultural produce and finished products. In a National Socialist Germany the interests of the German producers would come first and the economy would be completely controlled by Germans, Hitler insisted.[107] After 1930 the NSDAP continued to press for a massive resettlement program in eastern Germany. Party leaders argued that a resettlement program offered *workers* as well as farmers, merchants, and artisans the opportunity to climb the social ladder in a colonial setting.

The centerpiece of the Nazi economic policy before 1933 was unquestionably the NSDAP's Immediate Economic Program (Wirtschaftliches Sofortprogramm). Through this program the NSDAP showed itself to be the only major German party eager to assimilate the ideas of the economic reformers and willing to experiment economically.[108] In a May 1932 Reichstag speech, Gregor Strasser outlined the party's program to deal with the Depression. The NSDAP Immediate Economic Program called for an about-face from the deflationary policies of the Brüning administration. At the core of the NSDAP Immediate Economic Program were recommendations to establish full employment. The program called for a massive state-funded public works project, to include housing and highway construction as well as the establishment of new agricultural settlements, soil improvement programs, and land conservation. The program recommended expenditures of ten billion marks to employ nearly two million laborers. Housing construction alone would provide jobs for approximately a million unemployed workers. The NSDAP Immediate Economic Program called for the creation of a credit institution by the central bank to help finance the public works projects. Strasser placed much of the blame for Germany's current economic stagnation on exorbitant interest rates. Lower interest rates would free capital for productive investments. The program proposed (à la Keynes) that the public works projects would eventually pay for themselves because new jobs create savings through lower unemployment benefits and larger tax revenues.[109]

The NSDAP Immediate Economic Program also addressed autarkic economic development. Through an intensive development of Germany's own economic resources Germany would become self-sufficient and regain its economic self-determination. In the program the Nazis also recommended that Germany seek to gain access to key raw materials through bilateral trade with the individual states in Germany's continental economic zone. According to this scenario, Germany could exchange its finished industrial products for the raw materials of its neighbors in eastern and southeastern Europe.[110] Although many hard-pressed German workers welcomed the creative suggestions incorporated in the NSDAP Immediate Economic Program, the political establishment, and, one might add, the SPD and KPD, generally reacted with criticism, warning that the ideas contained in the Nazi program were too inflationary.[111]

The NSDAP's July 1932 electoral strategy focused heavily on the major themes of public works, job creation, and autarkic development. Party spokespersons declared that it was the duty of the state to guarantee that every German had a job. The Nazi Party called once again for a massive crash program of public works, to comprise housing, road, dam, and canal construction and the introduction of a compulsory labor service. Party leaders argued that reduction of the financial and psychological strain of unemployment far exceeded the cost to the state of providing jobs. Moreover, the contents of the Nazi Party's Immediate Economic Program were published by the party's official publishing house, Eher Verlag, and 600,000 copies were distributed at the time of the July 1932 Reichstag election. Before the July election Strasser broadcasted over the radio a summary of the Immediate Economic Program.[112]

The NSDAP's Immediate Economic Program was followed in November of 1932 with the Economic Reconstruction Plan (*Wirtschaftliches Aufbauprogramm*). In contrast to the Immediate Economic Program, which bore Strasser's indelible stamp, the newer program incorporated the thinking of Wagener, Feder, and Funk. The Economic Reconstruction Plan was less ambitious than the Immediate Economic Program: it called for three billion instead of ten billion marks to be spent on job creation. Principal themes of the Economic Reconstruction Plan were state intervention in financial matters and the restoration of the health of German agriculture. In particular, the program called for universal reduction in interest rates through nationalization of the credit system and state supervision of banks and currency exchange. The plan also contained an outline of the future Nazi Law for National Labor, along with a program of wage and price controls. But like the Immediate Economic Program, the Economic Reconstruction Plan clearly expressed the need for German financial independence and state management of currency, credit, wages, and prices.[113]

It becomes amply clear from even a cursory examination of the Nazi Party's 1930 employment program, the 1932 Immediate Economic Program, and the 1932 Economic Reconstruction Plan that the party had not abandoned its attempts to win over the working class. Many scholars have claimed that after the Nazi Party's disastrous electoral performance in 1928, Hitler steered the party away from its strategy of weaning the working class from the SPD and KPD. According to this way of think-ing, the influence of the party's left wing (the Strasser wing) on policy formulation waned dramatically. Kele, in his comprehensive examination of the Nazi Party's working-class politics, makes much of the Left-Right division within the Nazi Party leadership. Kele insists that Hitler and the Munich group advanced the rightist party line—a line intended to win over the middle class through attractive positions on business and private property; meanwhile, the Strasser brothers and Goebbels promoted the leftist position, aimed at gaining working-class support through a socialist program.[114] Childers likewise, echoing conventional wisdom, states that in 1928, in the aftermath of the party's electoral beating, the NSDAP shifted away from the labor-oriented electoral strategy that the Strasser wing had promulgated. Childers adds that after 1928 the party increasingly courted the middle-class electorate through emphasis on such major middle-class themes as anti-Marxism, support of private property, and opposition to department stores.[115]

The magnitude of Left-Right rivalry has been overstated; the distance between Hitler's and the Strasser brothers' positions was not substantial.[116] Although in 1926 Hitler personally chided Gregor Strasser and Goebbels for their support of the national plebiscite on the proposed expropriation without compensation of the German princes and for their pro-Russian view of foreign policy, that does not mean that Hitler and Munich head-quarters sought to steer the party away from working-class concerns but rather that there was more political capital to be gained by opposing the national plebiscite and the atheistic and anti-private property Soviet Union. Indeed Hitler probably chastised Strasser and Goebbels less on grounds of their working-class orientation than because the NSDAP, he insisted, must promote the interests of the *German* working class rather than those of the *international* working class.

Childers errs on two fronts in asserting that the party strategy gradu-ally shifted from pro–working class to pro–middle class. First, he ignores the pro-working-class measures embodied in the Nazi Party's 1930 em-ployment program, the 1932 Immediate Economic Program, and the 1932 Economic Reconstruction Plan. Second, he falsely assumes that the ma-jority of German workers opposed private property and were favorably disposed toward Marxism. Many German workers were attracted to the Nazi Party specifically because they perceived the party to be the only working-class party that promised to provide them with an opportunity to climb the social ladder.

BDC sample.

4.1   Nazi Party Joiners from the Working Class, 1925–1932

Additionally, Kele and others base their claims that the NSDAP had minimal labor support on evidence of close ties between Germany's unions and other political parties, especially the SPD. But these scholars apparently forget that nearly 60 percent of Germany's labor force in 1930 had no union affiliation at all.[117]

Did the Nazi Party between 1925 and 1932 attract a sizable working-class constituency, as I suggest? The data on Nazi Party joiners strongly support this claim. Figure 4.1 shows that the working class comprised about 40 percent of Nazi Party joiners for each year between 1925 and 1932. The Nazi Party membership data show clearly that the NSDAP drew substantial support from the blue-collar working class—male and female.[118] But we need to ask what kinds of workers should have been most attracted to the NSDAP.

First, in comparison with the SPD and KPD, the Nazi Party was clearly a more nationalistic party. Throughout the Weimar period the Nazis steadfastly opposed the government's policy of reparations fulfillment and German compliance with the stipulations of the Versailles treaty. Furthermore, in contrast to the Communists and Social Democrats, who avowed their sympathy for the international working class, the Nazis promoted the interests solely of the German working class and linked their opposition to reparations and the Versailles treaty to the economic interests of German workers. Therefore, more than the SPD and KPD, the NSDAP should have appealed to nationalistic German workers.

Second, throughout the Weimar era, the Nazis stood out as strong proponents of autarkic development. The party supported protective tariffs, the expansion of the domestic market, and the development of a continental economic zone in southeastern Europe. The Nazi positions on protectionism and autarkic development corresponded closely to the economic interests of workers in the import-oriented industrial sector. At the same time, the Nazis condemned free-trade policies and expressed no sympathy for improving relations with Germany's western European and North American trading partners. The Nazis' positions were at variance with the interests of many workers in the export-oriented industrial sector, however. Therefore, we should expect to find higher rates of Nazi Party affiliation among workers in industries producing primarily for the domestic market (food production, construction, mining, clothing, and woodworking) and lower rates of Nazi Party affiliation among workers in German industries producing primarily for the export market (chemicals, electrotechnology, machinery, and textiles).[119] Figures 4.2a through 4.2d list the seventeen principal industrial branches surveyed in the 1925 German census. For each branch I have calculated the proportion of Nazi Party working-class joiners eighteen years and older. These figures provide substantial support for the theory of interest-based adherence to the Nazi Party. They show that four of the five major import-oriented industrial branches (food production, construction, woodworking, and clothing) have significantly high proportions of Nazi Party membership, and two of the four chief export-oriented industrial branches (chemicals and textiles) have exceptionally low proportions of Nazi Party joining.

A critic might argue that the strong relation between particular industrial branches and Nazi Party joining was simply the result of a more general regional phenomenon, that is, that the Nazis did well in certain regions (such as Saxony, Thuringia, and northwest Germany) where some industrial branches were overrepresented and did poorly in other regions

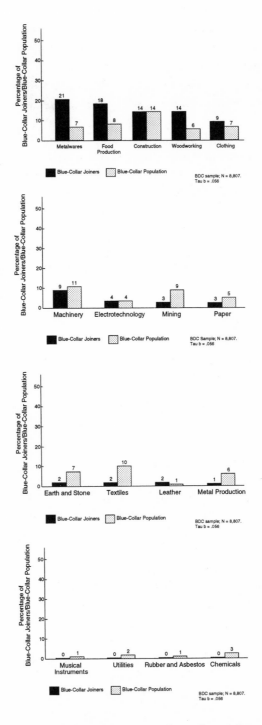

4.2 Blue-Collar Joiners of the Nazi Party, by Industrial Branch, 1925–1932

Table 4.1   Nazi Party Joiners Who Were Workers, by Industrial Branch and by Region of Germany

Branch	Region 1 (%)	Region 2 (%)	Region 3 (%)	Region 4 (%)	Region 5 (%)	Region 6 (%)	Nation (%)
Metalwares	20.6	19.2	19.6	19.7	21.3	25.4	20.5
Food Production	17.3	15.2	17.3	20.0	16.8	28.1	17.5
Construction	13.0	12.1	15.6	14.0	15.2	13.2	14.5
Woodworking	14.8	15.6	13.4	13.6	11.6	13.9	13.3
Clothing	9.4	10.1	7.6	8.5	9.9	6.7	8.9
Machinery	7.9	11.0	9.7	7.4	10.4	1.7	8.6
Electrotechnology	3.1	5.2	5.4	4.2	4.0	2.9	4.1
Mining	3.6	0.9	4.1	3.5	1.6	0.0	3.2
Paper	2.9	4.1	2.8	2.3	2.4	3.4	2.5
Earth and Stone	3.3	1.1	1.2	3.0	1.4	2.0	2.3
Textiles	1.7	1.8	1.1	0.9	2.6	0.1	1.9
Leather	1.5	2.5	1.7	2.1	1.1	1.8	1.7
Metal Production	0.6	0.5	0.5	0.5	0.5	0.0	0.7
Musical Instruments	0.1	0.0	0.0	0.1	1.1	0.0	0.4
Utilities	0.1	0.6	0.0	0.0	0.1	0.8	0.1
Rubber and Asbestos	0.0	0.0	0.0	0.0	0.0	0.0	0.0
Chemicals	0.0	0.0	0.0	0.0	0.0	0.0	0.0
n	3066	339	1235	1897	2042	228	8807

Region 1: Prussia, East Prussia, Brandenburg, Silesia, Berlin
Region 2: Saxony, Thuringia
Region 3: Schleswig-Holstein, Lower Saxony, Oldenburg
Region 4: Westphalia, Rhineland, Hesse, Pfalz
Region 5: Bavaria
Region 6: Baden, Württemberg

Source: Brustein-Falter BDC sample.
Note: We used O'Loughlin, Flint, and Anselin's regional categorization; see J. O'Loughlin, C. Flint, and L. Anselin, "The Geography of the Nazi Vote: Context, Confession, and Class in the Reichstag Election of 1930," Annals of the Association of American Geographers, 84 (1994): 351–80.

(Bavaria, Baden, and Württemberg) where the same industrial branches were underrepresented. In other words, region or religion rather than material self-interest may explain why domestic-oriented workers joined the Nazi Party. Table 4.1 presents a breakdown of NSDAP blue-collar joiners by industrial branch and region. It becomes clear from table 4.1 that region had little effect on Nazi Party joining. For instance, the mean proportion for Nazi construction workers in predominantly Protestant region 3 (northwest Germany) was 15.6 percent, compared with 15.2 percent in

Map 4.1   German Regions, 1930

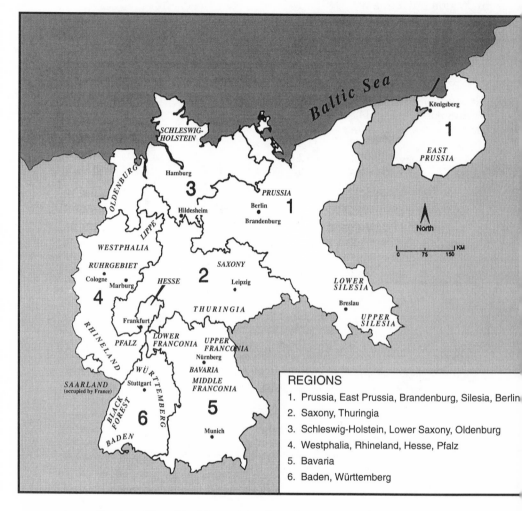

REGIONS

1. Prussia, East Prussia, Brandenburg, Silesia, Berlin
2. Saxony, Thuringia
3. Schleswig-Holstein, Lower Saxony, Oldenburg
4. Westphalia, Rhineland, Hesse, Pfalz
5. Bavaria
6. Baden, Württemberg

Source: Based on O'Loughlin, Flint, and Anselin, "The Geography of the Nazi Vote: Context, Confession, and Class in the Reichstag Election of 1930," *Annals of the Association of American Geographers,* 84 (1994): 355.

predominantly Catholic region 5 (Bavaria). The national mean for construction workers joining the Nazi Party was 14.5 percent.

Third, the NSDAP emerged in 1931 as a very forceful proponent of
pump priming and job creation. Consequently, we should expect that after
1931 the NSDAP should have recruited relatively well among employed
workers who feared the loss of their jobs and among the growing numbers of unemployed workers. In particular, because the NSDAP job creation program called for mass construction of public housing, highways,
dams, and canals, we should find that the party recruited especially successfully among workers in industrial branches who would get these new
jobs, principally workers in the construction and woodworking industries.
The evidence appears to support this conclusion. The highest unemployment levels between January and July 1932 occurred in the construction
industry (77.3 percent in January 1932 and 77.2 percent in July 1932) and
the woodworking industry (66.1 percent in both January and July 1932).[120]
These two industrial branches ranked among those with the highest proportion of Nazi Party working-class joiners. The lowest unemployment
levels were in mining (18.3 percent in January 1932 and 17.6 percent in July
1932). The mining industry ranked far below the woodworking and construction industries for Nazi Party affiliation.

Fourth, the Nazi Party was never a major proponent of unionization.
Hitler frequently admonished party leaders who wanted to replicate the
SPD's and Center Party's efforts to organize labor. Because many organized workers believed that their unions afforded them the best opportunity to maintain or improve their material position, they were likely
to support their unions' political patrons and unlikely to join the Nazi
Party. Nonetheless, many German laborers were unorganized, and others
were dissatisfied with their unions. Such workers may have looked at the
NSDAP as an attractive alternative to the traditional Weimar working-
class parties.[121] Thus, we should find Nazi Party membership higher in such
nonunionized industrial branches as clothing, leather, food production,
woodworking, and musical instruments and lower in such highly unionized industrial branches as mining, metal production, utilities, rubber, and
chemicals. Because of the absence of individual-level or industry-level data
on union membership for the period of 1925 to 1933, I employ Childers's
data on industrial plant size in 1925. Plant size is computed as ratio of employees (blue collar and white collar) to entrepreneurs. The assumption is
that the larger the ratio, the higher the level of unionization. Table 4.2 lists
the seventeen principal German industrial branches by their proportion of

Table 4.2   Nazi Party Joiners by Industrial Branch, with
Branch-Employee Ratio

Branch	% Nazi Party Joiners	Branch-Employee Ratio
Metalwares	19.7	600
Food Production	17.2	300
Construction	15.3	600
Woodworking	14.9	400
Clothing	8.6	100
Machinery	8.6	3,300
Electrotechnology	3.8	1,000
Mining	3.5	33,200
Paper	2.7	1,200
Earth and Stone	1.9	1,900
Textiles	1.5	800
Leather	1.5	300
Metal Production	0.4	9,900
Musical Instruments	0.3	400
Utilities	0.1	6,200
Rubber and Asbestos	0.0	6,100
Chemicals	0.0	3,300

Source: Brustein-Falter BDC sample; *Statistik des Deutschen Reichs,* vol. 402, pts. 1, 3; Childers, *Nazi Voter,* 275–76.
Note: Spearman's r = .493.

Nazi Party working-class joiners and plant size ratios. Though the data are not conclusive, it does appear that the branches with lower ratios of employees to entrepreneurs had the highest number of Nazi Party joiners, whereas industries with higher ratios generally ranked low in Nazi Party joining.

The finding that the Nazi Party recruited more successfully among workers in nonunionized industrial branches will probably not surprise scholars who hold to the view that blue-collar workers who joined the Nazi Party were primarily "atypical" workers—namely, blue-collar workers from the handicrafts, service, or agricultural sectors. But the theory of interest-based adherence posits that workers in big industry should have been well represented in the party since the NSDAP's working-class programs addressed the concerns of workers in big industry as well as those in handicrafts, service, and agriculture. If indeed Germans joined the party out of self-interest, we should find that Nazi Party working-class joiners from big industry were well represented in the party. Figure 4.3 presents the proportion of NSDAP blue-collar joiners by type of employment as

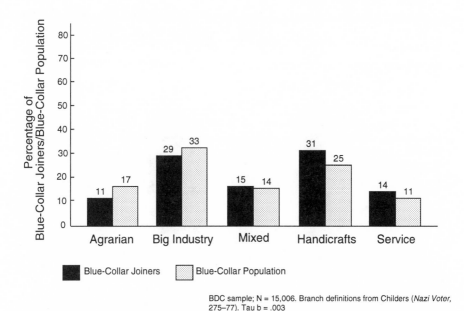

4.3 Blue-Collar Workers Among Nazi Party Joiners, Categorized by Structure of Branch, 1925–1932

a percentage of the total blue-collar population eighteen years and older. Handicraft workers comprised 31 percent of all NSDAP blue-collar joiners between 1925 and 1932, and workers in big industry constituted 29 percent of all blue-collar joiners. Thus, the results of figure 4.3 largely support the expectation that the NSDAP should have drawn workers successfully from each of the various types of employment rather than exclusively from handicrafts or service.

Fifth, and most important, alone among the working-class parties, the NSDAP subordinated an exclusively working-class orientation to a non-exclusive societal outlook. By promoting the interests of private property and small business, it is likely that the NSDAP turned off many workers who were convinced that private ownership and profit were unacceptable evils. But if many workers decided to stick with the SPD and KPD, the

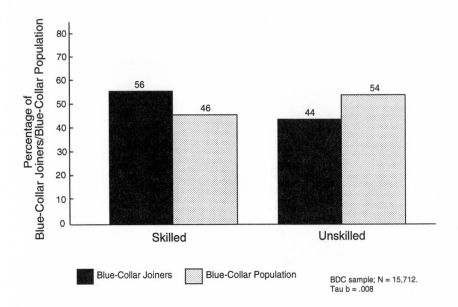

4.4   Blue-Collar Joiners of the Nazi Party, Skilled Versus Unskilled, 1925–1933

so-called "real" working-class parties, other workers who aspired to own homes, become salaried employees, or start their own businesses supported the NSDAP precisely because they perceived it as a working-class party that favored this social mobility. Turner has argued that the Nazi Party sought to achieve social equality through a process of upward leveling, that is, absorption of workers into the middle class.[122] In particular, skilled workers, more than semi- and unskilled workers, were likely to possess a strong aspiration for social mobility. Skilled workers thought of themselves as both socially and economically superior to semiskilled and unskilled laborers, and in contrast to semi- and unskilled workers should have believed that a middle class existence was a viable possibility for them.[123]

Some might claim that laborers in Weimar Germany had few prospects of social advancement. But for much of the Weimar period, German labor experienced a rise in its real hourly and weekly earnings. If we use an index of hourly and weekly earnings (1913 = 100), hourly earnings climbed from a level of 86 in 1924 to 125 in 1932; weekly earnings rose from a level of 70 in 1924 to a peak of 110 in 1929 and dropped to 94 in 1932.[124] The social and economic gains achieved by workers between 1924 and 1929 should have persuaded many workers that further social advancement was possible. Ironically, the SPD, by fighting for and winning improvements for the working class, may have prepared the ground for the Nazis to recruit workers. Many workers had prospered from the social and economic legislation of the mid-1920s and began to dream of a middle-class life. They found the SPD's opposition to private property and capitalism distasteful and may have turned to the NSDAP instead because they perceived that the NSDAP would help them up to the next rung of the social ladder. The desire for economic advancement and the perception that the NSDAP, alone among the working-class parties, responded to that desire made the NSDAP a likely choice for millions of German workers.

If the argument is correct that there is a link between social aspirations and the tendency to join the Nazi Party, then we should find that more skilled workers than semi- and unskilled workers joined the party. Skilled workers, by virtue of their social status and wage level, should have perceived social advancement as an achievable goal. Figure 4.4 compares the proportions of skilled blue-collar NSDAP joiners with semi- and unskilled blue-collar joiners for the period from 1925 to 1933. As predicted, skilled blue-collar workers were overrepresented in the NSDAP, and unskilled and semiskilled workers were underrepresented. Data by industrial branch on the proportion of skilled labor corroborate the individual-level findings on the relation between skilled workers and Nazi Party joining. Table 4.3 presents a comparison of skilled and semi- and unskilled Nazi Party joiners, by industrial branch. The findings show clearly that industrial branches with the highest proportion of skilled workers had the highest proportion of Nazi Party joiners. Skilled workers may have had an additional reason to join the Nazi Party between 1925 and 1932. German economic rationalization had the effect of replacing skilled jobs with semi- and unskilled ones. Skilled laborers, fearing the elimination of their jobs, may have viewed favorably the Nazi Party's position favoring protectionism and job creation.

Table 4.4 presents the results of a regression analysis of the proportion of Nazi Party joiners in fifteen industrial branches and provides additional

Table 4.3   Nazi Party Joiners by Industrial Branch, with Proportion of Skilled Labor to All Labor in Industrial Branches

Branch	% Nazi Party Joiners	% Skilled (1933)
Metalwares	19.7	60
Food Production	17.2	61
Construction	15.3	58
Woodworking	14.9	54
Clothing	8.6	64
Machinery	8.6	63
Electrotechnology	3.8	59
Mining	3.5	46
Paper	2.7	48
Earth and Stone	1.9	27
Textiles	1.5	17
Leather	1.5	35
Metal Production	0.4	30
Musical Instruments	0.3	50
Utilities	0.1	43
Rubber and Asbestos	0.0	20
Chemicals	0.0	25

Source: Brustein-Falter BDC sample; *Statistik des Deutschen Reichs*, vol. 402, pts. 1, 3: 458–93; Preller, *Sozialpolitik in der Weimar Republik*, 119.
Note: Spearman's r = .792.

evidence of the importance of skill level in explaining the kinds of workers who joined the Nazi Party. The findings of table 4.4 show that branch skill level is the strongest predictor (represented by the standardized "betas") of Nazi Party joining in the fifteen industrial branches between 1925 and 1932.[125]

And finally, many workers might have chosen the Nazis over the Socialists and Communists because the leftist lexicon and ideology were frequently too abstract and too far removed from the daily life of workers. George Orwell, an intellectual socialist, may have aptly captured socialism's and communism's failings in his *Road to Wigan Pier*, published in 1937. In his explanation of the European left's inability to counter the popular appeal of fascism Orwell states: "As for the technical jargon of the Communists, it is as far removed from the common speech as the language of a mathematical textbook. I remember hearing a professional Communist speaker address a working-class audience. His speech was the usual bookish stuff, full of long sentences and parentheses and 'Notwithstand-

Table 4.4

Regression of the Percentage of Nazi Party Joiners Working in Specific
Industrial Branches, on Branch Characteristics, 1925–1932

Variables	Unstandardized	t-values	Standardized
BSKILL	0.27+	2.70	.58
PROPROT	0.23 ns	1.18	.30
IMPORT	1.67 ns	0.54	.13
UNIONIZE	−0.00 ns	−0.37	−.10
Constant	−21.28 ns	−1.68	
$R^2 = .56$			

Source: Brustein-Falter BDC sample; data from 1933 *Statistik des Deutschen Reichs;* Abraham, *Collapse of the Weimar Republic;* Childers, *Nazi Voter;* Hoffman, *Wachstum der deutschen Wirtschaft;* Preller *Sozialpolitik;* Svennilson *Growth and Stagnation.*
Note: N = 15; +p < .05; ns = not significant at .05.
Variable Descriptions:
  BSKILL: percent skilled workers in each industry branch in 1933 (Preller, *Sozialpolitik,* 119)
  PROPROT: average proportion of all workers in specific branch who were Protestant
  IMPORT: a dummy variable whose value of one equals branches designated as import oriented; all other branches given a value of zero
  UNIONIZE: level of unionization in each branch via a branch ratio of employees to entrepreneurs (Childers, *Nazi Voter*)

ing' and 'Be that as it may,' besides the usual jargon of 'ideology' and 'class-consciousness' and 'proletarian solidarity' and all the rest of it." Socialists did not escape Orwell's wrath, either. He notes: "We have reached a stage when the very word 'Socialism' calls up, on the one hand, a picture of aeroplanes, tractors and huge glittering factories of glass and concrete; on the other, a picture of vegetarians and wilting beards, of Bolshevik commissars (half gangster, half gramophone), of earnest ladies in sandals, shock-headed Marxists chewing polysyllables, escaped Quakers, birth-control fanatics and Labour Party backstairs-crawlers. Socialism, at least in this island, does not smell any longer of revolution and the overthrow of tyrants; it smells of crankishness, machine-worship and the stupid cult of Russia." [126] By contrast, the Nazis wrapped their message in a simple, albeit sometimes crude, vocabulary.

The correlation between the Nazi Party's programs and the material interests of many Germans between 1925 and 1933 may explain in large part who joined the Nazi Party and why. But if material interests were all that was necessary to motivate Germans to become Nazi Party joiners, we should expect to find nearly fourteen million joiners in 1932. Material interests, by themselves, cannot tell the whole story. Why did only 10 percent of the Germans who voted for the Nazis in 1932 join the party? Joining the Nazi Party clearly involved greater costs than did casting a vote. In the following chapter I will focus on the role that selective incentives and disincentives played before 1933 in shaping the decision to join the Nazi Party.

5

Selective Incentives and Disincentives for Joining the Nazi Party

It is often believed that members of extremist movements constitute a separate subset of partisans: their fanaticism may predispose them toward physical confrontation or a desire for martyrdom. We should not doubt that zealotry characterized many Nazi Party joiners; nonetheless, I would maintain that most NSDAP supporters who decided to join the party were motivated largely by their perception of the costs and benefits associated with membership. Given the costs in time and money and the physical risks, the logical strategy for the average Nazi Party sympathizer would have been to vote for the party without joining it, or to catch a free ride, as discussed earlier. Had joining the NSDAP been cost-free, many more Germans would have joined the party before 1933. Still, why did more than 1.4 million Germans do so?

Nazi followers who joined the party before 1933 acted on their perception that the costs of membership had become acceptable because of an increase in the incentives and/or a reduction in disincentives to joining. Selective incentives and disincentives should also help explain why some groups were more likely to join the Nazi Party before 1933 than other groups. By way of illustration, disincentives help explain why farmers and civil servants who may have sympathized with Nazi Party programs were underrepresented as party joiners before 1933; positive incentives provide an important clue to why white-collar employees were overrepresented as party joiners before 1933.

Before examining individual incentives and disincentives affecting the decisions of Nazi sympathizers to joining the NSDAP prior to 1933, I need to digress briefly and describe the organization of the Nazi Party. The Nazi Party was organized on the basis of Gaue, or regions. In 1928 the thirty-five Gaue corresponded to the thirty-five Reichstag electoral districts. Below the Gaue were the *Kreise* (counties or districts) and within each *Kreis* were the *Ortsgruppen,* or local branches. Large local branches in big cities were frequently divided into sections. Hitler insisted that a local branch needed a minimum of fifteen members to be recognized.

The organizational structure of the Nazi Party was completely centralized: each new member had to accept the organization and the leader unconditionally, and local branches needed approval from party headquarters. Local branches were required to submit monthly activity reports to headquarters, and by 1931 each branch leader was expected to maintain a record on the performance of each branch member. *Gauleiter* (heads of regional branches) assigned inspectors to check on the performance of local branches.[1] Party finances were strictly monitored. Income and expenditures had to be logged, and each year audits were conducted on local and regional finances and the reports sent to party headquarters in Munich. The party treasurer in Munich had the power to examine the books of any branch without notification.[2]

Yet party headquarters afforded the branches a fair degree of independence with regard to recruitment and activities. The party favored granting independence to local organizations in the hope that greater latitude would allow them to fashion a strategy reflecting their local conditions. The party rewarded the most efficient locals, for instance, by sending them the most popular speakers who, by drawing a large attendance, could produce more money for the local party's coffers.[3]

Incentives to Join the NSDAP

What kinds of material incentives did the NSDAP offer joiners? Before the Nazi Party came to power, the party had few material rewards to parcel out. In this respect, the NSDAP differed greatly from Mussolini's Italian Fascist Party, which before its ascension to power succeeded in gaining control over the redistribution of some lands and the allocation of employment opportunities for agricultural laborers in north-central Italy.[4] Mussolini's party, consequently, found itself in a position to exchange material incentives for party membership. Unlike its Italian counterpart, the NSDAP constantly faced financial exigencies. The NSDAP obtained the bulk of its operating revenues from membership dues, sales of its newspapers, and entry fees charged for public rallies and meetings. Still, the Nazi Party possessed some tangible incentives to offer joiners. One was employment—by which I refer to both actual and future employment. It is likely that many Germans who joined the party after its initial electoral breakthrough in September 1930 saw Nazi Party membership as a ticket to employment or career advancement in a future National Socialist Germany. In late 1930, the party used membership as inducement to attract civil servants, by hinting that in a Nazi state civil service jobs would go only to registered Nazi Party members.[5] But even before Hitler's appointment as chancellor the NSDAP had jobs to offer. Between 1925 and 1933 the NSDAP had developed a government-in-waiting, comprising numerous specialized branches and departments. At both the regional and national levels, the party created bureaus staffed with members who were knowledgeable about legal, financial, agricultural, labor, medical, and cultural issues. This party apparatus created thousands of jobs. Unemployed or underemployed individuals with the requisite skills found job opportunities in the party that were unavailable elsewhere. Moreover, the party tried to establish contacts with local employers to hire party members and published a list of employment opportunities in the *Völkischer Beobachter.*[6]

One party employment program that has received some scholarly attention is the public speakers' program. The public speakers' program was important to the NSDAP because it helped the party disseminate its propaganda and recruit new members. The public speakers' program also became a valuable fundraiser because the party charged entrance fees. The NSDAP established a National Socialist Speakers' School (*Rednerschule der NSDAP*) for potential party speakers nominated by their *Gau* leaders, where speakers learned effective rhetorical skills and official party responses to standard questions. NSDAP public speakers also had to become knowledgeable about particular specialized topics, including local and regional economic concerns. The training normally took four months. Nearly six thousand party speakers had completed training at the school by January 1933.[7]

The job of public speaker was highly sought after by many party joiners as a means of gaining a satisfactory living, especially in periods of economic crisis. For each speech, a speaker received a fee, which by 1932 amounted to fifteen marks, plus free board and lodging and reimbursement for travel expenses. Speakers with a reputation for attracting large audiences commanded larger fees.[8]

Because of the clerical, service, and rhetorical skills required for many party jobs, the lion's share of NSDAP employment opportunities benefited the new middle class. In Chapter 3, I hypothesized that white-collar employees should have been underrepresented in the Nazi Party before 1933 because the party's economic positions largely failed to address white-collar concerns. The results of figure 3.6 showed, however, that white-collar employees were overrepresented as NSDAP joiners in comparison with the general German population of white-collar employees. Part of the explanation for the NSDAP's recruitment success among white-collar employees may have been the selective incentives (such as jobs) that the Nazi Party could offer this group.

Although most jobs that the party could provide to potential joiners before 1933 were geared toward the new middle class, the Nazis did attempt to create jobs for blue-collar workers. Evidence suggests that the Nazi S.A. (storm troopers) attracted many unemployed workers. Carsten reports that more than 60 percent of Nazi S.A. members were permanently unemployed. Kater finds that the unemployment rate of various S.A. organizations between 1931 and 1932 in parts of Bavaria ranged from 50 to 85 percent.[9] What kinds of material benefits could have attracted unemployed workers or financially hard-pressed groups to the S.A. and the NSDAP? The Nazi S.A. housed its members in hostels and barracks, where they received food and shelter. S.A. hostels frequently served as soup kitchens for unemployed members and on holidays distributed provisions to members' children. During 1932, in the depth of the Great Depression, the NSDAP established the *Winterhilfe* or Winter Relief program for party members. The S.A. provided free accident insurance to S.A. recruits injured in the line of duty and also found odd jobs for its unemployed members. Wherever possible, organizations of the Nazi Party assisted its faithful. Take the case of Hermann Wischner, who in late 1925, at the age of twenty-seven, joined the NSDAP and the S.A. At two different times between 1927 and 1933, the S.A. intervened on his behalf to provide him with housing, food, and employment. In 1927 Wischner had hoped to participate in a large Nazi Party rally scheduled to take place in Nuremberg. Unemployed and residing in Munich, Wischner lacked funds for the trip. He went to his S.A. leader for help, and thanks to his leader's efforts, Wischner and several other unemployed S.A. members obtained contacts with party members along the route from Munich to Nuremberg that enabled them to secure adequate lodging and food. In 1933 the S.A. found Wischner employment in the government's finance office.[10] Although one case does not prove a rule, it is likely that in many other instances the party employed its resources to assist its followers.

For the unemployed, largely young and working-class, the offer of employment, shelter, and food made joining one of the NSDAP's organizations all the more enticing. But I must emphasize that people probably did not join the party merely to obtain these benefits; the Communist Party, the Center Party, the Social Democratic Party, and the German Nationalist People's Party each had similar resources to offer the unemployed. What initially attracted them to the Nazi organizations was the similarity between their interests and the NSDAP program.

Incentives to join the NSDAP came as well from the preexisting social networks in which people lived, prayed, socialized, and worked together. For individuals ideologically predisposed to favor the NSDAP, social networks allowed division of the risks and obligations of party membership among many people and ensured uninterrupted access to desirable social benefits such as friendship and behavioral affirmation. Among the social networks that contributed significantly to individuals' decisions to join the NSDAP were family, friendship circles, and civic, occupational, and religious affiliations.[11] As was pointed out in Chapter 1, social networks reinforce both horizontal and vertical social ties and thus help overcome the impulse to ride free. The stronger the ties, the more likely ideologically predisposed individuals are to join the party.

The historical record buttresses the claim that horizontal social relations fostered Nazi Party recruitment. For instance, Mühlberger finds six policemen joining the party on the same day in Straubing; an overrepresentation of railway workers in the Kirchenlaibach party branch; and an extraordinarily high percentage of basket makers belonging to the NSDAP in the Bavarian villages of Oberlangenstadt and Küps.[12] Grill, in his detailed study of the Nazi Party in Baden, also mentions that family members of small communities joined the party en masse.[13] Moreover, what became obvious to me and my researchers in 1989 as we collected our sample of early Nazi Party members from the NSDAP master file was the extraordinary degree to which entire families and communities joined the Nazi Party en bloc on the same day—an occurrence seemingly highly inconsistent with the mass-society explanation of Nazi Party recruitment.

The significance of strong horizontal social networks was also apparent in the Nazi Party's success in mobilizing the predominantly rural Geest region of Schleswig-Holstein and Lower Saxony and in the party's relative difficulties in mobilizing the largely rural parts of Rhineland-Westphalia, Hesse, and southwest Germany. The Geest region exhibited many prerequisites for strong social solidarity. Like the Celtic regions of Scotland and Ireland, Geest villagers belonged to extended families and clans. Horizontal ties in the Geest region received an additional boost from its distinct field system. In contrast to the *Reihendorf* field system practiced in large sections of western, southern, and eastern Germany, the *Gewann-dorf* field system, which had existed in the Geest region since the early Middle Ages, relied heavily on communal cultivation and intercommoning of herds. Moreover, in the Geest region, farms were generally small or medium sized and family operated; there was no landless agricultural proletarian class.[14] The absence of agricultural proletarians and large farmers produced a fairly homogeneous social structure. Also, people in the Geest region resided in compact villages with close communal ties.[15] Bessel finds a similar social cohesiveness and strong Nazi recruitment effort in the rural southeastern corner of East Prussia.[16] Such factors all served to foster social solidarity and social control.

In contrast, the preconditions for strong social solidarity were less evident in many other German regions. Heberle and Noakes note that in particular areas of Schleswig-Holstein and neighboring Lower Saxony, large and small farms coexisted in certain districts and agricultural laborers were more common. These circumstances led to social heterogeneity.[17] Noakes further observes that the level of social conflict was high in these socially heterogeneous villages, in contrast to the socially homogeneous Geest region. Also, in many southern German localities with a relatively heterogeneous agricultural population, the absence of common property, joint work, and partible inheritance further hindered social solidarity.[18]

The historical record also suggests that strong vertical social relations nurtured Nazi Party recruitment. Members of groups and communities whose leaders had joined the NSDAP showed an inclination to follow the pattern of community leaders. Leaders generally tended to command respect from members by virtue of their authority and control over the distribution of resources. Zofka's brilliant study of Swabian villages depicts how the Nazis, by winning over important community leaders (*Honoratioren*), such as the mayor or village priest, captured the allegiance of entire villages. Zofka maintains that Nazi promises to improve villagers' economic well-being were not enough to ensure the party's success in parts of Swabia; the presence of a trustworthy and known local leader who favored the NSDAP appears to have been necessary to motivate villagers to embrace the party. Not surprisingly, Zofka finds minimal Nazi strength in such Swabian villages as Hafenhofen, Freihalden, Rettenbach, and Jettingen, where the local elite, the Catholic clergy, was anti-Nazi.[19]

Strong vertical social relations also help explain the NSDAP's successes in Kärle in Hesse. The community of Kärle was made up largely of a group of prosperous farmers and a group of dependent poor (goat) farmers. The

NSDAP succeeded in winning over the prosperous farmers, who through their social and economic authority had little trouble recruiting the poor farmers.[20] The NSDAP's infiltration and cooptation of preexisting networks, such as the various agricultural Landbunds and the Federation of German Retail Business, further exemplify the NSDAP's ability to mobilize an organization's rank and file successfully once it had won over its leadership.[21]

Disincentives to Joining the NSDAP

What is often ignored is that Nazi Party membership before 1933 entailed numerous costs and risks with relatively few material rewards. Party membership demanded numerous sacrifices on the part of joiners; they were obliged to pay membership dues, distribute party literature, attend party meetings, and participate in public rallies which took up time and financial resources.[22]

Before 1933, party membership dues constituted one of the principal sources of NSDAP revenues. Joiners usually paid an entry fee of 1 mark and monthly dues thereafter. Monthly dues for members climbed from 30 pfennigs in 1925 to 1.5 marks in 1932. Unemployed joiners were allowed to pay a lower rate.[23] The financial burden of monthly dues probably deterred many financially hard-pressed farmers, artisans, blue-collar workers, and service workers from joining the NSDAP. In our examination of the NSDAP master file we discovered that many membership records reporting an individual's departure from the party before 1933 noted as the cause the member's failure to pay dues.

As already noted, casting a vote for the NSDAP in a general election could not compare, in the demands it made on people's time and energy, with joining the party. Such party activities as attending meetings, planning events, distributing party literature, and selling subscriptions to party publications required considerable expenditure of time and effort. We can safely assume that many Nazi adherents decided against membership because they believed they could not meet the requirements for active participation.

Furthermore, joining the Nazi Party led in some instances to loss of business or employment. Weimar society consisted of many individuals and groups who disliked the Nazi movement and, as Abel notes, many shops and stores owned by NSDAP members were the target of boycotts, and membership in the party frequently led to members' dismissal by un-

sympathetic employers. In fact, Abel states that 12 percent of his infor-
mants reported that they had lost their jobs or had their business ruined
after they joined the NSDAP.[24] In his analysis of several personal accounts
of Nazi storm troopers, Fischer also finds that association with the Nazi
movement often led to dismissal from employment.[25] In the state of Baden,
Remmele, the anti-Nazi Interior Minister, was authorized by the state
cabinet in 1930 to initiate legal action against public schoolteachers sympathetic to the Nazis.[26] One of the most frequently cited examples of the
potential costs of joining the Nazi Party, as far as employment went, was
the government's pronouncement in 1932 that membership in the NSDAP
was incompatible with employment in the German civil service. All teachers and government employees, like public transport workers, had to sign
a declaration asserting that they were not members of the NSDAP and
had not participated in NSDAP activities. Thus, before 1933 many civil
servants who sympathized with the Nazis probably decided to vote for the
party and forgo joining it.[27]

Between 1925 and 1932, governmental policy often served as a major
impediment to Nazi Party recruitment. In particular, state and central governments frequently instituted bans on Nazi Party activities. Nazi Party
recruitment fared relatively ill in Prussia, Baden, and Bavaria, where governmental hostility toward the NSDAP eventuated in an array of official
bans on Nazi Party activities, active police enforcement of those bans, and
police harassment of Nazi Party activists. By contrast, party recruitment
fared best in Oldenburg, Saxony, Thuringia, Anhalt, Braunschweig, and
Mecklenburg, where (especially after 1930) numerous government officials
sympathized with Nazi goals. Consequently, in Oldenburg and Braunschweig official sympathy for the Nazis led to fewer bans on Nazi Party
activities as well as looser police enforcement of prohibitions against the
NSDAP.[28] Not surprisingly, on entering local and state governments before 1933, one of the NSDAP's first tasks was to gain control over, or at
least neutralize, the Interior Ministry and police bureaucracy.

Bans on Nazi Party activity took many forms between 1925 and 1933.
Table 5.1 provides a sample of governmental bans on Nazi Party activities
before 1933.

Voting for the NSDAP between 1925 and 1933 was unlikely to result
in imprisonment. Nonetheless, membership in the Nazi Party carried with
it some risk of arrest, which served as a clear disincentive to joining. The
local police generally kept extensive lists of NSDAP, S.A., and S.S. members. Both state and central government gave the police the authority to

Table 5.1   Bans on Nazi Party Activity, 1925–1932

Year	Location	Ban
1925	Bavaria, Baden, Prussia, Saxony Hamburg, Oldenburg, Anhalt, Lübeck, Hesse	Hitler's speeches
1927	Berlin, Pasewalk, Cologne, Neuwied	Nazi Party activities
1929	Prussia	NSDAP membership for public servants
1930	Germany	NSDAP membership for public servants
1930	Bavaria	Wearing NSDAP uniforms
1930	Prussia, Baden	Wearing of NSDAP brownshirts
1931	Baden, Prussia	Wearing NSDAP uniforms
1931	Berlin	S. A. sports festival
1931	Germany	Uniforms, press, meetings
1932	Saarland	NSDAP paramilitary groups
1932	Bavaria, Württemberg, Baden	S. A. uniforms and parades
1932	Germany	S. A. and S. S. military functions

Source: Childers, *Nazi Voter;* Pridham, *Hitler's Rise;* H. Volz, *Daten der Geschichte der NSDAP* (Berlin: A. G. Ploetz Verlag, 1939); Grill, *Nazi Movement;* H. A. Winkler, "Die Arbeiterparteien"; Bessel, *Political Violence;* Abel, *Why Hitler.*

disrupt political meetings and to arrest anyone who failed to abide by official bans on uniforms, demonstrations, and public meetings. For instance, in July of 1922 state authorities imposed a sentence of three months to five years on individuals failing to abide by the state ban on Nazi Party activities. The Baden Interior Minister, Remmele, established a special political police force to monitor the activities of groups such as the NSDAP and succeeded in arresting and sending to jail several Nazis.[29] During the early 1930s, Prussia's Social Democratic Interior Minister Severing developed a reputation for harassing members of the Nazi Party. In Prussia, the police on occasion disbanded Nazi Party meetings and rallies when speakers were perceived to have uttered offensive remarks about the state or the flag.[30] Between 1930 and 1932 in the states of Baden, Bavaria, and Prussia, the police frequently carried out surprise raids on Nazi Party offices and residences, hoping to intimidate party members and collect evidence of illegal activities such as the possession of weapons and violent propaganda.[31] For example, between 1930 and 1932 the Prussian police launched massive raids on Nazi Party offices, culminating in hundreds of arrests and jail terms for party activists. Some of those arrested, Abel notes after studying Nazi Party joiners' autobiographies, told of prison sentences as high as ten years.[32] In Prussia, in 1931 alone, 378 Nazis were arrested for their involvement in skirmishes with Communist and Social Democratic groups.[33]

If anxiety over being arrested did not deter many from joining the Nazi Party, the fear of physical injury or death did. When we think of the role of political violence in the rise of Nazism we usually associate it with the party's strategy to intimidate and destroy its enemies and to attract the elements in society to whom physical confrontation greatly appealed. We tend to forget that before 1933 the Nazi Party itself was frequently the target of political violence and that fear of physical punishment may have dampened the many sympathizers' desire to join the party. The principal adversaries of the NSDAP were the host of Communist Party paramilitary groups—the Red Front Fighters' League, Young Antifascist Guard, Fighting League Against Fascism, and the Anti-Fascist Action Group, for example.[34] Physical violence against Nazis usually occurred when the NSDAP attempted to stage rallies and marches in leftist strongholds. For example, in the East Prussian district of Oletzko, the SPD and KPD groups succeeded during the month of August 1930 in disrupting five of the twenty-three NSDAP rallies.[35]

Between 1930 and 1932, several hundred National Socialists were stoned, shot, or knifed to death by members of the Communist paramilitary organizations.[36] By recording the number of claims registered by the compulsory storm troopers' insurance plan, Bessel provides a potential measure of the violence inflicted on Nazis. According to Bessel, most of these S.A. insurance claims were made by S.A. members injured in skirmishes with political opponents or the police. We see the number of claims climbing from 110 in 1927 to 2,506 in 1930 and finally to 14,005 in 1932. The total number of claims for the period from 1927 to 1932 was 24,169.[37] Employing different sources, Rosenhaft reports that the Nazis suffered more than 2,500 injuries in 1930, 6,300 in 1931, and 9,715 in 1932.[38] One of the best sources for details (albeit somewhat tenuous) on Nazi casualties was the party itself. Among the records surviving World War II is the Nazi honor roll (*Ehrenliste der Ermordeten der Bewegung*), which contains the names of those who fought and died for the party before it came to power in January 1933. I gleaned from the honor roll the names of 170 individuals who died between January 1, 1925, and January 30, 1933. The honor roll lists three victims in both 1925 and 1926, five in 1927 and 1928, eleven in 1929, forty-two in 1931, and eighty-four in 1932. Between June 17, 1932, and July 31, 1932, thirty-two Nazis were killed and another thousand wounded. The bloodiest encounter for the NSDAP during this period occurred on July 17, 1932 (Bloody Sunday); three Nazis were killed and fifty seriously wounded in Altona, and three others died in Greifswald.[39]

In the face of so many disincentives associated with membership, it is certainly remarkable that the Nazi Party grew into a mass movement. To appreciate the hurdles the party had to overcome, one need only compare its trajectory with that of the Italian Fascist Party. More than two years before Mussolini's "march on Rome," the Italian Fascist Party began to enjoy an environment conducive to growth.[40] The literature on the rise of Italian Fascism abounds with examples of how the police and government abetted the activities of Mussolini's party. Italian magistrates received orders from the minister of justice to disregard records of Fascist crimes, and the police closed their eyes to Fascist acts of violence against socialist organizations.[41]

Finally, in discussing the role of social networks in the growth of the Nazi Party, I have concentrated in this chapter on how they served as an incentive for joining. But social networks also produced disincentives for joining the NSDAP. Many individuals who were sympathetic to the Nazi Party refrained from becoming members because their social networks (family, community, church) made the cost of joining unacceptable. Individuals who went against their group, whether family or social circle, probably incurred the loss of friendship, behavioral confirmation, and in some instances, employment. For instance, many organizations affiliated with the German Catholic Church frowned on membership in the NSDAP.[42]

If disincentives shaped people's decisions about joining the Nazi Party, we should find that the groups faced by the greatest disincentives were underrepresented in the Nazi Party. First, we should find a higher proportion of unmarried joiners than married joiners in the Nazi Party before 1933. We can generally assume that unmarried people had more disposable time to allocate to party activities than married people and that married people had to factor into their calculation of the potential costs of joining the NSDAP the consequences of their decision for their spouse and children. Furthermore, my theory projects that as disincentives associated with joining the NSDAP declined, married individuals who sympathized with the Nazi Party's programs would have been less reluctant to join the party. Figure 5.1 presents a comparison of married and unmarried (single, divorced, or widowed) Nazi Party joiners. I include only those joiners in my sample of 42,004 who listed a marital status on their membership cards. The results of figure 5.1 strongly support the proposition that party adherence was based on self-interest. More specifically, the proportion of married NSDAP joiners was 46 percent, as opposed to 54 percent unmar-

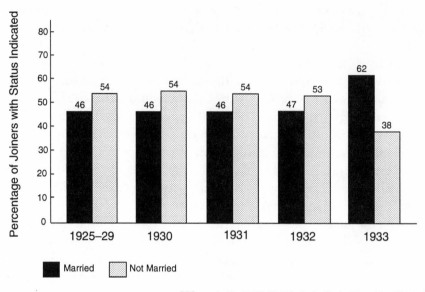

5.1   Nazi Party Joiners' Marital Status, 1925–1933

ried, for the years 1925 to 1929, 1930, and 1931. In 1932, the proportion of NSDAP married joiners rises to 47 percent and in 1933, the proportion jumps to 62 percent. That the proportion of married Nazis rose in 1932 and 1933 conforms to the argument that more married individuals joined the party as the costs associated with Nazi Party membership decreased. The risks associated with Nazi Party membership began to decline dramatically in the summer of 1932. With Brüning's exit from government in May 1932 and the end of the SPD-run state government in Prussia in June 1932, bans on Nazi Party membership disappeared. Moreover, the phenomenal electoral showing by the NSDAP in the July 31, 1932, Reichstag election demonstrated that the Nazi Party had a strong likelihood of gaining power. Hindenburg's appointment of Hitler as chancellor on January 30, 1933, eliminated most remaining risks associated with NSDAP membership.

Second, the high risk (death or imprisonment, for instance) of membership in a party engaged in violent activities should have dissuaded older Germans more than younger Germans from joining. Older individuals usually have more tangible assets (home, job, and family) to risk than young people. Figure 5.2a examines the age structure of NSDAP joiners between 1925 and 1933. As expected, it is skewed toward younger adults. The two youngest groups (eighteen to twenty-four years and twenty-five to thirty-nine years) are overrepresented in the party in comparison with their representation in the general population. The two oldest groups (forty to fifty-nine years and sixty years and older) are underrepresented in the party. Joiners eighteen to twenty-four years old are overwhelmingly overrepresented in the NSDAP. Concomitantly, we should expect to find that as the risks associated with Nazi Party membership declined, the average age of joiners should have climbed. The risks associated with Nazi Party membership began to decline dramatically in the summer of 1932. Figure 5.2b presents the average age of joiners by year from 1925 through 1933. Figure 5.2b confirms my claim that the average age of joiners increased as risks declined. The average age of joiners rose to thirty-three in 1932 and then jumped to thirty-six in 1933.

Third, disincentives to joining the NSDAP before 1933 were especially high for German civil servants. On numerous occasions between 1929 and 1932 the national government as well as various state governments prohibited civil servants from joining the NSDAP or KPD. Civil servants who joined the NSDAP, if caught, risked their careers. Therefore, we should expect civil servants to be underrepresented as NSDAP joiners before 1933. Figure 5.3 compares the proportion of NSDAP civil servant joiners with the proportion of civil servants in the general population for each year between 1925 and 1933. Civil servants are neither underrepresented or overrepresented in the party between 1925 and 1932. Considering the significant overrepresentation of the new middle class in the NSDAP (figure 3.5), however, the fact that civil servants were not overrepresented in the party would appear to support my claim that disincentives dissuaded many civil servants from joining the NSDAP before 1933. Clear substantiation of the claim that adherence was interest-based can be found in the jump at that point in civil servant NSDAP joiners: the proportion rose from 4 percent in 1932 to 10 percent in 1933. For German civil servants, 1933 brought an end to prohibitions against Nazi Party membership and ushered in a new era in which membership in the Nazi Party was a means to employment in the public sector.

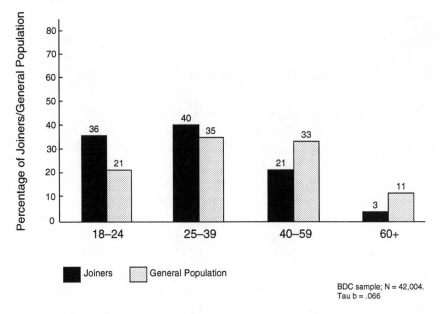

BDC sample; N = 42,004.
Tau b = .066

5.2a   Age of Nazi Party Joiners, 1925–1933

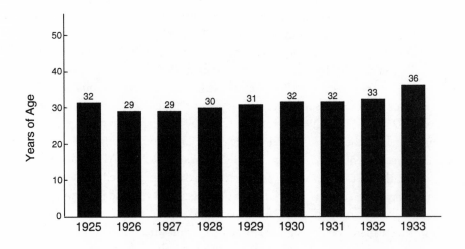

BDC sample; N = 42,004.

5.2b   Average Age of Nazi Party Joiners, 1925–1933

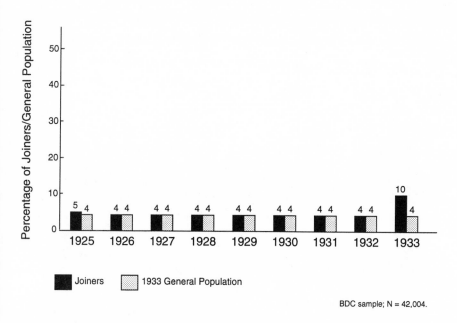

5.3 Nazi Party Joiners Who Were Civil Servants, 1925–1933

In this chapter I have examined a number of factors that help to explain why, of the Germans who viewed NSDAP programs as consistent with their interests (and probably voted for the Nazi Party), only 10 percent decided to join the party. For many pre-1933 Nazi sympathizers, compatibility of interests was an insufficient motivation to join the party. What made joining the party more attractive to these individuals was the offer of real or potential incentives, such as employment, money, and friendship, and the removal of disincentives, such as job dismissal, arrest, physical injury, and group ostracism. Once the Nazi Party came to power in January 1933, the equation changed dramatically. Incentives for joining the party became plentiful, and most disincentives evaporated. It is not implausible that if the Nazi Party had permitted all Germans who wanted to join the party after 1933 to do so, the ratio of voters to joiners would have approached one to one.

Though the compatibility of people's interests with the programs of the Nazi Party before 1933 cannot in itself explain why people decided to join, that factor nevertheless stands out as critical in explaining who joined the party and why. The persuasive power of incentives and disincentives should further elucidate why some people join high-risk political parties. It is highly unlikely that any positive incentives the German Communist Party or the Social Democratic Party might have offered to Nazi sympathizers would have sufficed to lure them away from the NSDAP. What brought Nazi sympathizers to the point of deciding to join the party was their perception that among all the Weimar political programs, the Nazi Party's most closely corresponded to their material interests. The production of positive incentives and the reduction of disincentives became a salient element in the decision to join the NSDAP only after people had already identified with the Nazi Party's political programs.

Conclusion

The goal of this study has been to provide answers to two questions: who became Nazis and why they became Nazis. The traditional explanations of the sociology of Nazism—the movement's irrationalist appeal, lower-middle-class backing, political confessionalism, and the NSDAP's status as a catchall party of protest—were found to be incomplete. Certainly many people were drawn to the Nazi Party for non-economic reasons (the NSDAP's racist and nationalist rhetoric, Hitler's charisma, or antipathy to the Weimar system). Indeed no single factor can explain why nearly 1.4 million Germans joined the Nazi Party between 1925 and 1932. Germans often had multiple reasons for joining the Nazi Party, though the dominant motivation for most was economic, I contend. I take issue with explanations that underscore the reactive and nonrational nature of people's response to Nazism, which have received disproportionate attention; the imaginative and proactive Nazi program, which appealed to the self-interest (particularly the material interests) of a broad section of German society, has been largely ignored. It is this shortcoming that I endeavor to remedy in the present study.

The principal axiom of the theory of interest-based political allegiance is that individuals are purposeful, goal-oriented actors. What are their goals? The assumption is that people prefer more wealth, power, and prestige to less wealth, power, and prestige. As long as individuals believe that one course of action will produce more of these desiderata, they will choose that course. To translate this assumption into political terms, people will vote for or join the party that they believe will increase their wealth, power, and prestige. Because we have no reliable systematic information about the preferences of Weimar-era voters, I have tested the empirical implications of party affiliation based on self-interest, that is to say, hypotheses about who should have joined the Nazi Party between 1925 and

1932. I posit that individuals who joined the party calculated that the expected benefits exceeded the expected costs. According to the theory of interest-based affiliation, the act of joining a party (especially an extremist party) is a two-stage process. Correlation of interests between individuals and party programs constitutes the first stage; the second stage consists of response to incentives or disincentives for joining.

The richness of this interpretation lies not in its prediction that the Nazi Party should have attracted votes from all social classes—that finding has received considerable attention elsewhere. Rather, this account offers an explanation for *why* the Nazi Party attracted voters from all classes and all professions and, equally important, an analysis of which groups within each class were overrepresented in the party and which ones underrepresented.

In this book I examine the political programs of the principal Weimar parties and the material interests of the German old middle, new middle, and working classes. I have postulated that the Nazi Party's emphases on protectionism, autarkic development, tax relief, resettlement, and mandatory application of impartible inheritance should have positioned the party to recruit successfully among the old middle class of artisans, merchants, and small independent farmers (especially livestock farmers). The results of the statistical analysis of Nazi Party joiners between 1925 and 1932 generally confirm predictions that the old middle class should have responded in accordance with its material self-interest. Interestingly, we have here a materialist explanation for the often cited (but seldom explained) relationship between a population's religious confession and its support for the Nazi Party. The absence of livestock farming and the use of partible inheritance in many Catholic communities, for example, strongly shaped attitudes toward the Nazi Party.

The dearth of specific Nazi Party programs engaging the interests of the new middle class of white-collar employees, in conjunction with party pronouncements equating manual and mental labor, should have hurt the party's recruitment efforts among white-collar employees. Furthermore, the Nazi Party's sexism should (according to my hypothesis) have impaired mobilization efforts among married white-collar women, as it bolstered those efforts among white-collar males. The findings fail to confirm both those expectations about white-collar employees but support the proposition that married female white-collar employees were underrepresented in the party by comparison with married male white-collar employees. Moreover, once the second stage in the decision to join the party, response to incentives and disincentives, is taken into account, the picture changes: compatibility of interests alone cannot adequately explain the representation of white-collar employees, but once we figure into the equation the incentives for joining (in this case employment), the findings are more consistent with those the theory would lead us to expect. Also, because the Nazi Party uniformly supported the interests of German civil servants, we might anticipate results showing successful Nazi recruitment within this group. The data yield only mild support for this prediction. Again, however, once we allow for the influence of disincentives, the data appear to confirm the claim of interest-based affiliation. More specifically, governmental bans on civil servants' participation in the Nazi Party before 1933 made joining too risky for many; however, the removal of bans in mid-1932 considerably lowered those risks. The data show a 250 percent rise in the proportion of civil servants joining the Nazi Party between 1932 and 1933.

Some of the most interesting and intriguing findings emerge when the theory of interest-based political affiliations is applied to the German blue-collar working class. In opposition to the conventional view that the Nazi Party never had a working-class strategy, or abandoned it after 1928, I hold that the Nazi Party consistently advanced programs for the German working class. The traditional explanations are based on a misinterpretation of workers' self-interest. The Nazi Party's working-class programs stressing protectionism, autarkic economic development, job creation, and social advancement should have strengthened the party's appeal, for instance, among workers who were especially patriotic, who were employed in the import-oriented industrial branches, or who were highly skilled. The findings strongly support my predictions. Between 1925 and 1932 the proportion of working-class Germans among all Nazi Party joiners averaged a healthy 40 percent. Moreover, the data reveal the highest proportions of Nazi Party joiners in import-oriented industrial branches; I have noted, too, the overrepresentation of skilled workers and the underrepresentation of semi- and unskilled workers.

The empirical findings show that the members of the old middle class, married male white-collar employees, workers in import-oriented industries, and skilled blue-collar workers constituted the backbone of the Nazi Party's membership before 1933. These groups found NSDAP programs particularly appealing. But if political membership is based on rational self-interest, why did the traditional Weimar parties not adapt their programs to address the interests of those same groups? In other words, why was the Nazi Party so adept at addressing the material interests of workers and other groups, whereas the traditional parties were inflexible or seemingly oblivious? To begin with, it is quite clear that parties besides the NSDAP captured support from large segments of the old middle class, new middle class, and working class. For instance, throughout the Weimar period the Catholic Center Party and the Social Democratic Party recruited particularly effectively among German blue-collar workers. It is also evident that the Nazi Party, like other parties, failed to enlist significant support from every social group in Germany. For example, the Nazi Party failed to recruit significant numbers of workers from the export-oriented industrial sector. These facts suggest that like other political parties, the Nazis were unable to adapt their political programs to address the material interests of every group in Germany.

Like other parties, though, the Nazis sought to construct a mass constituency; their positions, like those of other parties, were dictated by ideological factors and by leaders' calculations about what agenda would be effective and attract popular support. Thus, just as Weimar's two principal liberal parties, the German People's Party and the German Democratic Party, were unlikely to come out in favor of the socialization of the means of production, the Nazi Party was unlikely to abandon its steadfast opposition to reparations payments and non-German immigration.

In short, it would be unfair to suggest that the Nazis were successful in building a mass constituency because they were politically more astute than members of other parties, or even because other parties were more locked into their positions than the Nazis. The Nazi Party's phenomenal and precipitous rise can best be explained by the observation that in the depth of Germany's economic depression, the Nazi Party's positions answered the demands of various social groups better than those of any competing party. Let us not forget that the same party that gained nearly 38 percent of the vote in July 1932 had gained less than 3 percent in the elections of May 1928. What changed between 1928 and 1932 was not party positions so much as millions of Germans' perceptions about solutions to the perplexing problems brought about by the Depression.

The present study should hold wider implications concerning the rise of Nazism and the origins of evil. Three fallacies are widely believed about the means the Nazis used to gain a foothold in Germany. First, we are told, Hitler and the Nazis came to power surreptitiously. In his ascent to power, Hitler is portrayed as a thief coming through a broken window at midnight in the aftermath of a hurricane. Second, in an effort to make sense of the Nazis' genocidal campaign to exterminate European Jewry, some historians have advised us that a central component of the Nazi Party's popular appeal was the message of hate and in particular the depiction of the Jew as the personification of Germany's ills. Third, we have been led to believe that the Nazi Party could have succeeded only in Germany, because of Germans' particular national character. If the Germans had only been a rational and democratic people, they would have quickly put an end to this evil, poorly educated, ridiculous demagogue and his band of misfits. Thus, we, standing outside Germany and steeped in our democratic past, would have seen Hitler and his Nazi thugs for what they really were and would never have been duped.

But what if we have misconstrued the lessons of history? Let me first refute the three assumptions just listed.

First, Hitler's appointment as chancellor was neither illegal nor surprising. In a system of proportional representation such as that of Weimar Germany, when no party gained an electoral majority, it was customary for the leader of the largest party to become prime minister. Hitler did not sneak into power in January 1933; Hitler was appointed chancellor because he was the head of the Nazi Party, the single largest political party in Germany.

Second, and most important, we have overlooked the plausibility that millions of Germans may have consciously voted for or joined the Nazi Party because they believed the Nazi programs reflected their interests. It was not because they were evil that Germans flocked to the Nazi Party *before 1933*, nor did they perceive the NSDAP as representing evil. Rather, many Germans calculated that of the competing Weimar political parties, the Nazis offered them the best prospects for a better life. In particular, in the midst of the Great Depression, the Nazi Party alone crafted economic programs that in the perception of many Germans could redress their grievances or provide the means to greater social mobility.

Third, irrational leitmotifs such as anti-Semitism, hypernationalism, and xenophobia played a marginal role in the rise of the NSDAP. Because the collective result of Nazism was so horrific and irrational, the literature has naturally focused on the nonrational nature of Nazism and thus tended to overestimate the importance of nonrational themes to the rise of Nazism. In attempting to understand the Nazi phenomenon, we err if we fail to distinguish its origin from its outcome. The average German who voted for or joined the NSDAP before 1933 did not envision Auschwitz, World War II, or the destruction of Germany. Political opportunism led the Nazi Party to downplay its anti-Semitism, racism, xenophobia, and hypernationalism before 1933. Once in power, of course, the Nazis quickly abandoned their pre-1933 political strategy and pursued their hidden agenda of territorial expansion and racial persecution.

What if we have failed to register critical reasons for the rise of Nazism? Would we be able to detect a new Hitler or Nazi Party? I suggest that to a large extent we have neglected to recognize major elements of the Nazi success. If the argument is valid that the Nazis attracted a huge, broadly based constituency principally by appealing to people's material interests, then we can safely assume that German voters were like voters elsewhere — voting their pocketbooks. The absence of a deep tradition of democracy would have had little effect on Germans' calculations of the net benefits associated with support for the various Weimar parties. A corollary conclusion is that if the economic conditions, the electoral or political party system, and the political choices of Weimar Germany had existed in the United States, France, Sweden, or Britain, millions of people in those countries might have done exactly what millions of Germans did — vote for and join the Nazi Party.

Could another racist, xenophobic party come to power today? The logic of the argument presented here leads me to answer yes: evil may be the horrifying outcome of rational politics. If average Germans had known in 1932 what they knew in 1945 about the consequences of Nazism, the Nazi Party would never have attracted a mass following. The Nazi Party skillfully cloaked its aims until it had achieved power. Many present and future demagogues may similarly masque their message of hate. It is unlikely that we can always detect evil before it reveals itself. How should we judge the potpourri of xenophobic, racist, and hypernationalist movements and parties that are now in the news?

Fifty years have passed since the collapse of the fascist regimes in Europe. Though neofascist or neo-Nazi movements have arisen at other times since 1945, the late 1980s and 1990s are perhaps unrivaled both in the number of new radical-right parties and in the magnitude of popular support for these parties. Although the German Republicans, the Italian Northern Leagues Party, the Finnish Rural Party, the Swiss Auto Party, the Swedish New Democracy Party, and the Danish Progress Party have yet to obtain 10 percent of the popular vote in national elections, other new parties of the radical right have in the span of a few years surpassed the 10 percent mark. Some of the more successful right-wing European parties are the Norwegian Progress Party (13 percent of the votes in the 1989 general elections), the Flemish Bloc (12 percent of the votes in the 1992 Belgian parliamentary elections), the Freedom Party of Austria (16.5 percent of the votes in the 1990 general elections), and the French National Front (14.4 percent of the votes in the 1988 presidential election and 13.9 percent of the votes in the 1992 regional and departmental elections).

The recent popular success enjoyed by parties of the new radical right (NRR) can be attributed to a conjunction of structural conditions and political opportunism. The NRR has carved out a niche in the European political landscape by rejecting a multicultural society, by rebelling against perceived excesses of the welfare state, and by attacking the political establishment. These themes have struck a chord with growing numbers of Europeans during the past few years.

The NRR parties are not the direct descendants of the interwar German Nazi Party. If anything, the interwar analogue of an NRR party was the Belgian Rexist Party. Like the Belgian Rexist Party, new radical-right parties advocate conventional conservative policies such as economic liberalism, reduced government, and lower taxes. The Italian Fascist Party and the German Nazi Party do not fit the mold of a traditional conservative rightist party. In particular, in total contradistinction to the conservative right, the Nazi Party attacked economic liberalism and instead proposed economic autarky, in combination with an interventionist state industrial and agricultural policy, as measures to stimulate the economy and create jobs.

Despite these differences, the NRR and the Nazi Party do share important similarities. Both employ xenophobic appeals to build their core membership. The Nazi Party tempered its racist and xenophobic appeals between 1925 and 1933 because party leaders calculated that racism lacked sufficient allure for the electorate. The NRR highlights the racist and xenophobic elements of its program with the expectation that anxiety over the presence of foreign workers and the flood of immigrants and political refugees will benefit the extremist parties. Equally important, the NRR, like the Nazi Party, links racism and xenophobia to economic concerns. The Nazis used the Jews as a convenient target and played on the hatred among the old middle class of the department stores ("Jewish-owned department stores") and on workers' hostility toward international high finance (Jewish international monopolies). Hostility toward the French and the Belgians, among others, was frequently stirred up over oppressive reparations payments. The NRR blames high unemployment, inflation, and high taxes on the flood of political refugees and immigrants. In both cases, political opportunism shapes the use of racist themes. Also like the Nazi Party between 1925 and 1933, the NRR parties have embarked on an electoral strategy to win power.

How likely are the NRR parties to reach the level of success attained by the Nazi Party? As I have mentioned, few people in 1928 would have predicted that the Nazi Party, which had captured less than 3 percent of the vote in the 1928 national elections, would garner nearly 38 percent of the vote by 1932 and become the most popular political party in Germany. As I have stressed throughout, however, the Nazi Party did not gain its phenomenal mass constituency because of its emphasis on xenophobia but rather because the party designed a series of innovative programs that appealed to the material interests of a broad constituency overwhelmed by the Depression. Xenophobia alone could not have brought the Nazis to power. The shifting political economies of contemporary Europe and North America, however (with the concomitant internationalization of capital and especially labor markets), creates opportunities for NRR parties to exploit xenophobic sentiments in a manner not possible during the interwar period. The extent to which a contemporary extremist political party can successfully link public apprehension about the growing population of "cultural outsiders" to material interests such as jobs, taxes, crime, and AIDS may largely determine the size of that party's popular constituency.

What, then, should we conclude about evil from this examination of the social origins of the early Nazi Party? Should we deduce from this study that great evil may be brought into being when people do not examine the ramifications of choices made on the basis of rational self-interest? We certainly must. Yet any anticipation of the societal consequences of individual choice making is almost certain to fail. Evil may be wrought regardless of how deliberate people are in scrutinizing the potential consequences of their choices. It is highly unlikely that the millions of self-interested German citizens voting for or joining the Nazi Party in 1932 could have realized at the time that their decision would culminate in first dictatorship, then a world war, and finally the murder of millions of innocent people between 1939 and 1945. Thus, I must conclude that evil may have ordinary and rational origins. This applies to pre-1933 Germans as much as to all other peoples.

Social Ranking and Occupational Standing

In my examination of the social origins of Nazi Party joiners I have relied on three different occupational and class coding schemes. Each Nazi Party joiner's reported occupation has been assigned a code from the Mühlberger, Kater, and the Brustein-Falter coding systems.

Social Ranking According to Mühlberger

1. Lower Class

Agricultural workers
Unskilled and semiskilled workers
Skilled craft workers
Other skilled workers (not traditionally associated with artisanal occupation)
Domestic workers

2. Lower Middle and Middle Middle Class

Master craftsmen (independent)
Nonacademic professionals (specially trained, mostly self-employed)
Lower- and middle-level white-collar employees (not including public sector)
Lower- and middle-level civil servants (including public sector)
Merchants
Farmers (including self-employed in horticulture, forestry, and fishing)

3. Upper Middle and Upper Class

Managers (in private sector)
Higher-level civil servants
University and high school students
Academic professionals (usually self-employed)
Entrepreneurs

4. Status Unclear

Non-university students
Pensioners and retired persons
Housewives
Military personnel

Social Ranking According to Kater

1. Lower Class (Workers)

Agricultural, unskilled and semiskilled workers, domestic servants
Skilled workers, skilled craftsmen, dependent master craftsmen
Other skilled workers, specialized but not linked to the artisanal trades

2. Lower Middle Class

Independent master craftsmen (with assisting dependents)
Nonacademic professionals, artists, etc., mostly independent
Lower- and intermediate-level employees (private and public sectors)
Lower- and intermediate-level civil servants
Independent merchants, barkeepers, landlords (with assisting dependents)
Farmers (with assisting dependents)

3. Elite and Upper Middle Class

Managers and executives
Higher-level civil servants
Academically trained professionals (self-employed)
University and professional school students
Entrepreneurs and estate owners (with assisting dependents)

Social Ranking According to Brustein-Falter

Between 1990 and 1992 the Brustein-Falter research team developed a new occupational coding scheme for the BDC membership sample. The Brustein-Falter coding system is not a mere replication of Kater's and Mühlberger's occupational coding schemes. It is intended to correct for certain deficiencies in the Kater and Mühlberger schemes. In our coding scheme, each party member's listed occupation is coded according to the 1925 German Census (*Berufsordnung*) published in the *Statistik des Deutschen Reichs*, vol. 402, part 1. The 1925 *Berufsordnung* contains the most extensive list of German occupations and trades. An additional benefit of our coding scheme is that for each member's occupational location, our coding system includes a level of specification—that is, the level of probability that the member belongs in the assigned category. The rationale for including a level of specification is that we cannot unequivocally determine members' occupations and occupational categories solely by members' own reporting of occupation on their membership cards. For example, an individual might list the occupation of *Drechslermeister,* but we do not know whether that individual was self-employed or not; or an individual might list it as *Lebensmittelhändler,* but we do not know whether this person owned the grocery store or was simply an employee in the store. In such ambiguous situations we tried to include in our coding system additional information from members' cards, such as members' age, in order to assign occupational locations.

A final advantage of the Brustein-Falter coding system is that it includes information on skill level for each member's occupation. Skill levels include: academic, master, skilled, assistant, candidate or trainee, apprentice, helper, praktikant, and pupil.

1. Old Middle Class

Owners, self-employed persons, and entrepreneurs
Leaseholders
Administrators, directors, managers, and high-level civil servants
Door-to-door or street peddlers
Assisting dependents

2. New Middle Class

White-collar technical employees, civil servants, and specialized staff
Foremen and supervisory staff
Commercial employees, administrative officials, and office personnel

3. Working Class

Workers with specialized skills engaged directly in production process
Workers with specialized skills supporting the production process
Other workers
Domestic servants

4. Without Occupation

Brustein-Falter BDC Membership Sample Variables

1. "Core" Variables

Case	Fixed case number before deletion of doubled cases and foreigners' cases
Team	Berlin or Minneapolis team
Partyno	Official member's party number
Double	Official member's number existing twice
Kart	Blaue or Grüne or Franken Kartei
Famname	First letters of family name
Gend	Gender
Famst	Family (marital) status
Birthd	Birthday
Birthm	Month of birth
Birthy	Year of birth
Ent1d	Day of first entry into NSDAP
Ent1m	Month of first entry into NSDAP
Ent1y	Year of first entry into NSDAP
Entage	Member's age on first entry

2. Occupational Coding Variables

Occlab	Occupation label
Branch	Branch, referring to German occupational census of 1925
Skills	Skills, degree of training
Stell	"Stellung im Beruf" according to 1925 census
Stesp	Degree of specification of "Stellung im Beruf"
Kat	Social ranking according to Michael Kater (1983)
Müh	Social ranking according to Detlef Mühlberger (1991)
Civs	Status as civil servant
Agech	A check on member's age to specify occupational status

Spec   Degree of specification
Occint   Degree of interpretation

3. Location Coding Variables

Res1lab   Label of first residence
Res1no   Number of first residence*
Og1lab   Label of first NSDAP Ortsgruppe
Og1no   Number of first NSDAP Ortsgruppe
Gau1lab   Gau of first residence
Resint   Margin of interpretation referring to Res1no
Res2lab   Label of second residence
Og2lab   Label of second NSDAP Ortsgruppe
Res2no   Number of second residence
Gau2lab   Gau of second residence
Res3lab   Label of third residence
Og3lab   Label of third NSDAP Ortsgruppe
Res3no   Number of third residence
Gau3lab   Gau of third residence
Birthlab   Birthplace
Birthno   Number of birthplace
Birthint   Margin of interpretation referring to Birthno

4. Fluctuation Variables

Wdrawd   Day of withdrawal from NSDAP
Wdrawm   Month of withdrawal from NSDAP
Wdrawy   Year of withdrawal from NSDAP
Ent2d   Day of reentry into NSDAP
Ent2m   Month of reentry into NSDAP
Ent2y   Year of reentry into NSDAP
Rem2d   Day of relocation to second residence
Rem2m   Month of relocation to second residence
Rem2y   Year of relocation to second residence
Rem3d   Day of relocation to third residence
Rem3m   Month of relocation to third residence
Rem3y   Year of relocation to third residence

Note: Numbers given to member's residences and Ortsgruppe are location codes corresponding to location codes in the the Weimar Republic County Data Collection and the Weimar Community Data Set.

A Chronology of Significant Weimar Events

August 11, 1919	Announcement of Weimar Constitution
March 13–17, 1920	Kapp putsch in Berlin
March 27, 1920	Müller cabinet (SPD, Center, DDP)
March/April, 1920	Communist uprising in the Ruhr and central Germany
June 6, 1920	Reichstag elections (parties of Weimar coalition lose their majority)
June 25, 1920	Fehrenbach cabinet (Center, DDP, DVP)
March 20, 1921	Plebiscite in Upper Silesia
May 10, 1921	Wirth cabinet (SPD, Center, DDP)
August 26, 1921	Assassination of Center Party politician Erzberger by right-wing radicals
April 16, 1922	Treaty of Rapallo between U.S.S.R. and Germany
June 24, 1922	Assassination of Reich Foreign Minister Rathenau by right-wing radicals
November 12, 1922	Cuno cabinet (Center, DDP, DVP)
January 1, 1923	Occupation of the Ruhr by French and Belgian troops
January 13, 1923	Announcement of passive resistance against the Ruhr occupation
August 13, 1923	Stresemann cabinet (SPD, Center, DDP, DVP)
September 26, 1923	Abandonment of the Ruhr struggle by Stresemann government, declaration of martial law in Bavaria, answered by declaration by the government of a state of emergency in the Reich
October 22–23, 1923	Attempted communist uprising in Hamburg
November 8–9, 1923	Hitler putsch in Munich
November 15, 1923	New currency (end of inflation)
November 23, 1923	Collapse of Stresemann government

November 30, 1923	Marx cabinet (Center, BVP, DDP, DVP); Dawes Commission on reparations established
July/August 1924	Acceptance of the Dawes Plan by the London conference on reparations and by the Reichstag
December 7, 1924	Reichstag elections (radical parties lose ground)
January 15, 1925	Luther cabinet (Center, BVP, DDP, DVP, DNVP)
February 27, 1925	Nazi Party refounded
February 28, 1925	Death of Reichspresident Ebert
April 26, 1925	Field Marshal von Hindenburg elected Reichspresident
July 14, 1925	Evacuation of the Ruhr
December 1, 1925	Signing of Locarno Treaty
April 24, 1926	Signing of Berlin treaty between Germany and the Soviet Union
May 12, 1926	Luther cabinet resigns over "flag dispute"
May 16, 1926	Marx cabinet (Center, BVP, DDP, DVP) and then Center, BVP, DVP, DNVP
June 20, 1926	Referendum on expropriation of princely families
September 10, 1926	Entry of Germany into League of Nations
July 16, 1927	Unemployment Insurance Law
May 20, 1928	Reichstag elections (gains by SPD and KPD and losses by DNVP, DVP, DDP)
June 28, 1928	Müller cabinet (SPD, Center, BVP, DDP, DVP)
October 20, 1928	Hugenberg becomes head of DNVP
December 8, 1928	Prelate Kaas becomes head of Center Party
June 7, 1929	Young Plan finally settles reparations problem
October 3, 1929	Death of Foreign Minister Stresemann
October 25, 1929	"Black Friday" in New York City; beginning of world economic crisis
December 22, 1929	Referendum to reject Young Plan fails
March 12, 1930	Young Plan ratified by Reichstag
March 27, 1930	Collapse of Müller government over question of financing unemployment benefits
March 30, 1930	Brüning cabinet (presidential regime)
June 30, 1930	French troops leave the Rhineland ahead of schedule

July 16, 1930	Reichstag dissolved; first emergency degree by Reichspresident in the interest of "economic and financial security"
September 14, 1930	Reichstag elections (gains by Nazi Party)
May 11, 1931	Austrian Kreditanstalt collapses
June 20, 1931	Hoover moratorium on reparations
July 13, 1931	Bank crisis in Germany
October 11, 1931	Formation of Harzburg Front from ranks of the Nazi Party, DNVP, and Stahlhelm
April 10, 1932	Reelection of Reichspresident von Hindenburg
May 30, 1932	Resignation of Brüning Government
June 1, 1932	Papen cabinet (presidential regime)
June 16–July 9, 1932	Lausanne conference (reparations end)
July 20, 1932	Prussian government deposed by Papen
July 31, 1932	Reichstag elections (Nazi Party becomes largest party)
November 6, 1932	Reichstag elections (Nazi Party loses ground for first time)
November 17, 1932	Resignation of von Papen cabinet
December 3, 1932	Von Schleicher cabinet (presidential regime)
January 28, 1933	Resignation of Chancellor von Schleicher
January 30, 1933	Hitler cabinet

Sources: Questions on German History, 9th ed. (Bonn: German Bundestag, 1984), 460–61; D. J. K. Peukert, *The Weimar Republic: The Crisis of Classical Modernity,* trans. R. Deveson (New York: Hill and Wang, 1987), 284–89.

Notes

Chapter 1: Who Became Nazis and Why?

1. In Germany as compared to the United States, the ratio of party members to party voters is usually quite low, probably because joining a political party has different implications in the two countries. To vote in many state primaries in the United States, a person has to register as a member of a political party. In Germany, party membership or affiliation is not a prerequisite for voting. Also, unlike in the United States, party membership in Germany entails the payment of mandatory dues and a commitment of time to party activities.

For a more extensive review of the literature on the social origins of Nazism see P. Manstein's *Die Mitglieder und Wähler der NSDAP, 1919-1933: Untersuchungen zu ihrer schichtmässigen Zusammensetzung* (Frankfurt, 1988). While not treated here, other explanations of the rise of Nazism have been advanced in the literature. One of the better known theories of the rise of Nazism is that Germany took a particular path, or *Sonderweg*, toward modernization (B. Moore, Jr., *Social Origins of Dictatorship and Democracy* [Boston: Beacon Press, 1966]). The Sonderweg explanation emphasizes Germany's failed bourgeois revolution and the continuity of antidemocratic features in German politics throughout the period of the Second Reich (1871-1918) and Weimar (1919-1933). In other words, Hitler was a logical outcome of German history. J. Kocka ("German History before Hitler: The Debate about the German Sonderweg," *Journal of Contemporary History* 23 [1988]: 13) suggests that the Sonderweg thesis may have more to do with the collapse of Weimar than with the Nazis' coming to power.

2. J. B. Rule, *Theories of Civil Violence* (Berkeley: University of California Press, 1988), 93.

3. H. Arendt, *The Origins of Totalitarianism,* 2nd ed. (Cleveland: World, 1961); R. Bendix, "Social Stratification and Political Power," in *Class, Status and Power,* ed. R. Bendix and S. M. Lipset (Glencoe, Ill.: Free Press, 1953), 596-608; J. Ortega y Gasset, *The Revolt of the Masses* (London: Allen & Unwin, 1932); E. Lederer, *The State of the Masses* (New York: W. W. Norton & Co., 1940); W. Kornhauser, *The Politics of Mass Society* (Glencoe, Ill.: Free Press, 1959). Quite similar to the mass-society theorists' descriptions of the kinds of people who became Nazis are characterizations of Nazis by Lerner et al., *The Nazi Elite* (Stanford: Stanford University Press, 1951) as "marginal men" or "people of the social fringe"; J. Banaszkiewicz, "German Fascism and People of the Social Fringe," *Polish Western Affairs* 8 (August 1967): 251-88, as "abnormal people"; K. Heiden, *A History of National Socialism*

(New York: Knopf, 1935) as "failures at life"; and W. Shirer, *The Rise and Fall of the Third Reich* (New York: Simon & Schuster, 1960), as "psychopaths and social miscreants."

4. Arendt, *Origins*, 311.

5. E. Durkheim, *Suicide* (Paris: Felix Alcan, 1897).

6. Bendix, "Social Stratification and Political Power"; Kornhauser, *Politics*. Also, though a major advocate of the lower-middle-class theory of fascism, S. M. Lipset (*Political Man* [Baltimore: Johns Hopkins University Press, 1981], 178) observes a particular correspondence between adherents of political extremism and the disgruntled, psychologically homeless, socially isolated, unsophisticated, and uneducated masses.

7. For comprehensive reviews and critiques of the mass-society thesis see B. Hagtvet and R. Kühnl, "Contemporary Approaches to Fascism: A Survey of Paradigms," in *Who Were the Fascists*, eds. S. U. Larsen, B. Hagtvet, J. P. Myklebust (Bergen: Universitetsforlaget, 1980), 26-51; R. F. Hamilton, *Who Voted For Hitler?* (Princeton, N.J.: Princeton University Press, 1982).

8. J. W. Falter, "Radicalization of the Middle Classes or Mobilization of the Unpolitical?" *Social Science Information* 20 (1981): 389-430; F. L. Carsten (*The Rise of Fascism*, 2nd ed. [Berkeley: University of California Press, 1980], 121-59) notes that the unemployment figure in Germany climbed from 2,258,000 in March 1930 to 5,670,000 in December 1931 and to 6,128,000 in February 1932, while the Nazi vote jumped from more than 18 percent of the total vote in September 1930 to more than 37 percent in July 1932. Fischer, examining the Nazi paramilitary organization, the S.A. (*Sturmabteilung*), found an overrepresentation of workers, especially unemployed salaried employees and blue-collar laborers, between 1930 and 1933 (C. Fischer, "The Occupational Background of the SA's Rank and File Membership during the Depression Years, 1929 to mid-1934," in *The Shaping of the Nazi State*, ed. P. D. Stachura [New York: Barnes & Noble Books, 1978], 131-59). Also, though they do not explicitly subscribe to the mass-society thesis, B. S. Frey and H. Weck, "Hat Arbeitslosigkeit den Aufstieg des Nationalsozialismus bewirkt?" *Jahrbuch für Nationalökonomie und Statistik* 196 (1981): 1-31, and Z. A. B. Zeman, *Nazi Propaganda*, 2nd ed. (London: Oxford University Press, 1973), argue that the Nazi Party served as the principal refuge for many who feared unemployment.

9. G. Ritter, *The German Resistance*, trans. R. T. Clark (London: Allen & Unwin, 1958), 37-39.

10. P. D. Stachura, "Who Were the Nazis? A Socio-Political Analysis of the National Socialist Machtübernahme," *European Studies Review* 11 (1981): 315; R. G. Moeller, *German Peasants & Agrarian Politics, 1914-1924* (Chapel Hill: University of North Carolina Press, 1986).

11. D. Mühlberger, *Hitler's Followers* (London: Routledge, 1991).

12. K. Mannheim, *Ideology and Utopia: An Introduction to the Sociology of Knowledge*, trans. L. Wirth and E. Shils (New York: Harcourt Brace Jovanovich, 1946), 3-7.

13. M. Broszat, *German National Socialism*, trans. K. Rosenbaum and I. P. Böhm (Santa Barbara: Clio Press, 1966), 62.

14. Stachura, "Who Were the Nazis?" 285.

15. Ibid., 299, 315.

16. R. Bessel, "The Rise of the NSDAP and the Myth of Nazi Propaganda," *Wiener Library Bulletin* (new series, nos. 51-52) 33 (1980): 28-29. See also W. Schieder ("Die NSDAP vor 1933: Profil einer faschistischen Partei." *Geschichte und Gesellschaft* 19 [1993]: 142-43) on the absence of a solid and coherent Nazi Party program.

17. J. P. Madden, "The Social Composition of the Nazi Party, 1919-1930," Ph.D. diss., University of Oklahoma, 1976, 270.

18. A. Bullock, *Hitler and Stalin* (New York: Alfred A. Knopf, 1992), 224.

19. I am led to this conclusion partly by P. D. Stachura's comment (in "The Political Strategy of the Nazi Party, 1919-1933," *German Studies Review* 3 [1980]: 262) that the irrational emotionalism of Weimar politics contributed to the growth of Nazism.

20. G. D. H. Cole, *A History of Socialist Thought: Socialism and Fascism (1931-1939)*, vol. 5 (London: Macmillan, 1960), 3, 5.

21. H. Kohn, *The Twentieth Century: The Challenge to the West and Its Response*, 2nd ed. (New York: Macmillan, 1959), 50.

22. L. S. Dawidowicz, *The War Against the Jews, 1933-1945* (New York: Holt, Rinehart & Winston, 1975), 47.

23. T. Geiger, "Panik im Mittelstand," *Die Arbeit* (1930): 654.

24. Lipset, *Political Man*, 172-73. For an excellent analysis of Lipset's lower-middle-class theory, see Falter, "Radicalization of the Middle Classes or Mobilization of the Unpolitical?"

25. Hagtvet and Kühnl, "Contemporary Approaches to Fascism," 30.

26. H. A. Winkler, "German Society, Hitler and the Illusion of Restoration 1930-33," *Journal of Contemporary History* 11 (1976): 11. R. Lepsius (*Extremer Nationalismus: Strukturbedingungen vor der nationalsozialistischen Machtergreifung* [Stuttgart: Kohlhammer, 1966], 9-18) points to the Nazis' embrace of German middle-class morality.

27. D. Petzina, "Germany and the Great Depression," *Journal of Contemporary History* 4 (1969): 71-72.

28. C. Loomis and L. P. Beegle, "The Spread of Nazism in Rural Areas," *American Sociological Review* 11 (1946): 725.

29. J. K. Pollock, "An Areal Study of the German Electorate, 1930-1933," *American Political Science Review* 38 (1944): 89-95; R. Heberle, *From Democracy to Nazism* (Baton Rouge: Louisiana State University Press, 1945); Loomis and Beegle, "The Spread of Nazism in Rural Areas"; Carsten, *The Rise of Fascism;* W. T. Angress, "The Political Role of the Peasantry in the Weimar Republic," *Review of Politics* 21 (1959): 530-49; G. Stoltenberg, *Politische Strömungen im schleswig-holsteinischen Landvolk, 1918-1933* (Düsseldorf: Droste Verlag, 1962); Z. Zofka, *Die Ausbreitung des Nationalsozialismus auf dem Lande* (München: Stadtarchiv München, 1979); Moeller, *German Peasants;* Hamilton, *Who Voted,* 229.

30. Pollock, "An Areal Study."

31. A. Gerschenkron, *Bread and Democracy in Germany* (Berkeley: University of California Press, 1943), 3.

32. W. D. Burnham, "Political Immunisation and Political Confessionalism: The United States and Weimar Germany," *Journal of Interdisciplinary History* 3 (1972): 30.

33. Richter's work may be seen as an attempt to elucidate the Burnham thesis. Richter suggests that within the Protestant population, unlike within the Catholic and Marxist camps, the Nazis found strategic opportunities in the fragmentation into electorally weak and short-lived splinter parties, the lack of profound programmatic differences between the Nazi Party and other Protestant bourgeois parties, and the absence of defensive organizations that could counter Nazi appeals (M. W. Richter, "Resource Mobilisation and Legal Revolution: National Socialist Tactics in Franconia," in *The Formation of the Nazi Constituency, 1919-1933,* ed. T. Childers [Totowa, N.J.: Barnes & Noble Books, 1986], 112). Much evidence suggests that German Protestants were indeed more predisposed toward the Nazis

than German Catholics (W. S. Allen, "Farewell to Class Analysis in the Rise of Nazism: Comment," *Central European History* 17 [1984]: 57; Hamilton, *Who Voted;* J. W. Falter, *Hitlers Wähler* [Munich: C. H. Beck, 1991]; N. Passchier, "The Electoral Geography of the Nazi Landslide," in *Who Were the Fascists,* eds. S. U. Larsen, B. Hagtvet, and J. P. Myklebust [Bergen: Universitetsforlaget, 1980], 283–300). For instance, Hamilton reports that in the July 1932 Reichstag elections in which the Nazis gained approximately 38 percent of the national vote, the party won between 71 and 83 percent of the popular vote in such predominantly Protestant Franconian communities as Rothenburg ob-der-Tauber, Uffenheim, Neustadt, Ansbach, Dinkelsbühl, and Gunzenhausen and more than 87 percent of the vote in the equally Protestant Schleswig-Holstein county of Norderdithmarschen (*Who Voted,* 39).

34. M. Kater, *The Nazi Party* (Cambridge: Harvard University Press, 1983); T. Childers, *The Nazi Voter: The Social Foundations of Fascism in Germany, 1919-1933* (Chapel Hill: University of North Carolina Press, 1983); Hamilton, *Who Voted;* J. W. Falter, *Hitlers Wähler;* P. H. Merkl, *Political Violence Under the Swastika: 581 Pre-1933 Nazis* (Princeton, N.J.: Princeton University Press, 1975); Madden, "Social Composition"; Mühlberger, *Hitler's Followers.* Falter and Zintl have tried to attach a causal mechanism to the label of Nazism as a catchall party. Explaining the heterogeneity of Nazi support, Falter and Zintl point to different "subjective situations operating among various social groups: radicalization explains middle-class support" ("The Economic Crisis of the 1930s and the Nazi Vote," *Journal of Interdisciplinary History* 19 [1988]: 61–62).

35. Childers, *Nazi Voter,* 178–88.

36. Stachura, "Political Strategy," 282–83.

37. Mühlberger, *Hitler's Followers;* J. P. Madden, "The Social Class Origins of Nazi Party Members as Determined by Occupations, 1919-1933," *Social Science Quarterly* 68 (1987): 263–80.

38. Kater, *Nazi Party.*

39. S. G. Payne, "The Concept of Fascism," in *Who Were the Fascists,* ed. S. U. Larsen, B. Hagtvet, J. P. Myklebust (Bergen: Universitetsforlaget, 1980), 16; Rule, *Civil Violence,* 109; A. Oberschall, *Social Conflict and Social Movements* (Englewood Cliffs: Prentice Hall, 1973), 111; Hamilton, *Who Voted,* 433.

40. According to Falter, the Nazis won landslide victories across the board, irrespective of regional unemployment patterns. Falter adds that the relation between mass unemployment and Nazi electoral success was indirect. He cites a so-called transfer effect: voters for the Nazi Party may have been mainly people who, while not directly affected by unemployment, felt threatened by it and by the radicalization of the unemployed (J. W. Falter, "Unemployment and the Radicalization of the German Electorate, 1928-1933: An Aggregate Data Analysis with Special Emphasis on the Rise of National Socialism," in *Unemployment and the Great Depression in Weimar Germany,* ed. P. D. Stachura [New York: St. Martin's Press, 1986], 206). In another study, J. W. Falter, J.-B. Lohmöller, A. Link, and J. de Rijke found that unemployment correlated significantly with Nazi votes, particularly in areas marked by a sizable Protestant population and a rightist voting tradition; by contrast, Nazi votes and unemployment did not correlate strongly in areas with industry, strong union organization, and a radical-left tradition (J. W. Falter et al., "Hat Arbeitslosigkeit tatsächlich den Aufstieg des Nationalsozialismus bewirkt?" *Jahrbücher für Nationalökonomie und Statistik,* vols. 200-202 [Stuttgart: Fischer Verlag, 1985], 133).

41. Childers suggests that the ever-lengthening lines of jobless workers and the con-

comitant threat of social unrest may have prompted some nervous shopkeepers to support the staunchly anti-Marxist Nazi Party (Childers, *Nazi Voter,* 185).

42. Hamilton, *Who Voted,* 43.

43. Falter and Zintl, "The Economic Crisis," 73; J. W. Falter, "Economic Debts and Political Gains: Electoral Support for the Nazi Party in Agrarian and Commercial Sectors, 1928–1933," unpublished paper presented at the 85th annual meeting of the American Political Science Association, Atlanta, Georgia, 1989; T. A. Tilton, *Nazism, Neo-Nazism and the Peasantry* (Bloomington: Indiana University Press, 1975), 46. In his examination of Nazi Party membership data, Kater reveals that the party's cumulative compound rate of growth was higher in the more stable economic phase (1925–1930) than in the severest phase of the depression (1930–1933); his study thus lends support to Tilton's and Falter's claims that the connection between lower-middle-class economic decline and Nazi Party support is questionable (Kater, *Nazi Party,* 156–57, 365).

44. Zofka, *Ausbreitung;* G. Pridham, *Hitler's Rise to Power: The Nazi Movement in Bavaria, 1923–1933* (New York: Harper & Row, 1973); J. E. Farquharson, *The Plough and the Swastika: The NSDAP and Agriculture in Germany 1928–45* (London: Sage, 1976); J. Noakes, *The Nazi Party in Lower Saxony, 1921–1933* (London: Oxford University Press, 1971); K. Rohe, *Wählen und Wählertraditionen in Deutschland: Kulturelle Grundlagen deutscher Parteien und Parteisysteme im 19. und 20. Jahrhundert* (Frankfurt: Suhrkamp, 1992).

45. Z. Zofka, "Between Bauernbund and National Socialism: The Political Reorientation of the Peasants in the Final Phase of the Weimar Republic," in Childers, *Formation of the Nazi Constituency,* 48.

46. Pridham, *Hitler's Rise,* 139–40. Noakes and Pridham together observed that the Nazis established an electoral foothold in both the heavily Catholic industrial region of Silesia and the predominantly Catholic rural Palatinate (J. Noakes and G. Pridham, ed., *The Rise to Power 1919–1934,* vol. 1. *Nazism 1919–1945* [Exeter, Eng.: University of Exeter Press, 1983], 82).

47. Noakes, *Nazi Party,* 154; Farquharson, *Plough,* 40–41.

48. E. Faris, "Takeoff Point for the Nationalist Socialist Party: The Landtag Election in Baden, 1929," *Central European History* 8 (1975), 140–71.

49. Hamilton, *Who Voted;* Childers, *Nazi Voter;* Falter, *Hitlers Wähler.*

50. W. S. Robinson, "Ecological Correlations and the Behavior of Individuals," *American Sociological Review* 15 (1950): 351–57; W. P. Shively, "Ecological Inference: The Use of Aggregate Data to Study Individuals," *American Political Science Review* 63 (1969): 1183–96; E. T. Jones, "Ecological Inference and Electoral Analysis," *Journal of Interdisciplinary History* 2 (1972): 249–62; A. J. Lichtman, "Correlation Regression and the Ecological Fallacy: A Critique," *Journal of Interdisciplinary History* 4 (1974): 417–34; A. J. Lichtman and L. I. Langbein, "Ecological Regression Versus Homogeneous Units: A Specification Analysis," *Social Science History* 2 (1978): 172–93; M. Susser, *Causal Thinking in the Health Sciences: Concepts and Strategies of Epidemiology* (New York: Oxford University Press, 1973).

51. Hamilton, *Who Voted;* Falter, *Hitlers Wähler.*

52. Fischer, "The Occupational Background"; H. F. Ziegler, *Nazi Germany's New Aristocracy* (Princeton: Princeton University Press, 1989), 102–6. Interestingly, in contrast to the considerable scholarship that characterizes the Nazi movement as lower middle class or as a catchall party of protest, both Fischer's and Ziegler's studies emphasize the working-class nature of the Nazi movement.

53. Childers, *Nazi Voter,* 194; Mühlberger, *Hitler's Followers.* Of the roughly 1.4 million individuals who joined the Nazi Party by January 30, 1933, approximately 40 percent also left the party before that date. Consequently, party membership was about 850,000 at the time of Hitler's accession to power.

54. *Partei-Statistik,* 3 vols. (Munich: Reichsorganisationsleiter der NSDAP: 1935). There are some rather good local and regional examinations of NSDAP Party membership (see W. Böhnke, *Die NSDAP im Ruhrgebiet 1920–1933* [Bonn-Bad Godesberg: Verlag Neue Gesellschaft, 1974]; L. D. Stokes, "The Social Composition of the Nazi Party in Eutin, 1925–32," *International Review of Social History* 23 [1978]: 1–32; and, especially, Mühlberger, *Hitler's Followers*).

55. T. Abel, *Why Hitler Came Into Power* (Cambridge: Harvard University Press, 1986).

56. Merkl, *Political Violence.*

57. *Partei-Statistik.* The number of German *Gaue* varied between 1928 and 1933.

58. Mühlberger, *Hitler's Followers;* Ziegler, *Nazi Germany's New Aristocracy.*

59. For a fuller discussion of the strengths and weaknesses of the *NSDAP Partei-Statistik* and other sources on Nazi Party membership, see Mühlberger, *Hitler's Followers.*

60. The master file contains approximately 10.7 million original membership cards. We estimate, however, that these cards represent only 7.6 to 7.8 million members. The additional 3 million cards in the master file were cards issued to lapsed members on their readmittance to the party or follow-up cards for members who had experienced life course changes (such as a change of residence). Also, approximately 500,000 of the cards are for Austrian party members.

61. This is the conclusion arrived at by H. D. Andrews, "The Social Composition of the NSDAP: Problems and Possible Solutions," *German Studies Review* 9 (1986): 301. The Berlin Document Center staff corroborates his conclusion, provided that the two different files are taken together. Kater's estimate that the master file is 80 percent complete is based on his examination of the contents of just the Ortskartei.

62. The Ortskartei was rearranged alphabetically by surname for the purposes of judicial investigation after World War II. In October 1993 the U.S. State Department agreed to relinquish jurisdiction over the BDC files to the Germans.

63. One potential problem with the Master File is that the information on each card was furnished by the member. Thus, there is always a concern regarding the reliability of the information.

64. I will not deal with Gerhard Botz's study because Botz was strictly interested in a study of Austrian Nazis.

65. Madden, "Social Composition of the Nazi Party"; Madden, "The Social Class Origins," 263–80; Kater, *Nazi Party.*

66. Also, Kater's Nazi Party sample comes exclusively from the larger Ortskartei file. Kater's decision to rely on the Ortskartei file poses a particular problem. Though each of the two files is partially incomplete, missing cards from the Ortskartei may pose a more serious problem than missing cards from the Reichskartei. Since the Nazis had originally arranged the contents of the Ortskartei alphabetically by *Gau,* missing cards are more likely to disproportionately represent particular German regions. In particular, it appears that Bavaria is underrepresented in the Ortskartei (this is understandable given that the cards were held in Munich and the local Nazis probably decided to destroy cards from their own region first).

67. Madden's sample of pre-1930 Nazi Party membership was drawn solely from the

less extensive Reichskartei. Madden selected cards for members whose last names began with the letters *C, D, E, I, P, R, U, V,* and *Z.*

68. For instance, Madden translated the occupation *Stepperin* as step dancer while the common definition of *Stepperin* is a sewing-machine operator or seamstress.

69. *Brustein-Falter Sampling Technique:* From these files we took two different samples. In our first sample we drew a two-stage proportional random sample for the years 1925 to 1933, with more than 27,000 cases, using both membership files. Our primary goal was to assess the growth of the party during the period from 1925 to 1933. Our secondary goal was to gather the necessary information to weight our larger, disproportionate sample properly to be able to generalize to the whole period from 1925 to 1933. The second sample contains 42,004 cases, again from both files. Our second sample is a random sample stratified by year in order to get enough cases for each year of entry, including the years 1925 to 1928, when the party was minuscule. Regarding our second sample, we began with a systematic sampling of boxes (every twenty-fifth box of the geographical and every thirteenth box of the alphabetical file) after a randomly selected starting number. All told, there are 4,853 file drawers in the Ortskartei and 2,610 file drawers in the Reichskartei. We completed four runs through the Ortskartei and three runs through the Reichskartei. Subsequently, we employed cluster sampling for the years 1925 to 1929 and a systematic sample (every fifth card, with changing starting points within each box) for the years 1930 to 1932. For a more detailed description of our method of sampling see Torsten Schneider-Haase, "Beschreibung der Stichprobenziehung zu den Mitgliedern der NSDAP vom 27. März - 7. September 1989 im Berlin Document Center," *Historical Social Research* 16 (1991): 113-51.

70. In the set of raw data there were more than six thousand different occupational labels. After correcting for misspellings and variations in spelling, we ended up with nearly two thousand occupational labels, ranging from simple summary statements (*blue-collar worker* or *educator*) to highly specific designations (*brewery apprentice* or *middle-school headmaster*). The raw occupational data were also classified according to industrial branch, degree of vocational training, civil service status, occupational category, and social rank. We employed three different schemes for occupational category and social rank: one based on the official German census of 1925—a horizontal ranking scheme—and two others based on Michael Kater's and Detlef Mühlberger's earlier classification schemes—hierarchical or vertical ranking schemes (see Appendix A). In instances where we encountered ambiguous information regarding occupational category and social rank, we tried to resolve the ambiguity by using circumstantial evidence such as age (very young members would normally not have been independent proprietors or civil servants). Consequently, our data on occupational rank include variables on the degree of specification and interpretation (see Appendix B). Our coders followed absolute consistency in applying our rules. Two different teams of German coders were employed. There were no mistranslations, because native German speakers did the coding, transforming the raw data into German; and our coders drew on the literature of occupations from the Weimar period and relied on the definitions of occupations in the German census.

71. The Weimar Republic County Data Collection consists of demographic, economic, social, and political information on 865 German counties for the period from 1924 to 1933, whereas the Weimar Community Data Set includes demographic, economic, social, and political information on roughly five thousand German communities. The raw data for these two collections were taken from volumes of *Statistik des Deutschen Reiches* (Berlin, 1920-

1934) and printed sources such as unemployment statistics and fiscal reports. The task of identifying localities and combining them with Falter's community and county data sets required tremendous effort as well. The virtue of this enterprise is that we are able, for example, to differentiate between blue-collar workers living in a working-class environment and blue-collar workers living in middle-class communities.

72. This is a huge data set which occupies about twenty-five megabytes as a Statistical Package for the Social Sciences systems file even in condensed form with only a very few contextual variables added; in its full-sized version it may easily take up more than eighty megabytes. Research teams from the University of Berlin and the University of Minnesota spent more than three years preparing the data for analysis.

73. All population figures are for Germans eighteen years or older. In selecting the comparable population, we wanted to maintain consistency with the rules that governed Nazi Party membership: to be considered for membership in the Nazi Party between 1925 and 1932, the only requirements were that you be eighteen years or older and not Jewish (Jews made up roughly 0.5 percent of the German population). Because members came from the population of Germans who were eighteen years or older, that was the population we used as our base. Although it is true that the party membership between 1925 and 1932 was 94 percent male, the Nazi Party neither placed obstacles in the way of women's joining the party nor refrained from seeking female membership. In having a primarily male membership base, the Nazi Party was like virtually all political parties of the period. A few colleagues have recommended that we use a different base population for our analysis, such as the population of gainfully employed males. If we were to use the population of males who were gainfully employed rather than the population of Germans eighteen years or older as our base population, we would be forced to leave out those who were unemployed, dependent, and retired. The unemployed, the retired, and the dependent (including housewives) were able to join the Nazi Party and did so in sizable numbers.

74. Middle class consists of both old and new and lower and upper middle class. The classifications intersect each other. The categories lower middle class and middle middle class consist of small and mid-size independent farmers, artisans, shopkeepers, free professions, salaried employees and civil servants. The lower class consists of all skilled, semiskilled and unskilled blue-collar workers in addition to domestic servants. The upper class comprises the elites, including very high civil servants, managers of big industries and owners of large estates. The upper class accounted for roughly 2 percent of Weimar Germany's population in 1925. Thus, for practical purposes, I combine the upper class with the upper middle class of academic free professions, high-ranking civil servants and managers.

75. Unfortunately, our Nazi Party membership data provide no clues about individuals' religious confession. We are therefore obliged to rely on contextual data to test the relation between Nazi Party membership and religious confession. But I am quite confident of my results, because when we test the correlation between Nazi Party joiners and people of a particular religious confession on communities 99 percent or more Catholic and on communities 99 percent or more Protestant (nearly homogeneous religious communities), we find virtually the same correlation between party membership and religious confession as we did in communities with 75 percent or more Catholics and in communities with 75 percent or more Protestants. Interestingly, my finding regarding the relation between Nazi Party joiners and religious confession contrasts with the relation between aggregate-level voting for the Nazi Party and religious confession. Studies of Weimar voting have consistently pointed to the Nazi Party's inability to attract support from Catholic communities (Falter, *Hitlers Wähler*),

whereas our party membership data show that though the Nazi Party was underrepresented in Catholic communities, the party recruited a higher percentage of joiners than the voting studies would lead us to believe. Part of the explanation for the weaker relation between party membership and religious confession may be the result of the stepwise growth of the Nazi Party from its origins in the Catholic south and west into the Protestant north and east.

76. My theory of political behavior draws heavily on a rich social scientific tradition. Rational-choice theory (sometimes described as the theory of strategic decision making at the individual level) offers means to resolve certain theoretical and methodological problems inherent in explanations of political choices (M. Levi, *Of Rule and Revenue* [Berkeley: University of California Press, 1988], 9). Karl-Dieter Opp (*The Rationality of Political Protest* [Boulder: Westview Press, 1989], 11) proposes an important qualification to the "rational" in rational-choice theory. Opp suggests that individuals are rational insofar as they choose the behavioral alternatives that are relatively advantageous. Opp adds that *rational* implies calculation. In this sense, individuals are often not rational. A behavior is called rational, however, if a person adopts it after considering the relative costs and benefits of the range of available choices. Also, rational-choice models take many different forms. Social scientists who employ them generally agree about the importance of methodological individualism, preferences, opportunity costs, and institutional constraints, diverge over the kinds of incentives that motivate individuals to act. See D. Friedman and M. Hechter, "The Contribution of Rational Choice Theory to Macrosociological Research," *Sociological Theory* 6 (1988): 201–18; Opp, *Rationality*. Finally, since we cannot know the subjective interests of people who joined the Nazi Party between 1925 and 1932, we are obliged here to infer those interests from the joiners' objective—that is, social, economic, and political—situation.

77. M. Olson's focus on the logic of collective action is indeed appropriate for the study of Nazi Party membership, because participation in a party—especially an extremist party like the NSDAP—involves high personal risks (including physical injury, loss of employment, public ostracism, and arrest). M. Olson, *The Logic of Collective Action* (Cambridge: Harvard University Press, 1965); Opp, *Rationality*, 45.

78. For an interesting critique of Olson's theory that collective action is based on private interest, see S. E. Finkel, N. Mueller, and K.-D. Opp, "Personal Influence, Collective Rationality, and Mass Political Action," *American Political Science Review* 83 (1989): 885–903; Opp, *Rationality*. These rational-choice theorists argue in part that a desire to advance the public good can in itself motivate rational actors to overcome their urge to hitch a free ride.

79. At first glance, the theory of rational-choice or interest-based political behavior appears to be of questionable value. In his classic study of politics, A. Downs (*An Economic Theory of Democracy* [New York: Harper & Row, 1957]) suggests that a rational individual should not be expected to vote, for the costs of voting outweigh the benefit of voting. Downs asserts that it is highly unlikely that rational individuals would invest the time and energy to familiarize themselves with the specific contents of the programs of competing political parties when they know that by the time of the election each party, hoping to increase its chances of winning the most votes, will adopt a middle-of-the road position on the major issues. In a recent work that is highly critical of models of interest-based political behavior, G. Brennan and L. Lomasky (*Democracy and Decision: The Pure Theory of Electoral Preference* [Cambridge: Cambridge University Press, 1993]) posit that individuals' decisions and preferences concerning both voting and candidates reflect "expressive" rather than "utilitarian" behavior. Following Downs, Brennan and Lomasky argue that because the chance that one vote will be decisive in an election is minuscule, the rational individual will not vote

simply for her own utilitarian gain (*Democracy and Decision,* 37, 77, 185–86). I have argued earlier (W. Brustein, *The Social Origins of Political Regionalism: France, 1849–1981* [Berkeley: University of California Press, 1988], chapter 2) that whereas the model may tell us little about why individuals vote or join political parties, it can help explain why individuals who do vote or join a party select one party over another. Brennan and Lomasky (*Democracy and Decision,* 36), however, question the logic of theoretically separating the decision to vote from the decision to vote for someone. They point out that the motives for which individuals presumably go to the polls should carry over to the particular choices they make at the polls. Downs' and Brennan and Lomasky's objections appear more appropriate for a majoritarian or a two-party electoral system (for example, the U.S. majoritarian system) than for the European proportional representation and multiparty systems. In a system of proportional representation such as the Weimar Republic's, each vote for a party or a candidate matters, because a party need not win a majority of the votes to obtain representation. The proportion of votes a party obtains will determine its share of seats in government (except where parties need to surpass a threshold to be represented). Each additional vote for the party will increase the party's share. Thus, contrary to the assertions of Downs and of Brennan and Lomasky, in an electoral system with proportional representation, the rational individual has an incentive to vote for a preferred candidate, because her vote does matter. Moreover, in the proportional representation system, rational individuals realize that they have to familiarize themselves with the various parties' positions; parties are less likely to adopt indistinguishable positions on the key issues; instead, they try to attract the support of specific political constituencies.

80. Friedman and Hechter, "Contribution," 214–15.

81. Brustein, *The Social Origins of Political Regionalism,* chapter 2.

82. Ibid.

83. W. Brustein and M. Levi, "The Geography of Rebellion: Rulers, Rebels, and Regions, 1500–1700," *Theory and Society* 16 (1987): 467–95; J. Tong, "Rational Outlaws: Rebels and Bandits in the Ming Dynasty, 1368–1644," in *Rationality and Revolution,* ed. M. Taylor (Cambridge: Cambridge University Press, 1988), 98–128.

84. This obviously depends on the kind of electoral system. Voters are more likely to choose a party that they perceive to have a high probability of success in an electoral system with proportional representation than in a winner-take-all system. Also, I do not completely agree with Tong ("Rational Outlaws"), who appears to see a strictly positive relationship between individuals' support for a movement and the probability of the movement's success. Indeed, if the probability of success is low, individuals will not want to incur the costs of participation. If the probability of success is too high, however, individuals will decide to catch a free ride, believing that with the movement's success, everyone will gain access to the benefits. Any discussion of the relation between participation in a political movement and the probability of its success must address the degree to which the movement can enforce compliance by selectively withholding access to goods.

85. S. Popkin, *The Rational Peasant* (Berkeley: University of California Press, 1979), 262.

86. Olson, *Logic;* G. Tullock, *The Logic of the Law* (New York: Basic Books, 1971); M. Silver, "Political Revolution and Repression: An Economic Approach," *Public Choice* 17 (1974): 63–71; M. Hechter, *Principles of Group Solidarity* (Berkeley: University of California Press, 1987).

87. J. C. Jenkins and C. Perrow, "Insurgence of the Powerless: Farm Worker Movements (1946–1972)," *American Sociological Review* 42 (1977): 249–68; J. D. McCarthy and M. Zald,

"Resource Mobilization and Social Movements: A Partial Theory," *American Journal of Sociology* 82 (1977): 1212–41. Also, I choose to rely principally on the ways external rather than internal selective incentives shape people's desire to participate. Internal incentives, according to Opp (*Rationality*), include norms of participation, norms on violence, intrinsic value, entertainment, and cathartic value. Moreover, anticipated private goods such as employment or property, to which individuals believe they will have access when the party gains power, can serve as a realistic incentive to join. The incentive of anticipated goods is especially high for leaders and early joiners (B. Salert, *Revolutions and Revolutionaries: Four Theories* [New York: Elsevier, 1976], 38).

88. Olson, *Logic of Collective Action;* Opp, *Rationality,* 45; W. A. Gamson, *The Strategy of Social Protest* (Homewood, Ill.: Dorsey Press, 1975); C. Tilly, *From Mobilization to Revolution* (Reading, Mass.: Addison-Wesley, 1978).

89. Hechter, *Principles,* 281.

90. B. Markovsky and E. Lawler, "Sources and Consequences of Group Solidarity," unpublished paper presented at the 83rd Annual Meeting of the American Sociological Association, Atlanta, 1988.

91. Opp, *Rationality,* 56.

92. M. Olson, *The Rise and Decline of Nations* (New Haven: Yale University Press, 1982); J. S. Coleman, *Foundations of Social Theory* (Cambridge: Harvard University Press, 1990), 275–77.

93. M. Taylor, *Community, Anarchy and Liberty* (Cambridge: Cambridge University Press, 1982); R. Hardin, *Collective Action* (Baltimore: Johns Hopkins University Press, 1982); A. Sen, "Choice, Orderings and Morality," in *Choice, Welfare and Measurement,* ed. A. Sen (Oxford: Blackwell, 1982), 74–83; S. Lindenberg, "Social Production Functions, Deficits, and Social Revolutions: Pre-Revolutionary France and Russia," *Rationality and Society* 1 (1989): 51–77.

94. Taylor, *Community.*

95. D. McAdam, "Recruitment to High-Risk Activism: The Case of Freedom Summer," *American Journal of Sociology* 92 (1986): 87; M. Taylor, "Rationality and Revolutionary Collective Action," in *Rationality and Revolution,* ed. M. Taylor (Cambridge: Cambridge University Press, 1988), 63–97. For a superb discussion of the power of vertical ties in southern Italy see P. Bevilacqua, "Uomini, terre, economie," in *La Calabria,* ed. P. Bevilacqua and A. Placanica (Turin: Giulio Einaudi, 1985), 305–9, and F. Piselli and G. Arrighi, "Parentela, clientela e comunità," in *La Calabria,* ed. P. Bevilacqua and A. Placanica (Turin: Giulio Einaudi, 1985), 389–91. Another excellent example of a social arrangement based on vertical ties is Popkin's *Rational Peasant,* 259–61. Popkin presents a study of the role played by political entrepreneurs in Vietnam. Popkin found that political entrepreneurs (elites) could encourage active local political participation by introducing measures to overcome conditional cooperation—that is, people's natural inclination to make their participation contingent on the participation of others.

96. G. Tullock, *The Social Dilemma: The Economics of War and Revolution* (Blacksburg: Center for the Study of Public Choice, 1974), 39.

97. J. De Nardo, *Power in Numbers: The Political Strategy of Protest and Rebellion* (Princeton: Princeton University Press, 1985), 56.

98. Salert, *Revolutions and Revolutionaries;* Oberschall, *Social Conflict;* Tilly, *Mobilization;* Tong, "Rational Outlaws"; McAdam, "Recruitment"; White, "Rational Rioters."

Chapter 2: Weimar Political Parties

1. The German Democratic Party (DDP) would reorganize as the German State Party (DStP) in mid-1930. The Center Party's Bavarian wing was the Bavarian People's Party (BVP). The BVP tended to be more politically conservative than the Center Party and at certain intervals during the Weimar era pursued an independent political program.

2. D. Orlow, *Weimar Prussia, 1918–1925* (Pittsburgh, Pa.: University of Pittsburgh Press, 1986), 15–17; W. Mommsen, *Deutsche Parteiprogramme* (Munich: Isar, 1952).

3. Orlow, *Weimar Prussia*, 15–17.

4. Ibid., 18–19.

5. Ibid., 20–21.

6. Hamilton, *Who Voted*, 233.

7. A. Pfenning, *Das deutschnationale Agrarprogramm und seine Realisierung* (Itzehoe, Germany: Emil Friese, 1933), 57.

8. A. Milatz, *Wähler und Wahlen in der Weimarer Republik* (Bonn: Schriftenreihe der Bundeszentrale für politische Bildung, 1965), 102–6; Hamilton, *Who Voted*, 235; Childers, *Nazi Voter*, 147–48.

9. Carsten, *The Rise*, 134–35; Milatz, *Wähler und Wahlen*, 131–32.

10. Carsten, *The Rise*, 134–35.

11. *Vossische Zeitung*, April 16, 1930.

12. Milatz, *Wähler und Wahlen*, 131–32.

13. Pfenning, *Deutschnationale Agrarprogramm*, 58; A. Stupperich, *Volksgemeinschaft oder Arbeitersolidarität* (Göttingen: Musterschmidt Verlag, 1982), 189.

14. Mommsen, *Deutsche Parteiprogramme*, 135–36.

15. B. B. Frye, *Liberal Democrats in the Weimar Republic* (Carbondale: Southern Illinois University Press, 1985), 59–61.

16. L. E. Jones, *German Liberalism and the Dissolution of the Weimar Party System, 1918–1933* (Chapel Hill: University of North Carolina Press, 1988), 49–53; Milatz, *Wähler und Wahlen*, 98–101.

17. Orlow, *Weimar Prussia*, 26–28.

18. H. Lebovics, *Social Conservatism and the Middle Classes in Germany, 1914–1933* (Princeton, N.J.: Princeton University Press, 1969), 33–34.

19. Mommsen, *Deutsche Parteiprogramme*, 129–31; J. B. Holt, *German Agricultural Policy, 1918–1934: The Development of a National Philosophy toward Agriculture in Postwar Germany* (Chapel Hill: University of North Carolina Press, 1936), 107.

20. Jones, *German Liberalism*, 288–89; Lebovics, *Social Conservatism*, 33–34; P. Gourevitch, *Politics in Hard Times: Comparative Responses to International Economic Crises* (Ithaca, N.Y.: Cornell University Press, 1986), 22–23, 142.

21. Carsten, *The Rise*, 125–26.

22. Jones, *German Liberalism*, 295–96; M. Vogt, "Parteien in der Weimarer Republik," in *Die Weimarer Republik, 1918–1933*, ed. K. D. Bracher, M. Funke, and H.-A. Jacobsen (Bonn: Bundeszentrale für politische Bildung, 1987), 134–57; Mommsen, *Deutsche Parteiprogramme*, 129–31.

23. Jones, *German Liberalism*, 95–96; D. Abraham, *The Collapse of the Weimar Republic*, 2nd ed. (New York: Holmes & Meier, 1986), 298–302.

24. Jones, *German Liberalism*, 349; Abraham, *The Collapse*, 298–302.

25. Jones, *German Liberalism*, 349; Milatz, *Wähler und Wahlen*, 98–101; Hamilton, *Who Voted*, 240–42.

26. Jones, *German Liberalism*, 417–29; Milatz, *Wähler und Wahlen*, 98–101.

27. Jones, *German Liberalism*, 453–59; Hamilton, *Who Voted*, 244–45; Abraham, *The Collapse*, 302.

28. Frye, *Liberal Democrats*, 59–61; Jones, *German Liberalism*, 22; H. Fenske, *Der liberale Südwesten* (Stuttgart: Kohlhammer, 1981), 216.

29. Hamilton, *Who Voted*, 247.

30. Frye, *Liberal Democrats*, 59–61.

31. Ibid., 83; Jones, *German Liberalism*, 35–43.

32. Mommsen, *Deutsche Parteiprogramme*, 121–23.

33. Jones, *German Liberalism*, 44, 60; Hamiliton, *Who Voted*, 247; Frye, *Liberal Democrats*, 102.

34. Mommsen, *Deutsche Parteiprogramme*, 121–23.

35. Frye, *Liberal Democrats*, 83; Jones, *German Liberalism*, 246.

36. Mommsen, *Deutsche Parteiprogramme*, 148–52.

37. E. L. Evans, *The German Center Party, 1870–1933: A Study in Political Catholicism* (Carbondale: Southern Illinois University Press, 1981), 316–24; Frye, *Liberal Democrats*, 83–84.

38. *Berliner Tageblatt*, November 3, 1928.

39. Jones, *German Liberalism*, 282–83; *Vossische Zeitung*, June 16, 1927; Mommsen, *Deutsche Parteiprogramme*, 121; *Vossische Zeitung*, September 19, 1928.

40. Jones, *German Liberalism*, 294–95, 299–300.

41. *Berliner Tageblatt*, January 1, 1929.

42. Frye, *Liberal Democrats*, 156.

43. *Vossische Zeitung*, October 2, 1930.

44. Hamilton, *Who Voted*, 251.

45. Mommsen, *Deutsche Parteiprogramme*, 153.

46. Hamilton, *Who Voted*, 248.

47. Frye, *Liberal Democrats*, 157–58; Jones, *German Liberalism*, 372; Hamilton, *Who Voted*, 249.

48. Jones, *German Liberalism*, 381.

49. Ibid., 401–46.

50. W. Mommsen, *Deutsche Parteiprogramme* (Munich: Olzog, 1960), 485; Frye, *Liberal Democrats*, 83–84.

51. Mommsen, *Deutsche Parteiprogramme* (1952), 123–27.

52. Evans, *German Center Party*, 318; *Germania*, January 27, 1927.

53. Evans, *German Center Party*, 316–18, 353; *Germania*, May 6, 1928.

54. *Germania*, November 5, 1929; *Germania*, November 11, 1929; Evans, *German Center Party*, 307.

55. Mommsen, *Deutsche Parteiprogramme* (1952), 123–27; Mommsen, *Deutsche Parteiprogramme* (1960), 485.

56. *Germania*, August 5, 1927.

57. Evans, *German Center Party*, 262.

58. *Germania*, October 19, 1926.

59. *Germania*, November 11, 1929.

60. *Germania*, October 15, 1927; *Germania*, March 6, 1930; *Germania*, September 8, 1930; *Germania*, June 27, 1930.

61. Evans, *German Center Party*, 263.

62. Ibid., 264; *Germania*, January 27, 1927; *Germania*, April 14, 1927; *Germania*, May 15, 1928; *Germania*, August 11, 1928.

63. Evans, *German Center Party*, 346-49; Stachura, "Who Were the Nazis?" 306; Moeller, *German Peasants*, 153.

64. Evans, *The German Center Party*, 357-65; *Germania*, September 11, 1930; *Germania*, July 28, 1932; *Germania*, July 30, 1932. Oddly, although Brüning had use of Article 48 to implement his programs during his tenure as chancellor, he decided not to push through the Center Party's agenda with regard to the national school bill and the national concordat (Evans, *German Center Party*, 369).

65. Milatz, *Wähler und Wahlen*, 94-98; Evans, *German Center Party*, 370-73.

66. K. Schönhoven, *Die Bayerische Volkspartei, 1924-1932* (Düsseldorf: Droste, 1972), 279-84; Evans, *German Center Party*, 267-69; Mommsen, *Deutsche Parteiprogramme* (1952), 127-29.

67. Schönhoven, *Bayerische Volkspartei*, 279-84; Evans, *German Center Party*, 268, 297-98, 319. The BVP was particularly irritated by a public pronouncement by Erzberger, Reichsminister of finance and Center Party notable, calling for the abolition of the German Länder (states). See Evans, *German Center Party*, 269.

68. H. James, "Economic Reasons for the Collapse of the Weimar Republic," in *Weimar: Why Did German Democracy Fail?* ed. I. Kershaw (London: Weidenfeld & Nicolson, 1990), 48; Schönhoven, *Bayerische Volkspartei*, 222-29; Milatz, *Wähler und Wahlen*, 98. The Center Party ultimately supported the Young Plan, and the BVP opposed it (Evans, *German Center Party*, 360-61).

69. Schönhoven, *Bayerische Volkspartei*, 243-69.

70. Mommsen, *Deutsche Parteiprogramme* (1960), 453-56.

71. *Volkswacht*, July 6, 1927.

72. R. Breitman, *German Socialism and Weimar Democracy* (Chapel Hill: University of North Carolina Press, 1981); Lebovics, *Social Conservatism*, 35; *Volkswacht*, September 22, 1930.

73. Mommsen, *Deutsche Parteiprogramme* (1952), 118-21; Milatz, *Wähler und Wahlen*, 86-91.

74. *Volkswacht*, July 28, 1925; *Volkswacht*, August 11, 1925; Mommsen, *Deutsche Parteiprogramme* (1960), 467. There was, however, one tax the SPD wanted eliminated. The SPD called for the removal of the turnover sales tax, which it claimed was the most oppressive of all taxes (*Volkswacht*, September 1, 1930).

75. *Volkswacht*, April 4, 1931.

76. Breitman, *German Socialism*; Mommsen, *Deutsche Parteiprogramme* (1960), 456-58, 461-72; Holt, *German Agricultural Policy*, 107.

77. The SPD saw the reintroduction of compulsory military service as a means to lower unemployment.

78. *Volkswacht*, September 3, 1926; *Volkswacht*, September 16, 1926; *Volkswacht*, September 4, 1930.

79. *Volkswacht*, March 31, 1930.

80. *Vossische Zeitung*, April 3, 1930; Evans, *German Center Party*, 363-64.

81. *Volkswacht,* October 2, 1931; *Volkswacht,* October 3, 1931; Breitman, *German Socialism.*

82. *Volkswacht,* September 1, 1930; Breitman, *German Socialism.*

83. *Volkswacht,* November 2, 1932.

84. O. K. Flechtheim, *Die KPD in der Weimarer Republik* (Frankfurt: Europäische Verlagsanstalt, 1969), 329; Milatz, *Wähler und Wahlen,* 109–10.

85. Flechtheim, *Die KPD in der Weimarer Republik,* 329; Mommsen, *Deutsche Parteiprogramme* (1952), 115–18.

86. Fischer, *German Communists,* 18; Flechtheim, *Die KPD in der Weimarer Republik,* 191–92.

87. *Die Rote Fahne,* August 28, 1930; *Die Rote Fahne,* July 16, 1932.

88. Fischer, *German Communists,* 104–6.

89. Ibid., 104–6; Hamilton, *Who Voted,* 287–308; *Die Rote Fahne,* September 26, 1929; Flechtheim, *Die KPD in der Weimarer Republik,* 259–60.

90. Flechtheim, *Die KPD in der Weimarer Republik,* 260–69; *Die Rote Fahne,* August 24, 1930.

91. H. A. Winkler, "Die Arbeiterparteien und die Republik von Weimar," in *Weimarer Republik,* ed. G. Schulz (Freiburg: Ploetz, 1987), 109–10; H. Mommsen, "Die Sozialdemokratie in der Defensive: Der Immobilismus der SPD und der Aufstieg des Nationalsozialismus," in *Sozialdemokratie zwischen Klassenbewegung und Volkspartei,* ed. H. Mommsen (Frankfurt: Athenäum Fischer Taschenbuch, 1974), 106–9.

92. Fischer, *German Communists,* 102–3; Flechtheim, *Die KPD in der Weimarer Republik,* 260–61.

93. Carsten, *The Rise,* 95. Hitler first came into contact with the German Workers' Party through his employment in the German army. Hitler's humble social origins and his fiery oratory brought him to the attention of members of the officer corps of the Bavarian Reichswehr, who ordered him to attend meetings of the German Workers' Party.

94. Lebovics, *Social Conservatism,* 206.

95. Carsten, *The Rise,* 130.

96. H. Gies, "The NSDAP and the Agrarian Organizations in the Final Phase of the Weimar Republic," in *Nazism and the Third Reich,* ed. H. A. Turner, Jr. (New York: Quadrangle Books, 1972), 56.

97. A. Bullock, *Hitler and Stalin* (New York: Alfred A. Knopf, 1992), 168.

98. I. Kershaw, "Ideology, Propaganda, and the Rise of the Nazi Party," in *The Nazi Machtergreifung,* ed. P. D. Stachura (London: Allen & Unwin, 1983), 167; J. Farquharson and J. Hiden, *Explaining Hitler's Germany: Historians and the Third Reich,* 2nd ed. (London: Bratsford Academic & Educational, 1989), 114.

99. Lebovics, *Social Conservatism,* 206–10.

100. Farquharson and Hiden, *Explaining Hitler's Germany,* 151.

101. A. Barkai, *Das Wirtschaftssystem des Nationalsozialismus* (Frankfurt: Fischer, 1988).

102. W. D. Smith, *Ideological Origins of Nazi Imperialism* (New York: Oxford University Press, 1986), 210.

103. Farquharson and Hiden, *Explaining Hitler's Germany,* 147; J. B. von Kruedener, "Could Brüning's Policy of Deflation Have Been Successful?" in *Economic Crisis and Political Collapse: The Weimar Republic, 1925–1933,* ed. J. B. von Kruedener (New York: Berg, 1990), 98.

104. A. Barkai, *Nazi Economics: Ideology, Theory, and Policy,* trans. R. Hadass-Vashitz (New Haven: Yale University Press, 1990), 87; D. Calleo, *The German Problem Reconsidered* (Cambridge: Cambridge University Press, 1978), 69.

105. Barkai, *Das Wirtschaftssystem,* 86–87; Smith, *Ideological Origins,* 210.

106. Smith, *Ideological Origins,* 109; Barkai, *Das Wirtschaftssystem,* 64–67, 85–86; Calleo, *The German Problem,* 104.

107. Smith, *Ideological Origins,* 93–107.

108. Barkai, *Das Wirtschaftssystem,* 89–90, 93–96, 100.

109. Gourevitch, *Politics in Hard Times,* 128; Barkai, *Nazi Economics,* 67.

110. Calleo, *The German Problem,* 101; Barkai, *Nazi Economics,* 57; Gourevitch, *Politics in Hard Times,* 128.

111. Barkai, *Nazi Economics,* 103.

112. G. Feder, *Das Programm der N.S.D.A.P. und seine weltanschaulichen Grundgedanken,* Nationalsozialistische Bibliothek 1, 136th ed. (Munich: Eher, 1934), 10–15; B. Miller Lane and L. J. Rupp, *Nazi Ideology before 1933: A Documentation* (Austin: University of Texas Press, 1978), xii–xiii.

113. Calleo, *The German Problem,* 104; Barkai, *Das Wirtschaftssystem,* 28–29; Smith, *Ideological Origins,* 242–45.

114. Barkai, *Das Wirtschaftssystem,* 56–60; Lane and Rupp, *Nazi Ideology,* xvi–xx.

115. Barkai, *Das Wirtschaftssystem,* 56–60. Barkai claims that many of Gregor Strasser's ideas on autarky and job creation probably derived from the writings of the half-Jewish German economist Friedländer-Prechtl—a debt never acknowledged by Strasser. Also, P. D. Stachura (*Gregor Strasser and the Rise of Nazism* [London: Allen & Unwin, 1983], 99) asserts that few of the notions found in Strasser's May 1932 speech on the Immediate Program actually originated with Gregor Strasser.

116. Abel, *Why Hitler,* 172–73.

117. Childers, *Nazi Voter,* 188–89.

118. Ziegler, *Nazi Germany,* 90–91.

119. Ibid., 66–67.

120. Noakes and Pridham, *Nazism,* 78. Also, for a more detailed account of the Nazi Party's particular appeal to German youth, see D. J. K. Peukert, *The Weimar Republic: The Crisis of Classical Modernity,* trans. R. Deveson (New York: Hill and Wang, 1989), 89–95.

121. Kershaw, "Ideology," 167.

122. Carsten, *The Rise,* 127; L. Stokes, ed., *Kleinstadt und Nationalsozialismus: Ausgewählte Dokumente zur Geschichte von Eutin, 1918–1945* (Neumünster: Karl Wachholtz, 1984), 276.

123. Winkler, "German Society," 12.

124. Dawidowicz, *War Against the Jews,* 4–5.

125. Lane and Rupp, *Nazi Ideology,* xiii–xv; S. Gordon, *Hitler, Germans and the "Jewish Question"* (Princeton, N.J.: Princeton University Press, 1984), 53–54.

126. K. D. Bracher, *The German Dictatorship: The Origins, Structure, and Effects of National Socialism,* trans. J. Steinberg (New York: Praeger, 1970).

127. Gordon, *Hitler, Germans,* 67.

128. Bessel suggests that possibly the most important purpose of National Socialist propaganda was to fashion the behavior of the party activists rather than to attract a mass electoral base ("The Rise of the NSDAP," 24–25).

129. Lane and Rupp, *Nazi Ideology,* xiii–xv, 45, 59.

130. Gordon, *Hitler, Germans*.

131. Ibid., 68-70; Kershaw, "Ideology," 168. Some scholars disagree that anti-Semitism becomes less pervasive in Nazi Party propaganda between 1925 and 1933. J. H. Grill's study of the Nazi Party in Baden (*The Nazi Movement in Baden, 1920-1945* [Chapel Hill: University of North Carolina Press, 1983], 115-16) points to the primacy of the theme of violent anti-Semitism among speakers at closed party meetings (*Sprechabend*) in 1925 and 1926, and M. Kele (*Nazis and Workers: National Socialist Appeals to German Labor, 1919-1933* [Chapel Hill: University of North Carolina Press, 1972], 145) sees a rise in Nazi expression of vicious anti-Semitism during the party's attempt to win over industrial workers between 1928 and 1930.

132. D. L. Niewyk, *The Jews in Weimar Germany* (Baton Rouge: Louisiana State University Press, 1980), 80; Kershaw, "Ideology," 167-68.

133. R. Zitelmann, *Hitler: Selbstverständnis eines Revolutionärs* (Stuttgart: Klett-Cotta, 1987).

134. Gordon, *Hitler, Germans*, 53-54.

135. C. Koonz, "Nazi Women Before 1933: Rebels Against Emancipation." *Social Science Quarterly* 56 (1976): 555; Kershaw, "Ideology." Merkl (*Political Violence*) suggests in his examination of the Abel biograms that even among the early activist core members (*alte Kämpfer*) anti-Semitism played a less important role than other factors.

136. Kershaw, "Ideology," 167-68.

137. Zofka, *Ausbreitung*, 126.

138. Z. Zofka, "Nazi Appeal in Countryside (Bavaria)," unpublished paper presented at the Conference on Elections, Mass Politics, and Social Change in Germany, 1890-1939, in Toronto, April 1990.

139. Gordon, *Hitler, Germans*, 60-63. For an informative account of the history of anti-Semitism in Vienna, see B. F. Pauley, *From Prejudice to Persecution: A History of Austrian Anti-Semitism* (Chapel Hill: University of North Carolina Press, 1992).

140. J. S. Conway, "National Socialism and the Christian Churches during the Weimar Republic," in *The Nazi Machtergreifung*, ed. P. D. Stachura (London: Allen & Unwin, 1983), 140-41.

141. Niewyk, *The Jews in Weimar Germany*, 68-69; Fischer, *German Communists*, 59.

142. Fischer, *German Communists*, 60.

143. Noakes and Pridham, *Nazism*, 73; T. Childers, "The Social Language of Politics in Germany: The Sociology of Political Discourse in the Weimar Republic," *American Historical Review* 95 (1990): 344; Richter, "Resource Mobilisation," 118. For a superb study of how the Nazi Party methodically organized its campaign to win power in a small town in northern Germany, see W. S. Allen's *The Nazi Seizure of Power* (New York: New Viewpoints, 1973).

144. Pridham, *Hitler's Rise*, 229-30; Noakes and Pridham, *Nazism*, 75.

145. Childers, *Nazi Voter*, 218.

146. Pridham, *Hitler's Rise*, 144; Noakes, *Nazi Party in Lower Saxony*, 157.

147. Zofka, "Between Bauernbund," 46.

Chapter 3: The Middle Class and Weimar Political Parties

1. Lebovics, *Social Conservatism*, 6.

2. W. Kaschuba, "Peasants and Others: The Historical Contours of Village Class So-

ciety," in *The German Peasantry*, ed. R. J. Evans and W. R. Lee (New York: St. Martin's Press, 1986), 235.

3. D. Gessner, "The Dilemma of German Agriculture during the Weimar Republic," in *Social Change and Political Development in Weimar Germany*, ed. R. Bessel and E. J. Feuchtwanger (London: Croom Helm, 1981), 138; M. Sering, *Deutsche Agrarpolitik: Auf geschichtlicher und landeskundlicher Grundlage* (Leipzig: Hans Buske, 1934), 26–30.

4. Sering, *Deutsche Agrarpolitik*, 89–91.

5. Gessner, "Dilemma," 138; Sering, *Deutsche Agrarpolitik*, 26–30.

6. Milatz, *Wähler und Wahlen; Statistik des Deutschen Reichs*, vols. 402–8 (Berlin: Verlag von Reimar Hobbing, 1927).

7. Ibid.; Gessner, "Dilemma," 139; A. F. Mutton, *Central Europe: A Regional and Human Geography* (London: Longmans, 1968), 240.

8. Milatz, *Wähler und Wahlen; Statistik des Deutschen Reichs*.

9. Ibid.; Mutton, *Central Europe*, 240–41; Sering, *Deutsche Agrarpolitik*.

10. Abraham, *Collapse*, 2nd ed., 55, 59.

11. Kater, *Nazi Party*, 58.

12. H. James, *The German Slump: Politics and Economics 1924–1936* (Oxford: Clarendon Press, 1986), 257–58.

13. G. D. Feldman, *The Great Disorder: Politics, Economics, and Society in the German Inflation, 1914–1924* (New York: Oxford University Press, 1993), 840; D. Petzina, "Germany and the Great Depression," 59.

14. M. Tracy, *Agriculture in Western Europe* (New York: Praeger, 1964), 198; Farquharson, *The Plough and the Swastika*, 235–36.

15. Kater, *Nazi Party*, 58.

16. W. G. Hoffman, *Das Wachstum der deutschen Wirtschaft seit der Mitte des 19. Jahrhunderts* (Berlin: Springer Verlag, 1965), 634–49.

17. Tracy, *Agriculture in Western Europe*, 198.

18. Gessner, "Dilemma," 136.

19. K. Schaap, "Die Regierungsübernahme durch die Nationalsozialisten in Oldenburg, 1932: Ursachen, Hintergründe und Lehren," in *Oldenburg und das Ende der Weimarer Republik*, ed. Stadt Oldenburg Kulturdezernat (Oldenburg: Heinz Holzberg, 1982), 31–32.

20. R. Heberle, *Social Movements* (New York: Appleton-Century-Crofts, 1951), 227–28; Loomis and Beegle, "The Spread of Nazism in Rural Areas," 727.

21. Noakes, *Nazi Party in Lower Saxony*, 114–15.

22. James, *German Slump*, 257–58; Kruedener, "Could Brüning's Policy," 97.

23. Petzina, "Germany and the Great Depression," 59.

24. Moeller, *German Peasants*, 15–16.

25. Pfenning, *Deutschnationale Agrarprogram*, 13–14.

26. H. Kretschmar, *Deutsche Agrarprogramme der Nachkriegszeit* (Berlin: Junker & Dunnhaupt Verlag, 1933), 46.

27. James, *German Slump*; Lebovics, *Social Conservatism*, 40–41; Childers, *Nazi Voter*, 146.

28. Childers, *Nazi Voter*, 144–47; James, *German Slump*, 281.

29. Childers, *Nazi Voter*, 146–47.

30. Noakes, *Nazi Party in Lower Saxony*, 108–11.

31. Kater, *Nazi Party*, 39–40.

32. Sering, *Deutsche Agrarpolitik*, 127–32.

33. Childers, *Nazi Voter*, 146–47; James, *German Slump*, 281; Noakes, *Nazi Party in Lower Saxony*, 108–11; Angress, "Political Role," 531; D. Abraham, *The Collapse of the Weimar Republic: Political Economy and Crisis* (Princeton: Princeton University Press, 1981), 63.

34. Tilton, *Nazism*, 52 (quoted); Abraham, *Collapse*, 1st ed., 92.

35. Farquharson, *The Plough and the Swastika*, 237.

36. Childers, *Nazi Voter*, 217. Interestingly, before World War I the German livestock farming community joined with the export-oriented high-technology industry (for example, chemicals and electrical equipment) to support free-trade policies (Gourevitch, *Politics in Hard Times*, 22–23).

37. Stoltenberg, *Politische Strömungen*, 144–55.

38. Feldman, *The Great Disorder*, 840; Petzina, "Germany and the Great Depression," 59.

39. Sering, *Deutsche Agrarpolitik*, 115; Kater, *Nazi Party*, 58. Peukert (*Weimar Republic*, 65) asserts that farmers with mortgaged property who could pay off their debts with the hyperinflated marks benefited from the inflation crisis of 1922-1923. For a comprehensive analysis of the social, economic, and political consequences of the great inflation of 1922–1923, see Feldman, *The Great Disorder*.

40. Kater, *Nazi Party*, 39–40; Noakes, *Nazi Party in Lower Saxony*, 108–11.

41. Feldman, *The Great Disorder;* Pfenning, *Deutschnationale Agrarprogramm*, 49–51.

42. Noakes, *Nazi Party in Lower Saxony*, 108–11.

43. James, *German Slump*, 258–59.

44. Ibid., 257–58; Noakes, *Nazi Party in Lower Saxony*, 108–11.

45. Petzina, "Germany and the Great Depression," 59.

46. James, *German Slump*, 276.

47. Ibid.

48. Falter, "Economic Debts," 5. Lebovics and Abraham present different figures for farm mortgage foreclosures. According to Lebovics (*Social Conservatism*, 40–41), farm mortgage foreclosures rose from 3,173 in 1929 to 6,121 in 1932. Abraham (*Collapse*, 2nd ed., 75) reports that for farms of more than two hectares there were 2,292 foreclosures in 1928 and 6,200 in 1932.

49. Lebovics, *Social Conservatism*, 40–41.

50. Loomis and Beegle, "The Spread of Nazism in Rural Areas," 727.

51. Noakes, *Nazi Party in Lower Saxony*, 127.

52. Sering, *Deutsche Agrarpolitik*, chapter 2. Schleswig-Holstein had been an area of undivided inheritance since as early as 100 A.D. The common practice in Schleswig-Holstein was for the inheritance to go to the oldest son, who then on the death of his father would have authority over mother, children, and minor siblings. If possible, the other siblings would receive a cash payment as their inheritance.

53. Sering, *Deutsche Agrarpolitik*, 115.

54. Childers, *Nazi Voter*, 145–46.

55. Ibid., 145–46. Sering (*Deutsche Agrarpolitik*, 127–32) noted that the Weimar government offered some assistance in 1927 to German dairy producers by offering them access to an interest rate of five percent and government credit amounting to 71 million marks between 1927 and 1930. Sering does mention that the governmental assistance failed to ameliorate the problems besetting the dairy industry. Though much of the emphasis here has been on the

contrast between grain and livestock farming areas, other German farming regions suffered greatly from a decline in prices, high interest rates, and inadequate tariff protection. Grill (*Nazi Movement*, 137) mentions that farmers in the southwest state of Baden held similar concerns over taxes, tariffs, prices, and interest rates. See also Abraham, *Collapse*, 1st ed., 91–92.

56. Lebovics, *Social Conservatism*, 40–41; Angress, "Political Role," 544–45.

57. James, "Economic Reasons," 30–45.

58. Farquharson, *The Plough and the Swastika*, 237.

59. James, *German Slump*, 257–58.

60. Moeller, *German Peasants*, 17; Luebbert, *Liberalism, Fascism, or Social Democracy*, 300.

61. Gessner, "Dilemma," 145; Angress, "Political Role," 531–32.

62. Angress, "Political Role," 538–39.

63. Childers, *Nazi Voter*, 146; Angress, "Political Role," 538; H. Gies, "NSDAP und landwirtschaftliche Organisationen in der Endphase der Weimarer Republik," *Vierteljahreshefte für Zeitgeschichte* 15 (1967): 58.

64. Abraham, *Collapse*, 1st ed., 74; Kretschmar, *Deutsche Agrarprogramme*, 48.

65. Kretschmar, *Deutsche Agrarprogramme*, 48.

66. Stoltenberg, *Politische Strömungen*, 110–13; Noakes, *Nazi Party in Lower Saxony*, 108–20; Tilton, *Nazism*, 52; Angress, "Political Role," 540–41; Abraham, *Collapse*, 1st ed., 92; M. R. Lepsius, "From Fragmented Party Democracy to Government by Emergency Decree and National Socialist Takeover: Germany," in *The Breakdown of Democratic Regimes*, ed. J. J. Linz and A. Stepan (Baltimore: Johns Hopkins University Press, 1978), 53–54.

67. Kretschmar, *Deutsche Agrarprogramme*, 65; Angress, "Political Role," 543.

68. Kretschmar, *Deutsche Agrarprogramme*, 65, 73–74.

69. Ibid., 73–74.

70. Lebovics, *Social Conservatism*, 40–41.

71. Angress, "Political Role," 545.

72. Gourevitch, *Politics in Hard Times*, 145.

73. Kater, *Nazi Party*, 56. The restrictive credit policies of the Reichsbank in the spring of 1924 were a major blow to German independent artisans and shopkeepers (Jones, *German Liberalism*, 252).

74. Noakes and Pridham, *Nazism*, 1.

75. P. D. Stachura, "The Nazis, the Bourgeoisie and the Workers during the Kampfzeit," in *The Nazi Machtergreifung*, ed. P. D. Stachura (London: Allen & Unwin, 1983), 20; D. Orlow, *The History of the Nazi Party: 1919–1933* (Pittsburgh, Pa.: University of Pittsburgh Press, 1969), 194–95.

76. James, "Economic Reasons," 41–42; Stoltenberg, *Politische Strömungen*, 166–67.

77. Falter, "Economic Debts," 5. For the small-business sector, retail sales declined 30 percent between 1930 and 1931, and small-business bankruptcies increased by 20 percent (Jones, *German Liberalism*, 409–10).

78. Schaap, "Die Regierungsübernahme," 31–32.

79. Noakes, *Nazi Party in Lower Saxony*, 108–11.

80. Kater, *Nazi Party*, 64; Childers, "Social Language," 354.

81. Kater, *Nazi Party*, 64.

82. Ibid.

83. Noakes, *Nazi Party in Lower Saxony*, 113–14.

84. H. A. Winkler, *Mittelstand, Demokratie und Nationalsozialismus* (Cologne: Kiepenheuer & Witsch, 1972), 174.

85. *White-collar employee* is an imprecise translation of the German *Angestellte*, a term that conveys higher status than *white-collar*. Angestellte work in both the public and the private sectors. Similarly, *civil service employee* is an imprecise translation of the German *Beamte*, whose functions in fact entail more specific privileges and constraints than those of their counterparts in the U.S. civil service. Moreover, unlike civil servants, *Beamte* do not include any white-collar employees.

86. Kele, *Nazis and Workers*, 68-72.

87. Kater, *Nazi Party*, 43-44. Jones (*German Liberalism*, 251) states that one major consequence of the great inflation of 1922-1923 was that it reduced the income gap between salaried employees and blue-collar workers. Peukert (*Weimar Republic*, 157) notes that white-collar workers did on average receive greater pay than blue-collar workers.

88. Lebovics, *Social Conservatism*, 7.

89. Jones, *German Liberalism*, 251; Childers, *Nazi Voter*, 166.

90. Childers, *Nazi Voter*, 233; Jones, *German Liberalism*, 409.

91. Childers, *Nazi Voter*, 168.

92. Ibid., 93-94; Jones, *German Liberalism*, 251.

93. Lebovics, *Social Conservatism*, 46-47; James, "Economic Reasons," 41-42.

94. Childers, *Nazi Voter*, 169.

95. Kele, *Nazis and Workers*, 187-89; Childers, *Nazi Voter*, 229; Jones, *German Liberalism*, 409.

96. Childers, *Nazi Voter*, 229.

97. E. Rosenhaft, *Beating the Fascists? The German Communists and Political Violence, 1929-1933* (Cambridge: Cambridge University Press, 1983), 5; James, "Economic Reasons," 41-42; C.-L. Holtfrerich, "Economic Policy Options and the End of the Weimar Republic," in *Weimar: Why Did German Democracy Fail?* ed. I. Kershaw (London: Weidenfeld & Nicolson, 1990), 73.

98. Kele, *Nazis and Workers*, 68-72.

99. Pfenning, *Deutschnationale Agrarprogramm*, 3; Vogt, "Parteien," 134-57.

100. Pfenning, *Deutschnationale Agrarprogramm*, 18-22.

101. Ibid.

102. Ibid., 24-48.

103. Ibid.; Carsten, *The Rise*, 125-26.

104. Pfenning, *Deutschnationale Agrarprogramm*, 54.

105. Ibid., 37-42, 60-70.

106. There is some evidence that the DNVP gave preferential treatment to certain farmers as early as 1925. Theretofore, it had unswervingly advocated higher tariffs and rejected agricultural trade treaties as a means to lower tariffs, but once it was part of the government, the DNVP voted in 1925 for the ratification of a trade treaty with Spain. Many German wine producers charged that the treaty would lead to a flood of cheap Spanish wine and ruin Germany's wine industry (Pfenning, *Deutschnationale Agrarprogramm*).

107. Angress, "Political Role," 545-46; Pridham, *Hitler's Rise*, 119-21; Childers, *Nazi Voter*, 224; Pfenning, *Deutschnationale Agrarprogramm*, 60-70.

108. Jones, *German Liberalism*, 44-45; Mommsen, *Deutsche Parteiprogramme* (1952), 129-131.

109. Childers, *Nazi Voter*, 219-20.

110. Stoltenberg, *Politische Strömungen*, 69-73; Jones, *German Liberalism*, 300.

111. Abraham, *Collapse*, 2nd ed.

112. Mommsen, *Deutsche Parteiprogramme* (1952), 121-123.

113. Stoltenberg, *Politische Strömungen*, 69-72.

114. *Berliner Tageblatt*, May 23, 1925; Jones, *German Liberalism*, 283.

115. Frye, *Liberal Democrats*, 108; Jones, *German Liberalism*, 282-83.

116. *Vossische Zeitung*, June 16, 1927.

117. *Vossische Zeitung*, June 23, 1927.

118. Mommsen, *Deutsche Parteiprogramme* (1952), 113, 121; Vogt, "Parteien," 134-157; J. H. Grill, "The Nazi Party's Rural Propaganda Before 1928," *Central European History* 15 (1982): 184, footnote 123.

119. *Vossische Zeitung*, February 3, 1925.

120. Jones, *German Liberalism*, 77; Mommsen, *Deutsche Parteiprogramme* (1952), 148-49.

121. Jones, *German Liberalism*, 284, 295; Frye, *Liberal Democrats*, 108.

122. Jones, *German Liberalism*, 382-83, 402; Luebbert, *Liberalism, Fascism, or Social Democracy*, 282; Childers, *Nazi Voter*, 220.

123. Jones, *German Liberalism*, 386, 414, 435-36, 454; Luebbert, *Liberalism, Fascism, or Social Democracy*, 282; Childers, *Nazi Voter*, 220; Frye, *Liberal Democrats*, 185. Also, Jones (*German Liberalism*, 252) asserts that the DDP's defense of the Weimar Constitution significantly undercut the party's efforts to maintain its backing within the old middle class. I would insist that the party's failure to develop concrete economic proposals to improve the material situation of the old middle class damaged that backing more than did the DDP's defense of the Weimar Constitution.

124. *Germania*, May 14, 1925; Evans, *German Center Party*, 300-301.

125. *Germania*, October 19, 1926.

126. *Germania*, April 14, 1927.

127. James, *German Slump*, 268.

128. *Germania*, November 11, 1929.

129. *Germania*, June 24, 1930.

130. Kruedener, "Could Brüning's Policy," 83; Abraham, *Collapse*, 2nd ed.

131. Schönhoven, *Bayerische Volkspartei*.

132. James, *German Slump*, 276-77.

133. R. N. Hunt, *German Social Democracy, 1918-1933* (New Haven: Yale University Press, 1964), 138-40; Luebbert, *Liberalism, Fascism, or Social Democracy*, 298-99; N. Steinberger, *Die Agrarpolitik des Nationalsozialismus* (Moscow: Verlagsgenossenschaft Ausländischer Arbeiter in der UdSSR, 1935), 26-27.

134. Hunt, *German Social Democracy*, 138-40; M. Schumacher, *Land und Politik: Eine Untersuchung über politische Parteien und agrarische Interessen, 1914-1923* (Düsseldorf: Droste Verlag, 1978), 351-53; James, *German Slump*, 260.

135. *Volkswacht*, February 18, 1929.

136. Abraham, *Collapse*, 2nd ed., 82.

137. Gessner, "Dilemma," 146.

138. Abraham, *Collapse*, 2nd ed., 194.

139. James, *German Slump*, 260; Stoltenberg, *Politische Strömungen*, 115-16.

140. Schumacher, *Land und Politik*, 351-53; J. J. Linz, "Some Notes Toward a Comparative Study of Fascism in Sociological Historical Perspective," in *Fascism: A Reader's*

Guide, ed. W. Laqueur (Berkeley: University of California Press, 1976), 29; Gessner, "Dilemma," 146.

141. Pfenning, *Deutschnationale Agrarprogramm*, 30–34; Abraham, *Collapse*, 2nd ed., 61; Stoltenberg, *Politische Strömungen*, 69–72; Zofka, *Die Ausbreitung*, 120–25.

142. Abraham, *Collapse*, 2nd ed., 244.

143. James, *German Slump*, 267–68.

144. *Volkswacht*, February 22, 1929.

145. *Volkswacht*, September 4, 1930; *Vorwärts*, March 23, 1932.

146. *Die Rote Fahne*, December 10, 1927.

147. *Die Rote Fahne*, August 13, 1930.

148. *Die Rote Fahne*, August 22, 1930.

149. *Die Rote Fahne*, July 16, 1932.

150. Stoltenberg, *Politische Strömungen*, 174–75.

151. Orlow, *The History*.

152. H. A. Winkler, "Mittelstandsbewegung oder Volkspartei? Zur sozialen Basis der NSDAP," in *Faschismus als soziale Bewegung: Deutschland und Italien im Vergleich*, ed. W. Schieder (Göttingen: Vandenhoeck & Ruprecht, 1983), 100; Gies, "The NSDAP and the Agrarian Organizations," 46; Angress, "Political Role," 546; Gessner, "Dilemma," 150; Childers, *Nazi Voter*, 150; Grill, "Rural Propaganda," 164.

153. Barkai, *Das Wirtschaftssystem*, 28.

154. Sering, *Deutsche Agrarpolitik*, 83–86; Grill, "Rural Propaganda," 175–79.

155. Carsten, *The Rise*, 125–26.

156. Kele, *Nazis and Workers*, 43.

157. Childers, "Social Language." For a summary of Hitler's views on international capitalism, see Calleo, *The German Problem*, 90–91.

158. Grill, *Nazi Movement*, 151–52; Winkler, *Mittelstand*, 160, 174; Orlow, *The History*, 194–95.

159. Winkler, *Mittelstand*, 165–74; Winkler, "Mittelstandsbewegung," 103–104; Kater, *Nazi Party*, 56–57; Noakes, *Nazi Party in Lower Saxony*, 76.

160. W. Willikens, *Nationalsozialistische Agrarpolitik* (Munich: Boepple, 1931), 7–34; W. Frick, *Die Nationalsozialisten im Reichstag, 1924–1931*, Nationalsozialistische Bibliothek 37 (Munich: Eher, 1932), 117; Feder, *Das Programm der N.S.D.A.P.*, 14; Childers, *Nazi Voter*, 149.

161. H. Himmler, "Bauer, wach auf!" ["Farmer, Wake Up!"] *Der Nationale Sozialist für Sachsen*, August 1, 1926.

162. Lane and Rupp, *Nazi Ideology*, 94–97.

163. Stoltenberg, *Politische Strömungen*, 144–69; Frick, *Die Nationalsozialisten*, 106; Feder, *Das Programm der N.S.D.A.P.*, 10–15.

164. Lane and Rupp, *Nazi Ideology*, 117–18.

165. Ibid.; Pridham, *Hitler's Rise*, 124.

166. Pridham, *Hitler's Rise*, 125; James, *German Slump*, 261; Lipset, *Political Man*, 143.

167. Farquharson, *The Plough and the Swastika*, 57.

168. Holt, *German Agricultural Policy*, 204; Tracy, *Agriculture in Western Europe*, 200; Sering, *Deutsche Agrarpolitik*, 82; Farquharson, *The Plough and the Swastika*, 13–15, Childers, *Nazi Voter*, 218; Lane and Rupp, *Nazi Ideology*. Darré also disapproved of the *Anerbenbrauch*, whereby the actual inheritor of the land paid the other heirs for their shares. For Darré, the Anerbenbrauch created a problem: the heir who continued to farm the land often

had to assume debt, which began the destructive cycle of spending resources without improving the economy (W. Darré, *Neuadel aus Blut und Boden* [Munich: J. F. Lehmann, 1930], 75–76).

169. Lane and Rupp, *Nazi Ideology*, 120–21; Farquharson, *The Plough and the Swastika*, 13–15, 143–45.

170. Lane and Rupp, *Nazi Ideology*, 120–21; Farquharson, *The Plough and the Swastika*, 13–15; Pridham, *Hitler's Rise*, 124–25: Moeller, *German Peasants*, 143; Zofka, *Ausbreitung*, 120–25.

171. Lane and Rupp, *Nazi Ideology*, 121–22.

172. Ibid., 120; Farquharson, *The Plough and the Swastika*, 63–68; Zofka, *Ausbreitung*, 120–25.

173. Lane and Rupp, *Nazi Ideology*, 121–22; Farquharson, *The Plough and the Swastika*, 13–15.

174. Noakes, *Nazi Party in Lower Saxony*, 127; Farquharson, *The Plough and the Swastika*, 240). At the same time, in many parts of southern Germany, North Rhineland-Westphalia, and Hesse, farmers had a particular problem with the Nazi inheritance proposal. If implemented, the system of compulsory impartible inheritance would have terminated the practice of partible inheritance that was in effect in much of the region and guaranteed by regional laws. Because many farmers' children counted on inheriting their portion of fixed and movable property, the Nazi pledge to eliminate partible inheritance did not elicit their enthusiasm.

175. Grill, *Nazi Movement*, 228.

176. Lane and Rupp, *Nazi Ideology*, 130–34.

177. Stokes, *Kleinstadt und Nationalsozialismus*, 161–64.

178. Ibid., 306–9.

179. Loomis and Beegle, "The Spread of Nazism in Rural Areas," 733–34; Kater, *Nazi Party*, 55; Stoltenberg, *Politische Strömungen*, 165.

180. Winkler, *Mittelstand*, 175–82.

181. Richter, "Resource Mobilisation," 116; R. Bessel, *Political Violence and the Rise of Nazism: The Stormtroopers in Eastern Germany, 1925-34* (New Haven: Yale University Press, 1984), 81.

182. Bessel, *Political Violence*, 81; Stoltenberg, *Politische Strömungen*, 195–198.

183. Schaap, "Die Regierungsübernahme," 35.

184. Noakes, *Nazi Party in Lower Saxony*, 125.

185. Schapp, "Die Regierungsübernahme"; Stokes, *Kleinstadt und Nationalsozialismus*, 321–26.

186. Ibid.

187. P. Barral, *Les Agrariens français de Méline a Pisani* (Paris: Presses de la Fondation Nationale, 1968), 154; M. Dogan, "Political Cleavage and Social Stratification in France and Italy," in *Party Systems and Voter Alignments*, ed. S. M. Lipset and S. Rokkan (New York: Free Press, 1967), 179.

188. Barral, *Les Agrariens*, 155–56; G. Lefebvre, *Questions agraires au temps de la terreur* (La Roche-sur-Yon: Henri Poitier, 1954), 115.

189. R. Price, *The French Second Republic* (Ithaca: Cornell University Press, 1972), 202.

190. Price, *The French Second Republic*, 202; M. Gervais, M. Jollivet, and Y. Tavernier, *La Fin de la France paysanne de 1914 à nos jours*, vol. 4 of *Histoire de la France rurale*, dir. G. Duby and A. Wallon (Paris: Seuil, 1976), 404–5.

191. Brustein, *Social Origins.*

192. F. M. Snowden, "The Origins of Agrarian Fascism in Italy," *Archives Européennes de Sociologie* 13 (1972): 279; P. Corner, *Fascism in Ferrara, 1915–1925* (London: Oxford University Press, 1975); A. Lyttelton, *The Seizure of Power: Fascism in Italy, 1919–1929* (London: Weidenfeld & Nicolson, 1973); A. Szymanski, "Fascism, Industrialism, and Socialism: The Case of Italy," *Comparative Studies in Society and History* 15 (1973); F. J. Demers, *Le origine del fascismo a Cremona* (Bari: Laterza & Figli, 1979); P. Farneti, "The Crisis of Parliamentary Democracy and the Takeover of the Fascist Dictatorship: 1919–1922," in *Breakdown and Crisis of Democracies*, ed. J. J. Linz and A. C. Stepan (Baltimore: Johns Hopkins Press, 1979); A. L. Cardoza, *Agrarian Elites and Italian Fascism: The Province of Bologna, 1901–1926* (Princeton: Princeton University Press, 1982).

193. M. Vaini, *Le origine del fascismo a Mantova (1914–1922)* (Rome: Riuniti, 1961), 55–56; Cardoza, *Agrarian Elites,* 277.

194. Corner, *Fascism in Ferrara,* 162; C. Maier, *Recasting Bourgeois Europe* (Princeton: Princeton University Press, 1975), 310.

195. R. Zangheri, *Lotte agrarie in Italia: La Federazione nazionale dei lavoratori della terra, 1901–1926* (Milan: Feltrinelli, 1960), 401; Luebbert, *Liberalism, Fascism, or Social Democracy,* 243.

196. M. Magno, *Galanuomini e proletari in Puglia* (Foggia: Bastogi, 1984), 253.

197. M. Tasca, *The Rise of Italian Fascism, 1918–1922* (New York: Howard Fertig, 1966), 94.

198. Cardoza, *Agrarian Elites,* 336; *Il Popolo d'Italia,* April 1, 1921.

199. Luebbert, *Liberalism, Fascism, or Social Democracy,* 11, 278, 287–88, 310.

200. Ibid, 278.

201. *Partei-Statistik,* vol. 1.

202. R. Heberle, *Social Movements* (New York: Appleton-Century-Crofts, 1951); Loomis and Beegle, "The Spread of Nazism in Rural Areas"; Stoltenberg, *Politische Strömungen.*

203. Tilton, *Nazism,* 52; Pridham, *Hitler's Rise,* 124.

204. Moeller, *German Peasants,* 15–16; Kater, *Nazi Party,* 58.

205. Farquharson, *The Plough and the Swastika,* 63–68.

206. Ibid.

207. Ibid., 13–15; Noakes, *Nazi Party in Lower Saxony,* 124–25.

208. Heberle, *Social Movements;* Stoltenberg, *Politische Strömungen.*

209. Noakes, *Nazi Party in Lower Saxony,* 127; Farquharson, *The Plough and the Swastika,* 240.

210. R. Rietzler, *Kampf in der Nordmark: Das Aufkommen des Nationalsozialismus in Schleswig-Holstein (1919–1928)* (Neumünster: Karl Wachholtz Verlag, 1982), 14–15, 44.

211. Rietzler, *Kampf in der Nordmark;* Heberle, *Social Movements;* Stoltenberg, *Politische Strömungen.* Also, my theory of interest-based political allegiances has relevance for the study of the political geography of interwar rural fascism in Europe in general, not only in the case of Germany. In earlier studies I used the theory of interest-based political choice to account for the political geography of Belgian Rexism and Italian fascism. In both studies, the data strongly supported my argument (W. Brustein, "The Political Geography of Belgian Fascism: The Case of Rexism," *American Sociological Review* 53 [1988]: 69–80; W. Brustein, "The 'Red Menace' and the Rise of Italian Fascism," *American Sociological Review* 56 [1991]: 652–64).

212. For figure 3.2, if the "no occupation" category is excluded, the following compari-

sons are obtained: percentage of workers, 43–50–40–40–43–47–; percentage of new middle class, 22–20–49–12–23–17–; and percentage of old middle class, 35–30–11–48–34–36–.

213. For figure 3.3, the yearly male/female subsample sizes for all joiners are as follows: 1925, 2257/165; 1926, 1801/120; 1927, 1523/82; 1928, 2609/117; 1929, 5723/267; 1930, 7325/377; 1931, 7402/418; and 1932, 7287/502.

214. Hamilton, *Who Voted*, 234–35.

215. Childers, *Nazi Voter*, 178.

216. Jones, *German Liberalism*, 49, 78, 300; Childers, "Social Language," 348.

217. Childers, *Nazi Voter*, 178; Jones, *German Liberalism*, 418.

218. Jones, *German Liberalism*, 383–84; Childers, *Nazi Voter*, 178.

219. Jones, *German Liberalism*, 300.

220. M. Prinz, *Vom neuen Mittelstand zum Volksgenossen* (Munich: R. Oldenbourg, 1986), 81–91; Childers, "Social Language," 350.

221. Jones, *German Liberalism*, 437.

222. Hamilton, *Who Voted*, 252–53.

223. Evans, *German Center Party*, 365, 243–44.

224. Hunt, *German Social Democracy*, 137–38.

225. Ibid.

226. Childers, "Social Language," 348.

227. Childers, *Nazi Voter*, 97–98.

228. Ibid., 98, 175–78, 230–32.

229. Ibid., 172–78, 233–39.

230. Prinz, *Vom neuen Mittelstand*, 81–91; T. Childers, "National Socialism and the New Middle Class," in *Die Nationalsozialisten, Analysen faschistischer Bewegungen*, ed. R. Mann (Stuttgart: Klett-Cotta, 1980), 30–31.

231. Childers, *Nazi Voter*, 175; Prinz, *Vom neuen Mittelstand*, 81–91.

232. Prinz, *Vom neuen Mittelstand*, 81–91; Childers, "Social Language," 350. Nazi Party propaganda rarely differentiated between married and unmarried women with respect to employment. Nevertheless, that the Nazi Party campaigned vigorously against "double earners" and proposed that employed women with working husbands or fathers should be removed from the labor market makes the party's position on women and marital status obvious (C. Hahn, "Der öffentliche Dienst und die Frauen—Beamtinnen in der Weimarer Republik," in *Mutterkreuz und Arbeitsbuch: Zur Geschichte der Frauen in der Weimarer Republik und im Nationalsozialismus*, ed. Frauengruppe Faschismusforschung [Frankfurt: Fischer Verlag, 1981], 71–75; E. Kolinsky, *Women in West Germany: Life, Work and Politics* [Providence: Berg Publishers, 1989], 19; C. Koonz, "Mothers in the Fatherland: Women in Nazi Germany," in *Becoming Visible Women in European History*, ed. R. Bridenthal and C. Koonz [Boston: Houghton Mifflin, 1977], 454–55; J. Stephenson, *Women in Nazi Society* [New York: Barnes & Noble, 1975], 153, 158).

233. L. J. Rupp, *Mobilizing Women for War: German and American Propaganda, 1939–1945* (Princeton: Princeton University Press, 1978), 39–41; Childers, *Nazi Voter*, 236, 239.

234. Childers, *Nazi Voter*, 236, 239. The DHV leadership refrained from backing the NSDAP completely because the NSDAP failed to recognize the independence of organized labor.

235. For figure 3.5, the yearly male/female subsample sizes for all joiners are as follows: 1925, 2257/165; 1926, 1801/120; 1927, 1523/82; 1928, 2609/117; 1929, 5723/267; 1930, 7325/377; 1931, 7402/418; and 1932, 7287/502.

236. One might suggest that the overrepresentation of single females in the Nazi Party may be attributable to the perception that the party was a men's party: that for many married women it was enough to know their husbands were party members. See M. Kater, "Frauen in der NS-Bewegung," *Vierteljahrshefte für Zeitgeschichte*, vols. 31–32, 1983: 209. Though I do not doubt the truth of this supposition, I think it is equally plausible to argue that the Nazi Party's position on "double earners" helped shape both married and single women's attitudes toward joining the party.

237. Lepsius, in *Extremer Nationalismus*, 9–18, offers an alternative explanation for support from the new middle class for the Nazi Party before 1933. Lepsius focuses on the Nazi Party's noneconomic appeals to the middle class. In his view, the Nazi Party reached the middle class by denouncing class struggle and by affirming middle class societal norms (honesty, industriousness, achievement, frugality, national reliability and responsibility, and so on). Both the Nazi Party and the German middle class saw in communism a symbolic threat to middle class morality and German economic independence. Lepsius fails to explain, however, why certain groups within the middle class joined the Nazis while other groups did not and why these societal norms should have been more integral to German middle-class culture than to German working-class culture. See also J. Stephenson's *The Nazi Organization of Women* (London: Croom Helm, 1981) for the argument that many women chose the Nazi Party for its anti-Marxism, ultranationalism, or racist appeal.

238. Though I choose to concentrate on Germany's major political parties, I should mention that there existed smaller parties that emerged particularly to represent the interests of the old middle class. One such example is the Bauernbund in Swabia. The Bauernbund during the 1920s was an organization focusing on agricultural interests. In its propaganda the Bauernbund stressed its opposition to governmental economic and tax policies that unfairly discriminated against farmers but advocated the farming community's need for a political voice to represent its material interests (Zofka, "Between Bauernbund and National Socialism," 41). The best-known example of a smaller party devoted to the interests of the old middle class is the Wirtschaftspartei (Economic Party). The Wirtschaftspartei called for reducing governmental expenses, eliminating governmental meddling in business activity, and lowering taxes. Although the party referred to itself as a party of the entire middle class, it focused primarily on the economic demands of the self-employed middle class. The Wirtschaftspartei first appeared in government in the Prussian Landtag in 1921 and in the Reichstag in 1924. The party reached its zenith in 1930, winning twenty-three seats in the Reichstag. Two years later the party won only two seats. After 1930, the NSDAP took over the party's platform and captured a large part of its constituency (Milatz, *Wähler und Wahlen*, 101–2; Mommsen, *Deutsche Parteiprogramme* [1952], 131–32). Also, in my examination of the social origins of the Nazi Party I have decided not to include a study of the Weimar upper class or elite, because my goal is to concentrate on Germany's two principal classes, the middle class and the working class. Using Kater's (*Nazi Party*) definition of elite, there were 2,264 "elite" individuals in the Brustein-Falter BDC sample covering the period of 1925 to 1933. The percentage of upper-class joiners of the NSDAP ranged from a low of 5.2 percent in 1925 to a high of 9.2 percent in 1933. In general, the elite constituted approximately 6 percent of our sample, compared with 2 percent of the general population in 1925. Of the 2,264 "elite" individuals in our sample, 97 percent were male, 61 percent came from predominantly Protestant communities (communities comprising 75 percent Protestants or higher), and 56 percent came from communities with a total population of 20,000 or more. For those "elite" individuals in our sample who had a categorizable occupation (1,570), 55 percent were in

commerce, 34 percent in industry, and the remainder in agriculture. For a more detailed account of the social elite as a component of the Nazi Party, see Kater (*Nazi Party*).

Chapter 4: The Working Class and Weimar Political Parties

1. Abraham, *Collapse,* 2nd ed., p. 30.
2. Childers, *Nazi Voter,* 102–3; Abraham, *Collapse,* 2nd ed., 117. For a detailed account of the factors leading to the great German inflation of 1923, see Feldman, *The Great Disorder.*
3. Childers, *Nazi Voter,* 102–3.
4. Abraham, *Collapse,* 2nd ed., 26, 33, 119, 231–36.
5. Ibid., 236; Lebovics, *Social Conservatism,* 38; *Interrogeons l'histoire de l'Allemagne,* ed. Deutscher Bundestag (Bonn: Referat Öffentlichkeitsarbeit, 1988), 295.
6. *Volkswacht,* July 25, 1927.
7. L. Preller, *Sozialpolitik in der Weimarer Republik* (Stuttgart: Franz Mittelbach Verlag, 1949). For a detailed account of the process of industrial rationalization and its consequences for German industry before 1933, see R. A. Brady, *The Rationalization Movement in German Industry* (Berkeley: University of California Press, 1933).
8. *Wirtschaft und Statistik* 12 (1932): 147–48, 471–73; Childers, *Nazi Voter,* 180–81.
9. Childers, *Nazi Voter.*
10. Lebovics, *Social Conservatism,* 46–47; Kele, *Nazis and Workers,* 187–89; Childers, *Nazi Voter,* 244; Abraham, *Collapse,* 2nd ed., 267.
11. *Wirtschaft und Statistik* 12 (1932): 148; Childers, *Nazi Voter,* 244.
12. *Vorwärts,* September 4, 1932; Childers, *Nazi Voter,* 244.
13. Childers, *Nazi Voter.*
14. *Vossische Zeitung,* June 15, 1932; Abraham, *Collapse,* 2nd ed., 268.
15. *Vorwärts,* September 6, 1932; Abraham, *Collapse,* 2nd ed., 268.
16. *Volkswacht,* November 3, 1932.
17. Preller, *Sozialpolitik,* 119. Preller compiled his 1925 findings from the occupational census that reported on male and female workers, including apprentices, and his 1933 findings from the census of German firms reporting only males without apprentices. Though the two reporting procedures differed, the results support his overall finding of the effects of industrial rationalization.
18. My assumption regarding the relationship between plant size and unionization appears to contradict Luebbert's claim (*Liberalism, Fascism, or Social Democracy,* 181) that there was an inverse relation between plant size and unionization in Germany. According to Luebbert, organized labor comprised mainly skilled workers from smaller firms. Luebbert's claim, however, characterizes pre–World War I German labor, which I contend was vastly different from interwar German labor. German industrial rationalization and Weimar *Sozialpolitik* combined to boost the number of semi- and unskilled laborers and open the door to increased unionization.
19. Abraham, *Collapse,* 2nd ed.
20. Gourevitch, *Politics in Hard Times,* 142; Abraham, *Collapse,* 2nd ed.; Smith, *Ideological Origins,* 211.
21. Abraham, *Collapse,* 2nd ed., 140; Gourevitch, *Politics in Hard Times,* 22–23, 141–42; Calleo, *The German Problem,* 63.
22. Gourevitch, *Politics in Hard Times,* 141–42; Abraham, *Collapse,* 2nd ed.; Smith, *Ideological Origins,* 211.

23. Abraham, *Collapse*, 2nd ed., 139.

24. M. Sweezy, "German Corporate Profits, 1926–1938," *Quarterly Journal of Economics* 54 (1940): 384–98; W. G. Hoffmann, *Das Wachstum der deutschen Wirtschaft seit der Mitte des 19. Jahrhunderts* (Berlin: Springer Verlag, 1965), 522–23. For a detailed critique of Abraham's bipartite categorization and data, see P. Hayes, "History in an Off Key: David Abraham's Second *Collapse*," *Business History Review* 61 (1987): 452–72.

25. Abraham, *Collapse*, 2nd ed., 137. Gourevitch (*Politics in Hard Times*, 141–42) notes that foreign economic policy interests drove some German industrialists to establish more amicable relations with labor. Additionally, Gourevitch (*Politics in Hard Times*, 144) observes that by 1932 major elements of both German labor and domestic and heavy industry favored a policy of domestic reflation.

26. Stupperreich, *Volksgemeinschaft oder Arbeitersolidarität*, 53–57.

27. Fischer, *German Communists*, 88.

28. Stupperich, *Volksgemeinschaft oder Arbeitersolidarität*, 28, 53.

29. Ibid., 241–43, 176–86.

30. Frye, *Liberal Democrats*, 156; James, "Economic Reasons," 48; Jones, *German Liberalism*, 91.

31. Abraham, *Collapse*, 2nd ed., 302; Jones, *German Liberalism*, 429.

32. *Vossische Zeitung*, February 18, 1926.

33. *Volkswacht*, January 15, 1927.

34. *Vossische Zeitung*, June 1, 1927.

35. Frye, *Liberal Democrats*, 156.

36. *Vossische Zeitung*, November 1, 1931.

37. *Germania*, September 17, 1925.

38. *Germania*, January 27, 1927.

39. *Germania*, April 14, 1927.

40. Schönhoven, *Bayerische Volkspartei*, 223.

41. *Germania*, September 8, 1930; *Germania*, May 29, 1932.

42. *Germania*, September 11, 1930; Evans, *German Center Party*, 373–74.

43. *Germania*, May 29, 1932.

44. Luebbert, *Liberalism, Fascism, or Social Democracy*, 299–300; Pfenning, *Deutschnationale Agrarprogramm*, 16–22; Sering, *Deutsche Agrarpolitik*, 91.

45. Mommsen, *Deutsche Parteiprogramme* (1952), 118–21; Milatz, *Wähler und Wahlen*, 86–91.

46. Hunt, *German Social Democracy*, 34–35; *Volkswacht*, September 13–17, 1926.

47. *Volkswacht*, July 14, 1925.

48. *Volkswacht*, December 22, 1925.

49. *Volkswacht*, July 2, 1927; Luebbert, *Liberalism, Fascism, or Social Democracy*, 299.

50. Hamilton, *Who Voted*, 269–71.

51. *Vossische Zeitung*, September 21, 1929; *Volkswacht*, February 6, 1929.

52. *Volkswacht*, August 10, 1929.

53. James, "Economic Reasons," 48.

54. Mommsen, *Deutsche Parteiprogramme* (1960), 461–72.

55. *Volkswacht*, April 11, 1931; *Volkswacht*, October 2, 1931; *Vorwärts*, March 23, 1932.

56. Kele, *Nazis and Workers*, 190.

57. Hamilton, *Who Voted*, 271–72; Milatz, *Wähler und Wahlen*, 86–91; Kele, *Nazis and Workers*, 190.

58. Hamilton, *Who Voted,* 271-72.

59. Abraham, *Collapse,* 2nd ed., 226.

60. Mommsen, "Die Sozialdemokratie in der Defensive," 106-33; Childers, *Nazi Voter,* 250.

61. Breitman, *German Socialism;* Hamilton, *Who Voted,* 275-76. Also, for an extensive examination of the ideological variations within the SPD and the reasons underlying the party leadership's political immobility and inflexibility, see Mommsen's, "Die Sozialdemo-kratie in der Defensive," 108-13, 123-24.

62. *Vorwärts,* March 9, 1932.

63. James, "Economic Reasons," 49-50; Abraham, *Collapse,* 175. For an excellent ac-count of the contents of the WTB plan and its fate, see Michael Schneider, *Das Arbeits-beschaffungsprogramm des ADGB: Zur gewerkschaftlichen Politik in der Endphase der Wei-marer Republik* (Bonn-Bad Godesberg: Verlag Neue Gesellschaft, 1975).

64. *Volkswacht,* May 1, 1932.

65. Feldman, *The Great Disorder,* 853; Childers, *Nazi Voter,* 251; *Vorwärts,* September 4, 1932; *Vorwärts,* September 20, 1932.

66. Hamilton, *Who Voted,* 275-76; Breitman, *German Socialism,* 171; Barkai, *Nazi Eco-nomics,* 51-52.

67. Flechtheim, *Die KPD in der Weimarer Republik,* 217, 329; *Die Rote Fahne,* Septem-ber 26, 1929; *Die Rote Fahne,* August 24, 1930; Childers, *Nazi Voter,* 250.

68. Fischer, *German Communists,* 142.

69. *Die Rote Fahne,* January 13, 1926.

70. Abraham, *Collapse* 2nd ed., 231-32.

71. *Die Rote Fahne,* November 10, 1929; *Die Rote Fahne,* November 22, 1929.

72. *Die Rote Fahne,* June 23, 1932; Hamilton, *Who Voted;* Childers, *Nazi Voter.*

73. Hamilton, *Who Voted,* 276.

74. Flechtheim, *Die KPD in der Weimarer Republik,* 277; *Die Rote Fahne,* July 16, 1932.

75. Fischer, *German Communists,* 26-35.

76. E. D. Weitz, "State Power, Class Fragmentation and the Shaping of German Com-munist Politics, 1890-1933," *Journal of Modern History* 62 (1990): 294-95; Flechtheim, *Die KPD in der Weimarer Republik,* 215, 249-51, 260-66.

77. Childers, *Nazi Voter,* 250.

78. Hamilton, *Who Voted,* 302.

79. *Die Rote Fahne,* May 1, 1928.

80. Flechtheim, *Die KPD in der Weimarer Republik,* 259-69; Mommsen, "Die Sozial-demokratie in der Defensive," 132-33; *Die Rote Fahne,* August 24, 1930.

81. Kele, *Nazis and Workers,* 37-46.

82. Ibid. 91-92.

83. Böhnke, *NSDAP im Ruhrgebiet,* 212-21.

84. Kele, *Nazis and Workers,* 96-97; Carsten, *The Rise,* 125-26.

85. Kele, *Nazis and Workers,* 118-22, 138.

86. Böhnke, *NSDAP im Ruhrgebiet,* 204.

87. J. J. Spielvogel, *Hitler and Nazi Germany: A History* (Englewood Cliffs, N.J.: Prentice-Hall, 1988), 48-49; Kater, *Nazi Party,* 35-38. Kater (53-54) asserts, however, that owing to its radical demeanor and use of activist tactics the NSDAP began once again to attract working-class support between 1930 and 1933 that might formerly have gone to the KPD. Also, though the NSDAP was no great advocate of labor unions, it did establish the

Nationalist Socialist Shop-Cell Organization (*Nationalsozialistische Betriebzellenorganisation*, or NSBO), which had a membership of approximately 400,000 workers by January 1933 (M. Broszat, *Hitler and the Collapse of Weimar Germany* [Leamington Spa: Berg Publishers, 1987], 88; Kele, *Nazis and Workers*, 170).

88. Stachura, "Who Were the Nazis?," 305–6.

89. Kater, *Nazi Party*, 36.

90. Childers, *Nazi Voter*, 110–111; Noakes and Pridham, *Nazism*, 81.

91. Winkler, "German Society," 2.

92. Stachura, "The Nazis," 26–27.

93. Kele, *Nazis and Workers*, 37–38, 61.

94. Childers, *Nazi Voter*, 105–6.

95. Böhnke, *NSDAP im Ruhrgebiet*, 210–14.

96. Kele, *Nazis and Workers*, 57–58. Although the NSDAP frequently showed little sympathy for industrial strikes, it did advocate strikes against price hikes and tax increases (Kele, *Nazis and Workers*, 46) and even gave free reign to the NSBO to organize the participation of Nazi workers in work stoppages and strikes such as the November 1932 strike against the Berlin Transport Company (Broszat, *Hitler and the Collapse*, 88).

97. Kele, *Nazis and Workers*, 169.

98. Childers, *Nazi Voter*, 179.

99. Kele, *Nazis and Workers*, 143–44.

100. A. Tyrell, "Der Aufstieg der NSDAP zur Macht," in *Weimarer Republik 1918-1933*, ed. K. D. Bracher, M. Funke, and H.-A. Jacobsen (Bonn: Bundeszentrale für politische Bildung, 1988), 467–83; Gourevitch, *Politics in Hard Times* 26–27.

101. Kele, *Nazis and Workers*, 39–40, 189.

102. Childers, *Nazi Voter*, 111; Kater, *Nazi Party*, 55; Feldman, *The Great Disorder*, 854; Fischer, *German Communists*, 148 (quotation is from Fischer).

103. Lane and Rupp, *Nazi Ideology*, 129–30.

104. Holtfrerich, "Economic Policy Options," 73; Gourevitch, *Politics in Hard Times*, 26.

105. Holtfrerich, "Economic Policy Options," 72.

106. James, *German Slump*, 350.

107. Stokes, *Kleinstadt und Nationalsozialismus*, 161–64.

108. Farquharson and Hiden, *Explaining Hitler's Germany*, 133–34.

109. Lane and Rupp, *Nazi Ideology*, 139–44; Barkai, *Das Wirtschaftssystem*, 47–55; Childers, *Nazi Voter*, 245–47.

110. Barkai, *Das Wirtschaftssystem*, 42–44; Childers, *Nazi Voter*, 245–47.

111. Farquharson and Hiden, *Explaining Hitler's Germany*, 133–34.

112. Lane and Rupp, *Nazi Ideology*, 139–44; Barkai, *Das Wirtschaftssystem*, 47–55; Childers, *Nazi Voter*, 245–47; Stachura, *Gregor Strasser*, 100.

113. Barkai, *Das Wirtschaftssystem*, 42–44; Childers, *Nazi Voter*, 245–47.

114. Kele, *Nazis and Workers*, 96–97. For an extensive examination of Gregor Strasser's political philosophy, see also Stachura, *Gregor Strasser*.

115. T. Childers, "The Social Bases of the National Socialist Vote," *Journal of Contemporary History* 11 (1976): 26.

116. Stachura (*Gregor Strasser*, 42, 90–94) claims that Strasser was won over to many of Hitler's ideas after the 1926 Bamberg conference and that by 1930 Strasser appeared to have abandoned his opposition to private property and capitalism.

117. Abraham, *Collapse*, 1st ed., 236–37.

118. For figure 4.1, the yearly male/female subsample sizes for all joiners are as follows: 1925, 2257/165; 1926, 1801/120; 1927, 1523/82; 1928, 2609/117; 1929, 5723/267; 1930, 7325/377; 1931, 7402/418; and 1932, 7287/502.

119. My classification of industries as either import- or export-oriented is based on information from W. G. Hoffmann, *Das Wachstum der deutschen Wirtschaft seit der Mitte des 19. Jahrhunderts* (Berlin: Springer Verlag, 1965), 522-23; I. Svennilson, *Growth and Stagnation in the European Economy* (New York and London: Garland Publishers, 1983), 187, 335-36; Abraham, *Collapse*, 2nd ed. In examining the world market shares or total exports of seven major European countries and the United States for 1928, Svennilson shows that exports by the German chemical industry represented 42.8 percent of the world total, and German foodstuffs 9.3 percent (Svennilson, *Growth and Stagnation*, 187).

120. *Wirtschaft und Statistik*, vol. 12 (1932): 147-48, 471-73, 541-42, 740-41; R. A. Brady, *The Rationalization Movement in German Industry: A Study in the Evolution of Economic Planning* (Berkeley: University of California Press, 1933).

121. Gourevitch, *Politics in Hard Times*, 26.

122. H. A. Turner, Jr., *German Big Business and the Rise of Hitler* (New York: Oxford University Press, 1985), 64-65.

123. Kater, *Nazi Party*, 34-38.

124. Abraham, *Collapse*, 2nd ed., 248.

125. Only fifteen of the seventeen industrial branches could be used in the regression analysis presented in table 4.4, because my sample of the chemical and rubber and asbestos branches contained no Nazi Party joiners. I was unable to find a continuous variable measuring the export and import shares of each branch's total consumption. Because of the small number of cases and the limited value of the dummy variable measuring the "import" dimension, the results of table 4.4 are primarily suggestive and should be interpreted with a certain degree of caution.

126. G. Orwell, *The Road to Wigan Pier* (San Diego: Harcourt Brace Jovanovich, 1958), 175-76.

Chapter 5: Selective Incentives and Disincentives for Joining the Nazi Party

1. Noakes, *Nazi Party in Lower Saxony*, 65, 157-59.

2. Pridham, *Hitler's Rise*, 97.

3. Noakes, *Nazi Party in Lower Saxony*, 140; Pridham, *Hitler's Rise*, 140.

4. Tasca, *The Rise of Italian Fascism*, 109; Cardoza, *Agrarian Elites*, 338-39; Lyttelton, *The Seizure of Power*, 63; Demers, *Le origini del fascismo a Cremona*, 200-1; Vaini, *Le origini del fascismo a Mantova*, 15-19.

5. Pridham, *Hitler's Rise*, 193-94.

6. Kele, *Nazis and Workers*, 91-92.

7. Hamilton, *Who Voted*, 352; Orlow, *The History*, 158-59.

8. Noakes and Pridham, *Nazism*, 71, 75; Bessel, "The Rise of the NSDAP," 26; Noakes, *Nazi Party in Lower Saxony*, 143.

9. Carsten, *The Rise*, 139-40; M. Kater, "Sozialer Wandel in der NSDAP im Zuge der nationalsozialistischen Machtergreifung," in *Faschismus als soziale Bewegung: Deutschland und Italien im Vergleich*, ed. W. Schieder (Hamburg: Hoffmann and Campe, 1976), 32, 59, and n. 48.

10. The information on Hermann Wischner's life history obtained by Theodore Abel is

kept at the Hoover Institution. Further information comes from the NSDAP master file at the Berlin Document Center; his life history furnished his party number, which I used to locate his file among those in my sample of NSDAP members. Carsten, *The Rise*, 139–40; Fischer, *German Communists*, 144–45; Kele, *Nazis and Workers*, 191–92.

11. See Koshar's superb study of the role voluntary associations played in the rise of Nazism in the German towns of Marburg and Tübingen (R. Koshar, "Two 'Nazisms': The Social Context of Nazi Mobilization in Marburg and Tübingen," *Social History* 7 [1982]).

12. D. Mühlberger, "Germany," in *The Social Basis of European Fascist Movements*, ed. D. Mühlberger (London: Croom Helm, 1987), 72.

13. Grill, *Nazi Movement*, 158.

14. Heberle, *Social Movements*, 228; Noakes, *Nazi Party in Lower Saxony*, 4; Sering, *Deutsche Agrarpolitik*, 35–41.

15. Passchier, "The Electoral Geography," 290; Noakes, *Nazi Party in Lower Saxony*, 4.

16. Bessel, *Political Violence*, 39.

17. Heberle, *Social Movements*; Noakes, *Nazi Party in Lower Saxony*.

18. Noakes, *Nazi Party in Lower Saxony*.

19. Zofka, *Ausbreitung*.

20. J. H. Grill, "Local and Regional Studies on National Socialism: A Review," *Journal of Contemporary History* 21 (1986): 281.

21. Gies, "The NSDAP and the Agrarian Organizations," 64–65; Grill, "Local and Regional Studies," 229–30, 256; Noakes, *Nazi Party in Lower Saxony*, 166; D. Gessner, "Agrarian Protectionism in the Weimar Republic," *Journal of Contemporary History* 12 (1977): 771; H. A. Winkler, "German Society, Hitler and the Illusion of Restoration, 1930–33," *Journal of Contemporary History* 11 (1976): 8.

22. Abel, *Why Hitler*, 90.

23. Bessel, *Political Violence*, 55; Noakes, *Nazi Party in Lower Saxony*, 65.

24. Abel, *Why Hitler*, 99.

25. Fischer, *German Communists*, 95.

26. Grill, *Nazi Movement*, 204.

27. Abel, *Why Hitler*, 95; Pridham, *Hitler's Rise*, 193.

28. Pridham, *Hitler's Rise*, 208; Bessel, *Political Violence*, 29; Milatz, *Wähler und Wahlen*, 140–41; Koshar, "Two 'Nazisms,'" 41; Grill, *Nazi Movement*, 3–4; Noakes, *Nazi Party in Lower Saxony*, 28–29.

29. Grill, *Nazi Movement*, 70–71.

30. Bessel, *Political Violence*, 81.

31. Volz, *Daten der Geschichte der NSDAP*; Grill, *Nazi Movement*, 213–14; Pridham, *Hitler's Rise*, 189; Winkler, "Die Arbeiterparteien," 110–11; Bessel, *Political Violence*, 81.

32. Abel, *Why Hitler*, 95–96.

33. E. Rosenhaft, *Beating the Fascists? The German Communists and Political Violence, 1929–1933* (Cambridge: Cambridge University Press, 1983), 9.

34. Rosenhalt, *Beating the Fascists?* 3–4; Bessel, *Political Violence*, 77.

35. Bessel, *Political Violence*, 77–78.

36. Abel, *Why Hitler*, 105.

37. Bessel, *Political Violence*, 76.

38. Rosenhaft, *Beating the Fascists?* 6–7.

39. Volz, *Daten der Geschichte der NSDAP*, 42–43. For a detailed look at the violence between Nazis and communists in Berlin from 1930 to 1932 and a stimulating account of the

murders of Horst Wessel (Nazi S.A.) in 1932 and Herbert Norkus (Hitler Youth) in 1930, see J. W. Baird, *To Die For Germany: Heroes in the Nazi Pantheon* (Bloomington: Indiana University Press, 1990), chapters 4 and 5.

40. Demers, *Le origini del fascismo a Cremona*, 171.

41. Tasca, *The Rise of Italian Fascism*, 121-29; Maier, *Recasting Bourgeois Europe*, 315; C. G. Segre, *Italo Balbo: A Fascist Life* (Berkeley: University of California Press, 1987), 57; Snowden, *Violence and Great Estates*, 198-99.

42. In southern Germany the Catholic Church established Catholic youth associations (*Katholische Burschenvereine*) that provided Catholic youth with numerous activities while warning against involvement with the Nazi Party (Zofka, *Ausbreitung*, 168-69).

Index